SHIPWRECKS OF NOVA SCOTIA
Volume II

Volume II

SHIPWRECKS

OF

NOVA SCOTIA

BY JACK ZINCK

LANCELOT PRESS

Hantsport, Nova Scotia

DEDICATION

To Mrs. Pearl Beanlands

'Mrs. B.',

a kind and gracious lady

ISBN 0-88999-076-X

Published 1977

LANCELOT PRESS LIMITED, Hantsport, N.S.
Office and plant situated on Highway #1, ½ mile east of Hantsport.

ACKNOWLEDGEMENTS

I wish to express my appreciation to those who helped to make this book possible. My thanks to staff members of the Public Archives of Nova Scotia, the Public Archives of Canada, the National Maritime Museum in London, Lloyd's of London, the Ministere Des Armees of Paris, the Public Records Office in London, the Peabody Museum of Salem, Massachusetts, the Nova Scotia Legislative Library, and the Canadian Forces Photographic Unit in Ottawa. Special thanks to: Alex Storm of Louisbourg and Steve Giza of Halifax County, for kind permission to photograph artifacts they retrieved from sunken wrecks; Jerry Cobb for his photographic assistance; Charles Armour of the Killam Memorial Library; Joe Hattie for his kind contribution; the well-known photographers, Bob Brooks, Larry Boner, Budd Stacey, and Ned Norwood, for kind assistance and friendly advice; and my brother, Sonny Zinck, for sharing knowledge gained through his diving experiences and for his photographic support. A very special thank you to Anne Hyne, who was a great help at the start of this book and who guided me in the right direction.

CONTENTS

FOREWORD

We, as Nova Scotians, have learned a great deal from the sea, and undoubtedly will learn much more as time goes on. Our heritage as boat builders, sea merchants and fishermen, has played a great part in our daily lives. Over the years our protected harbours have seen many vessels come and go.

If we are to maintain a high quality environment, in so far as our coastline is concerned, then we must enact strong measures regarding shipping regulations. The old saying, "Once bitten twice shy!" should be heeded in the case of the *Arrow*. Looking back to the year 1970, the people of Cape Breton Island experienced a major oil spill, and with it an aftermath that will long be remembered.

Today it is almost commonplace to hear of an oil spill somewhere in the world. After a great deal of investigation it was learned that most of the oil spills were caused by Liberian tankers. It was discovered that these tankers were usually unsafe for navigation, ill equipped, poorly manned, and had generally outlived their usefulness.

Yet, with today's oil prices, there are those who will gamble and take the chance of transporting the "black gold". They will load these old vessels to capacity and try to cross the open sea without mishap, disregarding the possibility of endangering our environment. Should a shipwreck occur, there is very little we can do to prevent another 1970.

Looking into our past, when shipwrecks were a common occurrence, the only worry they had to contend with was the loss of the ship's cargo and any precious metal she may have carried. A fair number of ships have come to rest on our rugged coast. In most cases the sea will claim its victim by smashing and tearing it to pieces and once the anger of the sea has gone, there is nothing. All has disappeared below the surface or been tossed upon the shore of some lonely beach, distorted beyond recognition. Then there are those vessels which disappear without a trace somewhere along our coast.

The fate of many vessels has remained a secret to this day,

and unless they are found by the adventurous modern day wreck hunter, they will conceal their cargo forever. The present day scuba diver can now dive to greater depths, with more flexibility, and covei a great deal of ground in search of a wreck.

Because of the unspoiled waters that surround Nova Scotia, it is fast becoming a haven for divers from upper Canada and the United States. There are more and more young people taking to the water each year, and diving today is a great sport, as well as an enterprising business for some. It is a means of relaxation to some, while to others, it is a new form of experimentation. Using underwater camera equipment, divers can enjoy a new field of photography. Then there is the sport diver, with spear gun in hand, who can hunt the fish which abound in these waters. Last but not least, there is the ever present wreck hunter, a person full of adventure and eager to get his or her hands upon that lost vessel to find out what she was carrying.

With so much to offer in the way of reefs and shoals, we must remind ourselves that, although all this may sound intriguing to the underwater explorer, unknown areas can be very dangerous. Before you dive upon a reef or shoal, you should first survey the area, check the chart for depth of water, and find out how strong the currents are in that particuler spot. Before you carry out an initial dive in an unknown area, make sure that the person you are diving with is competent and be sure your confidence in each other is understood.

For those readers who have never experienced a dive upon a reef in search of a lost vessel, I will try to take you beneath the surface and give you an insight into what it is like. For the moment you can sit back and relax, close your eyes and picture a warm summer's day. Overhead the sky is a pale blue, with a gentle breeze blowing through your hair, and as you look out to sea, it is a mirror reflecting many colours. Now that we have set the scene, I will introduce you to Bill who will be my diving partner on this trip. Skipper is our man at the wheel of the large Cape Islander which will take us out to the reef. This particular boat was designed for fishing in our waters. It is the pride of our fishermen and a very seaworthy boat at that.

The reef which we will be diving on will remain anonymous and the area can be anywhere along the Nova Scotia coast. To start off, we are about four miles off shore, and situated on the south side of the reef. With the weather in our favour, and the sea relatively calm, we set the anchor. Now as we prepare for our dive, our excitment is expressed by our enthusiasm. Being extra cautious we go over our gear once more, checking the 'O' rings, our valves, regulators and the air pressure in the tanks.   With a working pressure of 2,200 pounds and a reserve of about 350 pounds of air, we are about ready.   Our vests check out all right, and a quick run over our masks, snorkel, weight belt, flippers, knife, depth gauge and wet suit prove out O.K.

Standing at the stern of the boat we slip into our wet suits and it feels good, until the sun's rays heat the outside surface of our suits and then we begin to sweat freely.   It is almost unbearable standing there in the boat, checking each other over once more before entering the water.   By now the cool water will feel great against our bodies and with one more glance over the reef, we turn and nod to Skipper.   He grins and shakes his head, for his expression shows that there is no way he will go under the water. Skipper has told us that he prefers to fish from the top and if he was supposed to be under water, then God would have given him gills.

A quick nod and a gentle roll backwards: the cool water feels refreshing.   At first the coolness chills our bodies, but within minutes the layer of water between our bodies and the suit warms up and it is very comfortable.   At the surface again, we bob up and down with the gentle rolling waves.   Placing the regulators in our mouths, we clear them and raise our thumbs in an upward motion to indicate that all is well.

With a kick of our flippers and a stroke of the arms, we begin a downward descent.   We are now entering a silent world, and the only sound we can hear is that of our regulators, which seem to echo in our ears.   If you were to hold your breath, all would be silent.   Now with each downward thrust of the flippers, we descend deeper and deeper.   The fish, which frequent the reef, out of curiosity come out to greet us.   Schools of pollock swim past and disappear into the large kelp beds.   The many coloured perch follow our every movement and hope that we will stir up food for them.   The plant life moves back and forth with the gentle action of the water portraying beauty in motion.

The sun's rays from above reflect pale greens and blues, adding to our adventure.   Visibility this day is exceptional and at a glance the depth gauge shows forty-eight feet.   We cannot help but take our time and enjoy the sea urchins that cover the rocks and the many starfish which appear everywhere.   The bright red and white sea anemones with their large tentacles are a sight to behold, moving back and forth with the action of the sea.

Soon we come to rest close to the ocean floor and at once we begin our search.   Motioning to Bill to spread out a little, we begin to work our way along the edge of the reef.   Coming across a large grey-blue wolffish, Bill stops suddenly. He watches as the wolffish eyes a fair sized lobster, which is about to come out of a small opening in the rocks. After a brief moment to see what would happen, we leave and veer to the left and descend deeper. We want no part of this creature, especially when he is waiting for his meal to emerge from the rocks.

A little while later much to our surprise we come across an old iron anchor. It is partly encrusted with coral and the remainder is badly eaten away from years of corrosion. Upon closer examination we find ballast rock and part of a chain. Full of excitment, we search the area by shifting rocks, digging and sifting through loose gravel. A sudden tug at my flipper startles me momentarily and I quickly glance over my shoulder. The sight of a small cannon ball in the hands of Bill is sign enough that we are in the midst of a wreck which probably occurred in the early 1800's.

Further diggings uncover grape shot, copper nails, a brass medallion and a silver coin. What seems like only a brief moment under the water is in fact close to forty minutes. The struggle for more air is the signal to pull our reserve and strike for the surface. A slight inflation of air into our vests helps to carry us upward with the newly acquired weight from the bottom.

With an easy stroke of the flippers, we follow our bubbles to the top. The nearer we get to the surface the warmer the water feels and before long the warm sun is bearing down on our hoods and reflecting a glare off the water into our face masks. It is almost blinding. We come within fifty feet of the Cape Islander, and Skipper is sitting at the stern looking at a passing cargo ship. A sharp whistle from Bill alerts him and he looks our way and waves.

Minutes later we are aboard the boat eager to display our find to Skipper. By now the tide is on the rise again, and after we remove all our gear and suits, we sit around for awhile talking about the find. Skipper is eager to come back and we agree to try this spot once more, to see if this wreck will yield any valuables with further searching.

—CEDAR GROVE—

On November 17, 1882, the steamship *Cedar Grove* left London, England, for Halifax and Saint John, New Brunswick, under Captain J. Fritz. During the entire trip across the Atlantic, the steamship had experienced rough weather. On Tuesday the 28th of November, Captain Fritz sighted the coast of Newfoundland and set his course for Cape Sambro.

With the weather against him all the way, the captain kept his ship on course as best he could. He kept a cautious eye on the coast of Cape Breton and made sure the ship was well off the land. As he neared the mainland of Nova Scotia, the weather changed and he found himself enshrouded in dense fog mixed with heavy mist. Once he lost sight of land, he relied entirely on his compass, but this was not enough. Because of the currents and strong tides, the ship drifted off its course. With each watch Captain Fritz ordered his men to keep a sharp eye for anything unusual. He had the engine room at peak efficiency in case the need should arise to come to a halt or reverse engines.

Early on the morning of the 30th the ship was moving slowly through the water when suddenly she struck heavily upon the ledges of Cape Island just off Canso. Upon impact the ship lurched and rolled upright again. The crew and passengers immediately rushed to the upper deck with fear in their hearts. They had no idea what had taken place and in the darkness they did not know what to expect.

From the wheel house Captain Fritz ordered all engines in full reverse and managed to get his ship off the reef. She moved out into ten fathoms of water with water spilling into the engine room. It was thought by the captain, engineer, and officers that she would stay afloat until daylight. But the water in the holds was rising very fast and it was impossible to control it. The chief officer, Mr. Masters, was given the order to let go with the port anchor in order to prevent further drifting. Within a short time the bulkheads gave way and the ship nosed towards the bottom. The crew and passengers scrambled for the life boats, while Mr. Masters attempted to go aft to speak with the captain, but the ship sank before he could reach him. After struggling for ten to fifteen minutes in the icy waters, the chief officer was picked up by the survivors in the starboard lifeboat which was manned by the fireman and crew members of the ship.

The chief officer took command of the life boat and ordered the men to make their way out of the heavy breakers. As they prepared to do this, they heard cries for help which came from the wreck. Apparently about ten feet of the stern remained above the water and when the men in the boat saw this, they turned and made for it. With much difficulty they reached the ship and rescued the chief steward and the third engineer.

In the early morning light the lifeboat was sighted by the schooner *Parole* and within a short time they were picked up. Once everyone was on board, the schooner proceeded on her course for Saint John, New Brunswick. Later that same day at 2:00 p.m., the schooner was run down by the steamer *Liddesdale*. The nightmare began all over for the survivors of the *Cedar Grove*. They, along with the men of the schooner, were removed from the water by the long boats of the steamer and, with much difficulty, were taken back to the *Liddesdale* and they were landed safely at North Sydney.

Due to the loss of Captain Fritz, Miss Farrel, and several others during the shipwreck, an investigation was held. On December 4th, 1882, an inquiry was set up to try to clarify what actually had taken place before and after the wreck occurred. Presiding over the inquiry was Captain Scott, R.N., and his first witness to the stand to give his testimony was John Griffin. He was the engine room operator and a native of Liverpool, England. He began by saying, "I shipped at London for this voyage. I have been going to sea eight years and I have been in Rankine and Gilmore's employ as donkey man. I was employed in the engine room and during my watch I attended the engines, being principally engaged in oiling them. When the vessel struck I was in bed. While I was getting up the third engineer came and told me that the ship was ashore. The second and third engineers, I noticed, were standing by the engines attending to orders by the telegraph.

"I saw the engines going both ahead and astern at different times. I think I was in the engine room an hour after the ship struck. I then came on deck, as all hands were called there. I think it was about three o'clock when the ship struck. When I came on deck I noticed that the life boats were swung out ready for lowering. I did not at that time think the ship was going to sink. Just at that time I saw no officer, but about ten minutes after I spoke to the chief officer who was giving orders to have provisions put into the port life boat. I asked him what he thought of the condition of the ship. He said he could not say for a certainty but matters looked bad. At that time it was blowing a light breeze off the land. I could see the sea breaking on the port bow about a ships length from us, but could see neither the shore nor any light. It was a little foggy. I heard no fog whistle and I did not notice any passengers on deck when I first went there. I think it was about six o'clock when I left the ship and it was still dark and foggy. The chief engineer called out, 'All hands on deck and hurry up.'

"The ship now listed heavily to port. When we came on deck the forward part was covered with water and the forward compartments were filling rapidly. When we took to the boats we tried to keep as near to the vessel as we could. I think it was the captain's gig that I got into. It was on the port side. There were in her two boys, the chief engineer and two seamen whose names I do not know.

"We remained near the ship and picked up a seaman and the male passenger. Mr. McAvity came from the engine room and jumped overboard. The wind drove us off shore but we pulled back toward the ship and kept close to her till after daylight. About seven o'clock we made out land on the starboard beam, but we did not pull immediately for it, as we could not see our way through the breakers. About ten o'clock we discovered a small cove and effected a landing. I heard that it was called Walker's Cove. About ten o'clock I saw the captain on the starboard side of the upper deck near the engine room hatch. I saw no passengers with him. I did not see the lady passenger, I saw the ship go down. She sank while we were pulling for the shore. All that was visible above the water were the topmasts. The starboard lifeboat with the second officer, the second steward, two firemen, the cook and cabin boy on board landed about the same time we did. Some of us went up on the hill to see if we could see any homes. In the afternoon two men came to us from Cranberry lighthouse and piloted us to Canso. I know of no reason why this ship went ashore, as there was no difficulty in getting the engines reversed, they worked well."

A seaman by the name of A.F. Wilson, who was a native of Finland, was called to testify. When he was sworn in, he began his version as follows, "I was at the wheel when the ship struck. The steering gear worked by steam and the course that we were sailing was west by south by the binnacle compass. The ship also had a pole compass, but I don't know whether the pole compass and binnacle agreed or not. I did not observe any compensating magnetic correcting the steering compass.

14

"The captain was on the bridge when the ship struck. He called out, 'Star board your helm,' and I did so. He seemed considerably excited. I think it was about three o'clock in the morning when she struck. I left the wheel as soon as she struck. Before she struck breakers were seen and the captain immediately ordered the engines stopped and reversed full speed, but the headway she had carried her forward till she struck. All hands were then called to clear away the boats. We then went forward and let go the starboard anchor. We saw Cape Race, but I do not remember what day it was. There were no soundings taken during the whole voyage. But between twelve and two o'clock on the morning of the accident I went with another man to get the leads and deep sea line. We looked for it for over an hour before we found it. The second officer sent us to look for it, I do not recollect what course we steered after we left Cape Race. It was snowing when the ship struck, but not very hard, it was very thick. It was raining and very foggy, but after we left Cape Race the weather was pretty fine. All day Wednesday the weather was clear. I saw the captain taking the sun on Wednesday, and I saw the lady passenger only once and this was just after the ship struck. She was running out of the cabin crying and I told her not to cry for I then thought she would be saved. The compasses worked very well. I do not know any reason for the ship running ashore.

"I saw the captain about a quarter of an hour before the ship went down. He was standing on the main deck talking with the first officer and the chief engineer. I think the lady was in the cabin at the time. I left the ship in the port gig."

On the witness stand, Joseph Dickens stated, "I am 26 years of age and belong to Berkshire, Great Britain. Been 15 years at sea, nine years as stoker and six as an ordinary seaman. I was in my bunk when the ship struck, I was awakened by being violently thrown out of my bunk when the ship struck. The first thing I said was, 'We are sinking!' and called all the others to turn out. The ship made no water in the engine roome for the first two hours; it ran in forward. I went on deck immediately and helped to get the boats ready for lowering.

"I saw the captain at that time. He was standing on the main deck just of the bridge giving orders. I saw the lady passenger standing at the companion door some time after the ship struck. After the boats were got out, the captain gave orders to sound the bell in the midship compartment under the bridge. He also gave orders for soundings to be taken.

"I think I heard some one say the leadsman got fourteen

15

fathoms.　Mr. McAvity told me to get some water for the boats, which I did.　After that I placed provisions in the two life boats. When this was done the third engineer came on deck and ordered all the firemen to go below and get the pressure up to eighty pounds.　I left the engine room about half an hour before the ship went down, and all the other firemen were called up.　When I got on deck, I observed that the bunker hatches had been forced off by the confined air.

"Just after this, orders were given by the captain to lower away the starboard life boat.　Some of the crew who were in the boat were directed to go on board again, as the captain thought the ship would not sink and might possibly hold together.　I heard an order sent to the engine room to start the engines, but whether it was ahead or astern I do not know, but I think it was ahead.　This was done, and shortly after this, when the engines were stopped, the ship went down head foremost.

"I then got into the starboard lifeboat, I saw the lady passenger just before this. The chief steward had her in his arms off the Jacob's ladder.　I was in the bow of the boat, but not having a boat hook could not keep her close to the ship, and a sea swept us back in the boat senseless.　The boat drifted astern and what became of the lady I do not know.　Our boat had only three oars, the others having been broken.　Our boat was disabled and we were unable to go back to the ship again.　I called out to the port life boat to go back and take in the men who were seen on the stern. They proved to be the third engineer and the chief steward. I did not see the land when the ship struck, as it was thick with rain and sleet, but after the day broke we saw it and pulled for it, landing at Walker's Cove with port cutter and the starboard life boat.　The second officer had charge of our boat.　I walked from where we landed and reported the news of the disaster to every one I saw.　I cannot account for the loss of the ship, as I was asleep and knew nothing about the course steered."

The fourth person to take the stand was Joseph Frank, a German who had been at sea for seven years.　He began his statement by saying, "When the ship struck I was on the look out on the top-gallant forecastle.　The weather was too thick to see far, I neither saw any light nor heard any sound from the whistle. Before the ship struck I reported breakers, but they were very close to us.　She struck about two minutes after I saw them.　I did not see the captain when the ship struck, but I saw him on deck afterwards.

"The second mate was officer on watch.　Orders were given,

16

after the ship struck, to let go the starboard anchor. I did not see the lady passenger until sometime after the ship struck. She was then at the door of the chart house. I never saw her afterwards. I have taken the wheel of the ship occasionally. I don't know anything about the course steered the day previous to the wreck. I got away from the ship in the port life boat. We had great difficulty in pulling the boat as we were short of oars. We had to go back to the ship to take in the steward and third engineer. We observed a schooner passing and went on board of her, she proved to be the *Parole* of Saint John, New Brunswick. After being on board of her for two hours, we were transferred to the steamer *Liddesdale* and landed at North Sydney."

When Charles White was questioned he said, "I belong to Hamburg, am 42 years of age and have served 27 years at sea. It was my watch from 10 p.m. to 4 a.m. and I was at the wheel from 12 to 2 a.m. I was sitting on the deck, near the funnel when the ship struck. I heard a cry from the lookout but did not know what was said. The captain gave orders but I know not what they were. I assisted in getting the boats ready, hoisted the jibs and let go the anchors. I saw the lady passenger standing at the door of the captain's cabin. I got into the captain's boat on the port side of the ship with the engineer, Mr. McAvity, and two seamen. The ship struck three times and I don't know anything about the course the ship was being steered."

Before adjourning until 9:30 that same morning, Harry Clements took the stand and said, "I was born at Hamburg. Am 22 years of age and have been six years at sea, I was at the wheel from 10 o'clock till midnight. The ship was being steered west by south, but the course was frequently changed while I was at the wheel. The captain ordered the course to be changed. We had clear weather after passing Newfoundland. I saw the captain taking observations on Wednesday morning and at noon. I went on deck at 2:45 the morning the steamer struck. The first thing we (the look party) did was to get the boats ready for lowering.

"We hoisted the jibs and hauled them down again. I landed in the starboard lifeboat, I was in charge of her at first, but afterwards the second mate took charge. We remained by the ship until she sank. The steward had the lady passenger in his arms when I saw her. This was when the ship was sinking. They were on the Jacob's ladder, I endeavoured to put my boat alongside the ship, but the second mate, having jumped off the ship's rail into the boat, caused her to sheer off, and before we could get to the ship again the sea had washed the lady passenger overboard with the

17

steward. The latter lost his hold of her and then made for the ship again as the boat was too far astern to reach. When we could save no more we pulled for the land, landing at Walker's Cove. Before the ship struck I hauled the patent log and it read 723/4 and 9½ by the common log."

When the investigation resumed again, they called to the stand Charles White. He was a German who had shipped from London for this particular voyage. Upon taking the stand he said, "The night was very dark and rainy and about 2 o'clock the vessel struck. When I took the wheel the first mate told me to steer straight, as they wanted to run along the coast, and as no lights were visible he said we would have to be careful not to get on the rocks. I thought once or twice that the water looked as though we were near land, but as it was not my place to speak to the officers about it I said nothing. The second mate who was on the bridge with the lookout noticed breakers directly ahead and immediately gave the order to have the engines reversed which was done instantly. About five minutes after the engines were reversed the vessel struck."

Joseph Dicker who was a fireman aboard the *Cedar Grove* stated, "The shock threw me out of the berth, the whole crew then rushed on deck and willingly went to work at the captain's orders to get out the boats. In the life boats were placed provisions and water. The story about the men refusing duty is altogether untrue, every man did as he was told. The men speak highly of the strenuous efforts of the chief engineer in attempting to save the vessel. After the anchors had been let go, and it was found they did not hold, the jib and staysail were hoisted for the purpose of keeping her head off the breakers.

"They failed to do this and were accordingly hauled down. It was not long after this that she went down bow first. She sank forward to the lower foretopsail yard and her stern stuck out of the water. The starboard lifeboat had by the captain's orders been lowered about half an hour previous to this, and was lying alongside. When the vessel went down Miss Farrel was standing alone in the cabin door. The next seen of her was when the chief steward was holding her over the windward side ready to drop her into the starboard lifeboat. While there, a giant wave washed them both overboard, and the lady was seen no more by any of the survivors. The steward was washed back on deck where he was picked up by the third engineer, and they were both taken off by the port life boat. The men assert that the captain was on the quarter deck when the vessel went down."

18

According to John Walsh who was the fourteen year old cabin boy, "I was with Miss Farrel during most of the time the vessel kept afloat. She was quite cool and did not seem to be in terror. The captain came into the cabin and told her to remain in the ship and there would be no danger. Had it been supposed that the vessel was going down, the lady could easily have been put in one of the life boats; but the prevailing opinion among the men was that the safest place was on board the steamer. Indeed some who were in the boat climbed on deck again thinking they were safer there."

When William Brown the chief steward was called to the stand, he began his statement by saying, "The *Cedar Grove* under Captain Fritz left London bound for Halifax with a general cargo. She had a crew of twenty-nine; also two passengers, Miss Farrel and Mr. McAvity. On the morning of the 30th about three o'clock, she struck between Cape Canso and White Head. The night was very dark and the breakers rolled over the vessel. The captain gave orders to have the boats ready and about two hours after striking the crew took to the boat with the exception of the captain, Miss Farrel, Sheppard, and myself. The first officer was washed overboard and was picked up by one of the boats. The boats remained alongside attempting to rescue those on board, but found it impossible from the high sea to get alongside.

"The steamer began settling down, and I attempted to save Miss Farrel and held her over the steamer's side for a quarter of an hour waiting for one of the boats. The sea was continually washing over us. The sea at last washed Miss Farrel from my arms and I went overboard but was washed on deck again. I did not see her again. The captain at this time could not be seen and must have been washed overboard, when the steamer settled down. I saw him last in the chart room examining some papers. The third engineer and I were holding onto the stern when the first officer's boat passed underneath. We both dropped and I fell into the boat and the engineer into the water. When he was rescued, we then pulled for sea and in about an hour were picked up by the schooner *Parole* of Saint John. Neither of the other boats were then in sight, we having lost sight of them before leaving the vessel. Shortly afterwards we saw a steamer and hailed her. She passed under the schooner's stern and crossed her bow, and while the schooner was in the act of luffing, the steamer struck her. All hands then took to the boats and got on board the steamer *Liddesdale* and landed at North Sydney.

"After the vessel struck, the captain asserted the compasses were out of order. The captain did not wish Miss Farrel to be placed in the boats at first as he thought she would freeze, and kept her wrapped up in the pilot house watching for a favorable opportunity to take her off."

When the mate took the stand, he gave his brief statement saying, "The captain and I were standing on the starboard side of the chart room when the captain sent me forward to let go the anchor, when the bow of the steamer went down, so went the lady and the captain. I managed to get into the boat with the crew but nothing was seen of the captain or the lady anymore. There was little or nothing floating to which they may have clung to until rescued."

The last to take the stand in conclusion of the evidence to be given was William Carey who said, "I am a fireman aged 24 of Southampton. Been following the sea for five years. I came off the fires at midnight and was asleep when the ship struck. I went on deck and remained there about half an hour assisting in getting out the boats ready for lowering. I then went below and put my clothes on. I returned to the upper deck and helped to provision the port life boat. It was blowing fresh with rain and mist. After this the second engineer came on deck and ordered all the firemen below. We then fired up for steam, as it had run down.

"I heard the gong strike several times at one time the engines were going ahead and at another astern. I then assisted to get the sluices clear to pump out the fore hold. I was in the engine room when the ship took a heavy lurch to port and slid to leeward. At this time the chief engineer called all hands up as the ship was sinking. Upon reaching the deck, I found the water up to the engine room hatches. Mr. McAvity, Mr. Pavey and I jumped overboard into the boat. I saw nothing further of Pavey after that. We landed in the cove at Andrew's Island."

When the trial was over and all the evidence weighed, it was evident that Captain Fritz had done his utmost to try to save his ship and those aboard it, at the loss of his own life. Mr. McAvity was praised for his valuable assistance; his past experience as second mate of the brigantine *A.L. Palmer* proved most valuable in the time of crisis. He had left his ship in London and had taken passage aboard the *Cedar Grove* for Saint John. The steamer was insured for $137,000 and it was learned later that a reward was offered for the recovery of Miss Farrel, who was a cousin of Mr. W.H. Farrel of Saint John. She had been on her way to visit him.

—S.S. DANIEL STEINMAN—

Slowly the coach pulled away from the jetty and headed overland away from the sea under a blanket of mist. As the horsedrawn coach twisted its way north in the direction of Halifax, the small village of Sambro faded into obscurity. Captain Schoonhovan peered through the open window, unaware of anything around him. He listened to the sounds of heavy waves crashing against the large granite cliffs, leading to the water's edge, until he could hear them no more.

Now there was nothing, except the sound of hoofs and the grinding of wooden wheels, as they pitched and rolled over the rough road ahead. All around him the landscape was shrouded in grey, darkened by the black spruce and tall fir trees towering above him. Within the confines of the coach, Captain Schoonhoven sought refuge from the sounds of human cries, echoing within his mind. He placed his head in his hands and closed his eyes, in the hope that sleep would come. But for him it would only be torment under the constant questioning of the reporter, who ventured to Halifax with him.

"Can you tell me, sir, what actually took place before the wreck occurred?" asked the reporter.

For the moment there was no reply. Captain Schoonhoven just sat there motionless. His face bore the marks of a shattered man of forty years. He was a mild mannered man with a fair complexion and of slight build. For twenty-four years he had been in command of a vessel, and for the first three years at sea he had been first mate. He never as much as had an accident until he entered the waters off Nova Scotia, and now he had lost his ship along with most of the passengers and crew. Again the piercing sound of the reporter's voice resounded in Captain Schoonhoven's ear, "Sir! Are you all right?"

Captain Schoonhoven raised his eyes and looked straight at the young reporter and replied, "Are you addressing me, young man?"

"Yes, sir, I was wondering if you could tell me your version of what took place?"

"You can learn all about if from the papers which I will

21

submit to the agency of this shipping line."

"But if I could get it first hand from you, then I can print the real facts and my editor would be very grateful."

For a few moments there was complete silence, except for the sound of hoofs and the occasional shout from the coachman. The captain straightened up in his seat and rested his back against the padded seat. He looked directly at the eager young reporter and said in a low voice, "Very well, if you insist on knowing the facts as they happened. Then I will tell you what you want to know, since this will be a long and tiring trip to the city."

"Could you begin from the day you set sail?" asked the reporter, as he removed a note book and pencil from his pocket.

So began the captain, recalling the past, "For several days we encountered bad weather. It was rough and foggy. I was on the bridge all Tuesday and Wednesday night. On the eve of Thursday a heavy blanket of fog enshrouded the ship, with occasional bursts of rain. The sea rolled heavily with flashes of lightning dancing about and by 6 o'clock what I thought to be Chebucto Light lay dead ahead. I bore west half degree south by the compass. I judged the light to be ten miles distant and then steamed ahead dead slow, steering west quarter degree south and taking soundings every hour. At twenty minutes past nine I saw through the mist a faint light, located two points on the starboard bow. It flashed at intervals. Still thinking it was Chebucto Head light, I kept the ship on her course accordingly, the soundings giving thirty fathoms. Between ten and twenty minutes later, I discovered that it was the fixed light at Sambro.

"It appeared clear and at the same time I made out a faint glimmer which I took to be Chebucto Light about four points on our starboard bow. The soundings then given was twenty-six fathoms and I was going dead slow when the steamer struck lightly, At that moment, the whistle sounded for the first time and I ordered the helm hard-a-port.

"A moment or so later she struck very heavily and refused to answer helm. The rudder and propeller were destroyed or carried away by the impact. By now all the passengers were on deck and I ordered the crew up. I told the first and second mate to launch the life boats and to get the women and children in them.

"After the ship struck the scond time, she drifted off into deep water and I ordered the anchor to be let go. We maintained proper order among the passengers and crew and the work went well. While all this was taking place, breakers were visible all around us. The anchor soon let go in twenty-six fathoms of water,

22

and the ship continued to drift.

"I then rushed down from the bridge to see if the chain cable had parted. Most of the passengers and crew had gone aft or were in the life boats. Without warning a tremendous wave broke over the ship and washed away scores of passengers. The vessel gave a violent lurch and like a heavy rock went to the bottom. I judged the time then to be about ten o'clock. I managed to grab hold of the rigging, but she sank so fast that I let go and rose to the surface. Finally I got on the yard arm which was above water. I had not been there long when a man swam up to the yard and he was also saved.

"He proved to be one of the passengers, a young man by the name of Saco Nikolo who was bound for New York. While we sat on the rigging, I removed my coat, vest, and boots in order that, if the worst came, I would be prepared to swim to the shore. But the masts held and we remained in our perilous position for seven hours, until rescued by the heroic Mr. Gilkie who came for us in one óf our own boats. Up to that time I had not been aware that anybody except myself and the passenger I rescued had been saved.

"I was very surprised to find these men here when we landed. I cannot account for how I managed to get so out of my course except on the following grounds: we had had foggy weather for several days previous to the accident, on the last two of which I had been unable to take any observations whatever; added to this there must have been an exceedingly strong easterly current and my compass must have been subject to some attraction. The passengers were all families with from four to six children, seventeen of whom were to land at Halifax. No one of any family was saved. While we were on the yard we did not observe any bodies floating past. I think the vessel has the projections of some ledge protruding through her at about her center. This keeps her in a steady position, as she sits on an even keel, the masts being perfectly upright.

"I do not think anything will happen to the freight, nor will the vessel break up unless a very strong easterly storm occurs. The facts which I have placed before you are correct. My log papers, etc., all went to the bottom with the ship."

With pen still in hand, the reporter waited for more information concerning the wreck of the *S.S. Daniel Steinman,* but Captain Schoonhoven remained silent. He sat back in a relaxed position with both eyes closed. He seemed as if a burden had been lifted from his shoulders. Now that the city of Halifax was in sight, the reporter knew it was pointless to continue questioning the captain. As far as he was concerned, he had a first hand report of what had taken place.

23

The following morning on April 7, 1884, the *Morning Herald* carried this headline: "UPWARDS OF 120 LIVES LOST, ONE OF THE WORST DISASTERS ON OUR COAST."

The people of Halifax were horrified by this and they demanded that the captain be brought before a formal inquest. But because this was a foreign ship with a foreign captain, there was nothing that could be done regarding an inquiry. A further protest was raised against the White Cross Lines who were the agents for this ship, but they could do nothing. The public was told that should there be no investigation into the conduct of the captain, then the facts could be elicited at an inquest with a coroner and a jury.

Because of the 120 lives that had been lost, the human cry was so great that pressure was brought against the government to see that an inquest be held. With Captain Schoonhoven in custody, an inquiry was set up under the proper authorities and so began the long process of trying to reach the right conclusion as to what actually had taken place aboard the *S.S. Daniel Steinman*.

The first witness to be sworn in and take the stand was Fred Keyworth of the Royal Artillery Signalmen who was stationed on Sambro Island. He gave his account of what he saw:

"I was on duty that Thursday night. At 9:30 I sighted a steamer from the look-out-house. She was about six miles from the lighthouse and making straight for the island from south-west. It had been foggy during the day and the whistle continually sounded, but toward night it began to clear up, and at that time it was so clear that I could see Chebucto Light.

"The whistle then ceased to sound, even though it was a little misty. There was quite a breeze with a heavy swell as the wind increased. I distinctly saw the port and mast head light of the steamer and at a quarter to ten she stopped. A few minutes later she continued on her course, straight for the light-house. I called attention to her position and got the engineer to start the whistle to warn her of her danger. The whistle started in three minutes. She was then about three miles off. I saw her stop and again go ahead at apparently full speed, going perhaps three quarters of a mile. Then she stopped again. She again moved slowly ahead and all at once came to a sudden stop, when about half a mile from the light-house. She then drifted back and appeared to strike again. Signals of distress were then hoisted. The steamer drifted toward the lighthouse and sank about half past ten within about 300 yards of the island.

"I could distinctly hear screams of women and children and

men calling for help, but we could do nothing. We had no life boats here, nor a boat of any kind except a small flat boat. Had there been a life boat there we could have launched it without difficulty and doubtless could have saved many lives, if not all on board. Later I assisted the life boat with the survivors and guided them around the island to a safe landing place. At daylight the following morning I put off with the others in the ship's lifeboat, in which the survivors had landed, and rescued the captain and passengers from the rigging."

The lighthouse keeper's report was presented to the court and it went as follows:

"April 3rd foggy, wind S.E., whistle going from 9:00 a.m. to 8:45 p.m. When it cleared up, we could see Chebucto Head and Devil's Island light. When one of the signal men saw a steamer approaching within dangerous proximity, although it was still clear enough to see the other light, we started the whistle and kept it going until 2:15 next a.m.

"The whistle was sounded as a warning and the ship was about one mile south by east of light."

Following the report which was examined by those presiding at the inquiry, a Mr. Florentine Von Geissel was asked to take the stand and give his account of what had taken place aboard the steamer. He apparently was the man on the lookout and, at the time of the wreck, had been at sea for fifteen years. He had been involved in several wrecks and the last aboard the *Maderin,* while enroute to Antwerp from Buenos Aires. He, along with three others, survived. While three hundred went down with the ship, he again escaped to tell his story:

"I was on the lookout at nine o'clock Thursday night. It was foggy, with rain, lightning, and a fair breeze. Previous to this the captain had been aloft himself to look at the light. He would not trust anyone else to go aloft on the mission. We were going slow when I saw the light a quarter of an hour after going on watch and reported it to the captain and the second mate. They said they had seen it and thought it was a revolving light.

"At 9:00 a.m. I threw the lead. It was 26 fathoms and immediately after I heard the fog whistle. We were going slow at the time when the ship struck lightly. We had stopped several times previously to this, and the captain was afraid to go ahead. When he heard the whistle, he shouted that we were in the wrong place and should get out. Fifteen minutes after the first striking, the ship again struck heavily, but soon floated off again. Then the captain called out to us not to get excited but to get the boats ready

25

and call up all hands.

"She struck a third time when we lost the rudder and broke the propeller. We then dropped anchor and at that moment the captain, doctor, and chief engineer were on the bridge. The boats were made ready just in case, even though they had not been used for quite sometime. In the darkness, excitment and terror sounded throughout the ship and slow progress was made. People were crowding around the boats and it was impossible to do much in the way of rescue.

"Just as we let go the anchor, the ship struck heavily amidships. All hands ran aft and many were swept off by a big wave, a number of people were in the life boat on the port side and nobody seemed to be in the other three boats. I ran to the second boat on the port side which was the jolly boat and jumped into it with Otto Crausse, a seaman. As the ship was sinking, we cut the painter with an axe and let her drop into the sea. We quickly pulled away from the sinking ship in order to get out of the suction. While we were doing this, a man who was a passenger jumped from the bridge into the boat head first.

"All this occurred within a short time before the ship went down. Only one davitt on all the life boats had been cut, and this life boat was full of people mostly made up of sailors who went down with the ship. As she sank, the boatswain, a boy, and a fireman leaped from the stern of a life boat into our boat.

"We managed to get out of the suction while most of the passengers and crew were struggling for their lives. Many of them made a grab for our oars but we beat them off. One man caught hold of the boat and we tried to get him on board, but two or three others were holding onto his legs. We had not choice but to let him go and he went under the water to get clear of the others. The next time he surfaced we got hold of him and helped him into the boat. He was an Italian passenger.

"I could hear the people in the water calling out to me by name to come and save them. There were twelve or so, hanging onto a spar, and I kept clear of them. Had we attempted to save them or the others who appealed to us, they would have swamped the boat and we would have all been lost. Those in the boat wanted to try and land on the rocks, but I was in charge and refused landing, knowing that to do so would be certain death. We could see the people on the island making signals to us with the use of fires and colored lamps. We were within 400 yards of the island all this time and could hear shouts but could not understand. However we followed the beacon lights and after three hours of battling waves, surf, and breakers, we rowed safely around

26

the island two miles to a little cove, where we landed and were taken care of.

"I don't think any bodies will be found in the ship, as everybody so far as I know was on deck, except the chief engineer. He ran down to the engine room to put on full steam just before the ship sank. I think the captain did his best under the circumstances. But few are equal to such terrible occasions. It is difficult to measure time under such conditions, but after mature consideration, I should say that it was fully an hour and a half from the time the ship first got on the rocks until she sank.

"During most of that time chaos, which no one could describe, reigned supreme. It is true our boat would have held thirty people or more. But it was half full of water after we got in it, for it had a hole in the bottom. It kept most of us bailing with hats and boots. Yes, perhaps fiteen could have been saved in its condition, but it was every man for himself, and any attempt to save others simply imperiled ourselves."

The next to take the stand was the boatwain by the name of Fritz Nich:

"The weather was bad on Wednesday and Thursday and I went on duty at eight o'clock Thursday night. It was foggy, blowing heavily, with rain and snow. About nine the rain held up, and it looked as though it was going to clear. The captain had been on the bridge two days and two nights. I saw the second mate take soundings at nine o'clock. He reported 35 fathoms, half or three quarters of an hour later he threw the lead and reported 26 fathoms. Just then I heard the fog whistle. After the first soundings were taken I saw the captain go aloft to see if he could make out the light. When he came down he ordered the mate to throw the lead immediately. That was the second time, and just as the lead was being hauled in, the ship struck lightly. The ship at this time was going dead slow. I was in the act of calling the first mate when the ship struck. All the passengers were below at that time, but they soon rushed on deck. The first mate ordered the boats to be got ready. Within fifteen minutes after the ship first struck, she struck the second time with great force and it became unmanageable. I then rushed to the bow to help get out the port anchor.

"All the crew had been called up after the ship struck the first time and were now on deck, and with the passengers at or near the boats, I was helping to get out the anchor. From the time she first struck, up to the time of throwing the anchor, I had been working at the first life boat on the port side. While the anchor was

27

running out, the ship struck violently the third time, and almost immediately afterwards went down. As soon as I left the anchor, I rushed back to the life boat and got in at the stern. Just at that moment a heavy wave swept over the ship. A number of the people jumped into the boat at the same moment. The ropes at the bow had been cut, but not those at the stern, with the result that the life boat went down bow first with the ship. As she went down I sprang out of her stern and into the jolly boat. I didn't know anything about the boats on the starboard side. When I called the first mate, I noticed that he put on his gold watch and a big ring on his finger. These had been presented to him at his marriage six months ago. But when his body was brought ashore on the island by the fishermen, they were both missing. I remember seeing the doctor and chief steward on the bridge as the ship went down. There was great excitment on the ship after she struck, as passengers and crew alike were shouting, crying, swearing and praying. In the confusion and excitement that prevailed, it is impossible for me even to form an idea of the time that elapsed between when the ship first struck and when she sank. I had worked on the *Daniel Stienman* for 18 months and I regard Captain Schoonhoven as a capable and thorough seaman."

Most of the passengers aboard the ship were of foreign tongue and could speak no English and those who could, did so in very broken English. It was therefore difficult to get an accurate story. With all the officers lost, except the captain, it was of course impossible to obtain any official authoritative report in corroboration of the captain's story. In order for the court to reach some kind of conclusion as to what actually had happened, it was necessary for them to ask some of the passengers to take the stand and give their story as best they could. The first of the passengers to take the stand and give his side of the story was Eischen Picolois from Luxembourg who had been on his way to visit in Chicago:

"I was in bed with my cousin, a young man of 23 who was coming with me. We were going to friends in Chicago. We were between decks, as all the passengers were then. The women and children were there, too, mostly in bed. When the ship first struck, a number of passengers got out of bed and went on deck. They didn't then know that there was danger. I put on my pants, and also went on deck. My cousin went to the baggage room to get some papers of value, and that was the last I saw of him. Between the time the ship first struck and the time she went down, the passengers were rushing round on deck in the greatest confusion.

28

After the ship struck the second time, I saw a man putting his wife and five children into a boat on the starboard side. I don't know what became of them! I went on the hurricane deck and watched two men cutting the jolly boat adrift as the ship was sinking. When she got properly in the water, I jumped into her and was saved."

Johanna Niedermann, aged 26, from Bavaria bound for New York took the stand and began his side of the story:

"I was in bed when she struck, as were most of the other passengers. I heard the ship strike the first time, but didn't get up. Two friends were sleeping with me. Most of the passengers were below when the vessel struck the second time, some asleep, while others were talking and telling stories.

"The second shock was not a very violent one. I judge that fully half the passengers were still in bed then. But I got up and dressed and rushed on deck. I left the others dressing. They were just then beginning to realize the danger. I went on the bridge. There were a number of passengers, including one women, and crew on the bridge when I got there. I was watching them getting a boat ready, and all of a sudden was carried off by a wave. Every one on the bridge was washed off at the same time. I was under water fully two minutes during which I got hold of the rigging and climbed up until I got above water. While I was under water I felt several people around me, one man caught hold of my leg but I kicked him off. I got on the foremast yard and found that the captain was on the mast above me. He was the only man I saw. We stood there all night. We saw the fires and lights on the island 200 yards distant. Both the captain and I shouted until we were tired, but no help came until daylight. The captain and I had no conversation while we were together on the mast, because I couldn't talk Belgian and he couldn't speak German. But both of us suffered greatly from numbness and exhaustion."

A young Italian passenger bound for New York, gave his brief account of what he saw:

"I was in my bunk when the ship struck and immediately went on deck. There were other Italians below with me, and all Italians went on deck together. After she struck the second time, I pulled off my coat and sea boots and prepared to jump overboard and swim. I am a good swimmer. After she struck the second time, she soon filled with water, and I saw that she must soon sink. With the third shock I jumped overboard and swam around till I saw the jolly boat launched. Then as I made for it, several drowning men caught hold of me, but I kicked them off and finally got aboard."

From the testimonies given by the survivors, it was quite obvious that Captain Schoonhoven did everything in his power to avoid the loss of his ship and those aboard it. If anything, the government of Nova Scotia should have been held responsible for the lives that were lost. Had there been a number of life boats on Sambro Island, a large portion of those who were lost would have been saved.

Life boats in such a dangerous area as Sambro Island should have been an absolute necessity. A thorough investigation should have been held regarding the marine department as to why there were no life boats on the island at the time of the wreck. Later it was brought to the attention of the officials of the marine department that the soldiers on the island heard women crying in the water for an hour after the accident, but they had no boats to try to rescue them.

They did not have any rockets and the fog whistle was not much of a success, because seamen listening for it, often as not, could not hear the sound until they were on the rocks. When questioned further, it was learned that the men on the island did not fire the warning guns when they saw the ship stop and take their last sounding outside the first reef. If they had heard the guns, they could have backed off. Once all the facts were presented, it was clear that Captain Schoonhoven was not at fault and if anything he should have received a public apology for being so unjustly accused before the truth was known.

For those persons interested in the location of Sambro Island, it lies about twenty miles from Halifax, at the western entrance of the harbour. It is considered one of the most dangerous areas on the coast. The island itself is surrounded for a mile in all directions by shoals and rocks. A vessel landing upon them has very little hope of getting off. The *Daniel Steinman* first struck on the Broad Breakers and later landed on Mad Rock Shoal where she sank. She now lies in an upright position with her stern in 13 fathoms of water. The two fore topsail yards were just above the water and part of the main top mast was visible as well as the peak of the fore gaff.

Fishermen in the area by the names of James Rogers, Alex Young of Sandy Cove, John Myatt of Ketch Harbour, Andrew Twohig, James Twohig, both of Pennant, brought thirteen bodies ashore from the scene of the wreck. Of the approximate 120 lives lost, only these thirteen bodies were found. The bodies retrieved were as follows: the chief officer, the lamp trimmer, two sailors and nine passenger.

When the bodies were brought ashore their faces were

disfigured almost beyond recognition from contact with the rocks. They were placed in boat houses, covered with canvas, and later buried on shore near where the ship went down. Among the articles found on the bodies were: a pipe and pen holder, a purse with 27 francs in gold, silver, and small coppers, a silver open faced watch and brass chain, a steel key, pocket knife, medicine vial, and a blonde memoranda book with a ticket from Amsterdam to New York in the name of August Richter, 37 years, a notice from Dusseldorf and Prussia, also a lottery ticket no. 45241 of the Royal Saacheische Landes Lottery, dated Leipzig July 4, 1883, were also found.

—VALENTINE—

Early one October Monday morning in the year 1884, wreckage from a vessel was discovered floating upon the water near an island at Bull Rock. The rock is located just off Cape Breton at a place known as Gabarus. Apparently the people of this area were expecting a vessel which was due to visit their port on Saturday night. That evening the weather was clear with a bright moon overhead, and there was absolutely no storm in sight.

The men of Gabarus were both puzzled and concerned. They had no idea as to what kind of vessel met its doom so close to their shore, and there were no bodies to be found. While walking along the shore close to his home, a man by the name of Henry Cann picked up a name plate with the inscription *Valentine*. He took the plate back to the authorities and they traced the vessel to its place of origin and found her to be the vessel which was due in at Gabarus.

The *Valentine* was under the command of John Ormiston, with a crew of two, consisting of John Gillis, twenty-one years of age, and Philip Cann, also twenty-one years of age. The ironic part of this tragedy is that Henry Cann, who picked up the name plate, later learned that his brother Philip was part of the crew of this mystery vessel, and now he was lost.

Today in a small, United Church cemetery in Gabarus, surrounded by an iron rail fence, is a monument with the inscription: 'In memory of John Ormiston, born at Edinburgh,

31

Scotland,
February 17th. 1813.   Lost at sea October 11th. 1884.'
Not far away are two stones bearing similar inscriptions.
The story of how this vessel was wrecked remains a mystery to this
day.

—MELMERBY—

On October 1, 1890, the Barque *Melmerby* had sailed from
Quebec for   Greenock, Scotland, with a cargo of Canadian white
pine above and below deck, with a full complement of twenty-one
hands.   She was a barque of four hundred tons and was mastered
by Captain Olsen.   She was owned by John Ross and Company of
Quebec and built in Liverpool, England.   The barque had sailed
the north Atlantic between the old and new world for twenty-six
years until her last voyage.   Misfortune followed the *Melmerby*
from the moment she left Quebec.   Not far down the St. Lawrence
River, a young English seaman, by the name of David Evans of
Liverpool, fell from the mizzen mast to the deck and sustained a
dislocated arm and head wounds.   Five days out in th Gulf, a heavy
gale of wind pounded the barque severely enough to open the
seams and force the crew to man the pumps.   The *Melmerby* was in
danger of foundering when the order was given to the mate,
Richard Carew, to jettison the deck load of timber.   When the deck
lashings were cut, the strong wind and high seas rolled the barque
sufficiently to cause the timbers on the deck and cargo to move
violently and smashed three of the *Melmerby's* four life boats.   The
deck house was also smashed by the threshing timbers and then
washed overboard taking most of the barque's provisions with it.
Seven days out of port, the barque was in distress, but when a
Norwegian vessel saw her and offered assistance, Captain Olsen
refused, declaring he would make Sydney.   The eighth day, a
schooner, the *Mary* from Prince Edward Island, recorded seeing
the *Melmerby's*   plight and stood by her.   The captain of the
schooner was Captain Boudrot and he advised Captain Olsen to
set a course for Port Hawkesbury.   She kept on course for Pictou
making slow headway.   On Saturday, October 11, a violent storm
arose and the schooner soon lost contact and, for her own safety,
she had to run before the wind for Pictou.   Saturday night the
32

Melmerby's three masts went overboard and the stricken barque's decks were awash and she no longer answered her helm. Early Sunday afternoon on October 12th she struck broadside in view of a half dozen farmers on shore, who had watched her drifting landwards for several hours.

Minutes after she struck, Captain Olsen gave the order to abandon the barque. The one remaining boat was put over the side and sixteen men crowded into her, including the master and mate. Almost at once the boat capsized and fifteen men drowned, among them the captain and the mate. Only one of the sixteen reached shore safely by clinging to the overturned boat. There were six men still on board the Melmerby, one of them the injured David Evans unable to do anything to help himself. Through the rest of Sunday afternoon and through the night the wind blew with a gale force and the barque began to break up. Monday the gale continued and by this time word of the wreck had spread from the country to the Pictou County towns. Hundreds of men on foot, horseback, and in carriages converged on the beach. They watched until darkness fell. Monday evening two of the men decided to swim ashore, Samuel Cook and James Fletcher, both strong swimmers. They rode out the waves to where the breakers were pounding and where a human chain was made by residents. Strengthened by the gathering crowd from New Glasgow and other towns, the rescuers pulled them from the water. By October 14th the waves still pounded the wreck and the barque was now nearly broken in two and timbers from the cargo were floating ashore mixed with planks from the barque's hull. Men from the schooner *Mary* heard of the wreck when they put into Pictou harbour and they joined the men from Pictou who crossed the harbour by rowboat and went the remaining ten miles overland to the wreck on foot. With this group was a young man, Alphonse Boudrot, the son of Captain Boudrot, who had left the schooner *Mary* to help pilot the *Melmerby*. More than a mile from the beach opposite the wreck, the lifeboat which had capsized and had washed ashore was found still intact and needing only minor repairs to a small hole in the bottom. Young Boudrot asked for volunteers from the crowd to man the boat with him to attempt to save the four men on the wreck, one of whom he had learned from the survivors was his father. Five Pictou county men agreed to go with young Boudrot. From the bow a dentist, by the name of Dr. McLean, placed oil ahead of the boat to smooth the sea and a veteran master mariner, Captain Peter Graham, steered in the stern. With Boudrot pulling on the oars was David Fraser, a machine shop foreman, Watkins Williams, a deck hand from a steamer ferry in Pictou Harbour and a fisherman-farmer from Big Island of Merigomish, James McGlashen. The small boat reached the *Melmerby's* side and sheltered in her lee, took aboard first the injured man, who was lowered by the others. Then the other three jumped in, one of them being Captain Boudrot who was reunited with his son. The return trip was relatively easy along the oil path until the little boat, with ten aboard, got into the breakers and again the human chain pulled them all to safety one by one. Twenty-one men had sailed from Quebec aboard the luckless barque and of that number only six were now alive two weeks after leaving Greenock. A seventh man was spared, Captain Boudrot, who piloted the barque. It has been many years since the barque washed ashore on the beach in the little harbour on the north shore of Nova Scotia near New Glasgow. That is how Melmerby Beach acquired its name.

—MARY JANE—

West of Tatamagouche Bay is a small Basin which at one time might have been called Malagash Bay by the farmers living in that area. Today the countryside around Malagash remains much as it was a hundred years ago, except for a slight increase in population and development. A passerby would look the area over and marvel at its beauty. Should he take but a few moments to visit a lonely cemetery which rises up from the sea at McNab point, there can be found a special marker. If the tombstone could speak, it would reveal to the listener the life story of an orphan boy, whose life was one of adventure upon the high seas.

During the late 1800's, a farmer by the name of Welwood MacNab (McNab) had taken under his wing a young boy by the name of Danny Gerrard. He and his wife raised the orphan boy as their own. They watched as he played about in the fields and were grateful for his help on the farm in later years. But in his youth he would always go down to the sea and watch the vessels sailing to and from the bay.

He enjoyed many hours as a lad of ten years playing in his father's dory. He rigged a make-shift sail and with the oar as a tiller, he sailed around the Basin. As he grew older, he ventured

34

out into the bay in all kinds of weather, where he soon learned to handle himself on the water. He would make sure his work was done at home, around the barn and the wood shed and what ever his foster father needed, which he would do without question.

Although the farm was his home and he loved his foster parents, there was always that one challenge which lured him away; the sea would reach out for him. His love for the water grew very strong and while working in the fields he would raise his head and gaze upon the passing vessel and yearn to be aboard her. He would often question his father on the different kinds of vessels and how much they would weigh and where woudl they sail to and from. Being a farmer Mr. MacNab could not answer all Danny's questions, he tried to persuade Danny to concentrate on the farm and forget his wild ideas of the sea, as that life was not for him. As fate would have it, Danny tired of the farm and of school. He only wanted to be near his first love so he ran away from hom at an early age and signed on a vessel bound for Saint John, New Brunswick. His first taste aboard a large vessel only helped to wet his appetite for more adventure and he soon joined a ship bound for England.

Upon his return to Nova Scotia, he went back to the farm to visit his parents. They were more than happy to see him and forgave him for running away. They knew he would never be happy working on the farm and that it would only be a matter of time before he was gone again, which later proved to be true. He bade them farewell and once more took to the sea, and this time he was gone eight years.

He travelled to various parts of the world and made the dangerous Cape Horn. He sailed up the west coast of North America and followed the south seas to Australia, than westward to India. During the eight years of travelling he returned home after each trip and visited with his parents. He told them many tales of the sea and how people lived in other parts of the world. His father offered him a farm of his own in order to persuade him to stay at home, but after much pondering Danny could not accept for he loved the sea too much to give it up. He could see that his father because of his Scottish heritage was a prosperous farmer. To Danny the land was only an anchor to hold him down and in order to keep peace with his parents he had to compromise. He let his father know how he felt about the idea and of his inner feelings,

"Father! I don't need a farm. Truly I appreciate your offer but I'd be a failure on a farm. You've always been so good to me and so has mother, more than most parents are to their own flesh and blood. I don't want to sound ungrateful for what you have done for me, but the sea is my life. If I could get me a schooner, I'd stay here and work. That way I could be home; that is close to home and not very far away. When the freeze came I'd be home 'til spring with the both of you."

It was plain to his father that Danny would never be a farmer and the only way to keep him close to home was to buy him a schooner.

"Very well, Danny, we'll get ya a schooner."

They both knew that because of the compromise a new life had opened for them creating a tie which would not be broken. Both he and his father searched the coast for a schooner that would carry a hundred tons or more, but at that time in 1890 when coastal trading flourished, it was hard to find a vessel. After a great deal of searching, they found a schooner called the *Mary Jane*. She was an old schooner but with beautiful lines and water tight and her planking was sound. Mr. MacNab paid the price of $1,000 for the schooner and Danny's day of true happiness had come to pass. He was now master of his own schooner and quickly located two men to work as crew on the *Mary Jane*. It was not long before he was sailing and he often took his father with him. The schooner was registered for 55 tons but could carry twice that amount. Under the watchful eye of Danny, the schooner earned back the $1,000 and showed a profit. Just when things were going so well for him at the age of twenty-four, lady luck left him. He was carrying a load of coal from Pictou to Miramichi, New Brunswick. The weight of cargo was around 120 tons. Then the weather turned cloudy. He had cleared Pictou Harbour and was headed into the Strait. It was October 5th and there was nothing to distinguish this trip from any other. He had sailed along the north shore of Malagash many times before and as usual the people watched as he passed by. That night the wind was light and off the land and on noon of the 6th, 1890, with all her sails set to catch the wind, she passed Cape Tormentine and a few hours of sailing would put her at her place of destination. Suddenly there was a change of wind. It died down and became very still. Danny knew what was in store for him as the wind shifted from a gentle off shore breeze to an on shore squall which would create hurricane winds. Soon it was more than the old sails could stand and it was not long before they went to pieces. Without her sails the schooner was useless and Danny with the other two men, Steve Clarke and Frank Seaman, dropped both anchors. The force of wind was too strong and the anchors dragged. She was now heading inward with the sea sweeping over her decks. The schooner began to drift much faster towards an ugly reef. They were now a short distance from Cape Tormentine when the schooner lurched and struck with a heavy crunching noise. She lifted and struck again, tearing away the bottom of the hull on the jagged rocks. The three of them tried to save their lives by climbing onto the rigging and lashing themselves to it in hopes of riding out the storm. Through the pouring rain and high winds, the people on shore could see their helpless state. Men volunteered to help at the risk of losing their own lives, but there was no boat in the area available and when one did arrive it was too late. The spars of the schooner broke and carried with them the shrouds to which the three had clung. All three drowned under the watchful eyes of those on shore and the dream of an orphan boy had ended.

—OTTAWA—

Christened in January of 1891, the *Ottawa* slipped into the water all new, sleek and shiny. She bore the marks of a well built steamer, Alex Stephen and Son of Linthouse, Glasgow. The steamer was designed for the trade between London and Nova Scotia. She was made of mild steel, at a length of 285 ft., width 35 ft. and a depth of 24 ft. She was schooner rigged and registered in at 1,145 tons. When not in full sail, the steamer was propelled by 25 horse power engines. The steamer at that time was valued at $165,000.

Under a proud new captain and a crew of 26, the *Ottawa* set her course for the new world. Her destination was the port of Saint John, New Brunswick, with 300 tons of general cargo. The voyage across the Atlantic was fairly good, with everything going well for the newly built steamer. Until she neared the waters off the coast of Nova Scotia it seemed as if she would live a long and prosperous life. During this time of year, the weather along the coast had a habit of changing without warning. Caught in unusual weather, the *Ottawa* drifted off her course. The captain thought he was going in the general direction of New Brunswick but was, in fact, heading directly for the dreaded Blonde Rock.

It came as a great shock to everyone on board the steamer, when on the 1st of November, 1891, she struck heavily on the great rock. Rising high out of the water, the steamer lurched and then slid back into the water. Her bow was caught in the grip of this large rock and unable to move, and she began to fill with water.

The captain was stunned, for he was in what seemed to be the middle of the ocean with no land in sight. His vessel was doomed. He knew by the way she hit the rock that it was only a matter of time before she would sink. The captain and crew knew that it was hopless and made ready with the life-boats. Under the guidence of the captain, everyone got into the boats and pulled away from the *Ottawa*. They watched as she slowly sank into deeper water, until she was no more. Once the weather cleared, the men sighted Seal Island, a small speck upon the horizon.

In their efforts to reach the island in heavy seas, one of the lifeboats overturned. Mrs. Lindsay, the stewardess, and three men found themselves in difficulty. Because of the rough water and strong tides the other boat had a hard time trying to reach those in the water. Two of the men managed to swim through the cold water in the direction of the other boat. They reached the boat and were pulled to safety, but by the time they could reach the stewardess and the man, who were caught under the boat, Mrs. Lindsay had died. The man was barely alive when they got to him.

Somewhere near Blonde Rock lies the watery grave of the *Ottawa* once owned by Christopher Furness.

—HILDA MAUDE—

The *Hilda Maude* was a schooner of thirty-seven tons register and sailed out of Lunenburg on the 18th of October, 1891. She sailed to the fishing grounds and filled her holds to capacity with six hundred and fifty quintals of fish. Returning with her catch of fish, she unloaded and engaged herself in the fall fishing on the banks off Ingonish. Needing more salt, she sailed for Sydney in the black of night.

When she reached the entrance to Sydney Harbour, she could not make it in due to the weather. She was then compelled to anchor in four fathoms of water off Cranberry Head. At eight o'clock the weather became worse and she lowered her two anchors and rode head into the storm, with forty fathoms of chain. The
38

crew worked all night and were drenched by the waves that broke clean over them from time to time. The *Hilda Maude* plunged, rolled, and pulled at her anchors until the chains gave way around five in the morning. She drifted for about half a mile close to Black Point, where she fetched up in shallow water. It was lucky for the schooner and all on board that she hit sandy bottom and not rock. All the crew could do was to take to the rigging. The nine men went up the stays, which were ratlined, and lashed themselves fast.

When she finally went ashore, it was not far from the famous old Sydney mine and some of the miners lived near the beach. When news got around that a schooner was aground, they came out of their houses in the foggy, rainy, stormy morning and lined the beach.

There were approximately a hundred people watching the nine men of the *Hilda Maude* as they tried to send a line ashore by fastening it to a trawl buoy. The big twenty gallon cask, which keeps the baited trawl line afloat upon the restless sea, might have worked except for the backwash of huge breakers which kept the buoy from getting within reach of the men on shore. If the plan had worked, the men on shore could have gotten hold of the line and dragged the men off the wreck one by one to safety.

John Cox and three others made an effort to try to launch a boat in order to reach the men on the schooner. But the boat was a sharp-pointed whaler and the huge rollers were smashing and roaring on the shore. They tried to lower a boat and found it impossible to launch the boat without it filling with water. Again they tried and failed. It would be dangerous even to get a boat afloat in such breakers with so much recoil and backwash. The undertow created a problem in trying to keep her in trim and to row her.

Aboard the schooner Captain Thomas Selig asked if any of his men could swim. The man who answered was Rufus Parks of Parks Creek, which is located on the east bank of the La Have river near the mouth. Rufus was a young strong lad of twenty-two and weighed two hundred pounds, made up mostly of bone and muscle. He had been hardened by the daily labour of deep sea fishing and the task he was about to carry out required all his strength. He stripped to his drawers and gave his clothes to George Herman, the mate who stood beside him in the fore-rigging. He watched for a chance between the waves then ran along the windward rail and leaped over the stern into the sea. As his feet touched bottom, he fell forward on his face unconscious. His strength was gone and his strong frame helpless. Two men from shore rushed into the icy breakers and pulled him up on the beach. He was soon helped to a house nearby and given clothing, food, and drink. In about an hour he regained his normal strength and went back to the shore to see what he could do to help his friends aboard the schooner.

The sharp pointed whale boat was useless and the four trawling dories had been hammered and broken against the shore. Three were utterly useless upon examination, but the fourth was not so badly damaged. One of the long strakes was split and Parks quickly procured a hammer and nails. He took pieces of the broken dories and patched up the boat with them. A couple of men helped him to caulk the gaping side and made it somewhat water tight. Rufus asked if anyone would go off with him in the eighteen foot long dory, as it required two men to handle it. Not one man of the hundred would risk his life to help try to save those men who remained on the schooner. Rufus turned away and, with all his strength, tried to push the dory into the on-coming waves. A few men, feeling a little ashamed, helped him to launch the dory and run her out on the reflux of a wave and into the towering combers which threatened to overwhelm the dory and man together.

A dory is the staunchest thing a man has ever built to contend with wind and wave. It will outlive a storm in which schooners have foundered. It is to the fisherman what the horse is to the cowboy. Rufus had to do the work of two men in the roughest kind of weather. It was necessary to keep the dory down in the water to prevent it from capsizing. He brought it as close as he dared to the schooner, and the men on the rigging watched their chance and jumped into the dory. Jumping into dories was part of their fishing routine and practice makes a man perfect. The first to take the hazardous leap was Uriah Smith. He and Rufus rowed back swiftly to shore and Rufus returned again to the schooner.

He made three trips in all and brought off every man. The captain was the last man to leave the wreck. He was injured by a piece of the wreckage. It was about three hours from the time Rufus jumped into the sea until he had the last man on shore. For his bravery he received a silver watch, which cost the government of Canada thirty dollars. The reward was given because an M.P. for Lunenburg urged the Canadian Minister of Marine to do something for the brave deed enacted by Rufus Parks. The Royal Humane Society gave him a silver medal for having preserved the life of a citizen.

Peter Stuart

—PETER STUART—

The ship *Peter Stuart* under the command of Captain Henry Hughes sailed out of Saint John, New Brunswick. She was bound for Liverpool, England, with a cargo of deals. On July 8, 1892, the *Peter Stuart* was south west of Yarmouth when she ran into rough weather.

Captain Hughes, unaware of his position, tried his best to keep his ship on course. Unknowingly he was headed for the dreaded Gannet Rock. Under stress of high winds and heavy seas, the ship tossed and rolled, but moved slowly forward. From the wheel house it was impossible to see in any direction, as the sea broke over the deck with a tremendous force.

The man on watch at that time heard breakers crashing dead ahead and he immediately gave warning that shallow water was in front of them, which meant a dangerous shoal. Before Captain Hughes could alter course, the ship struck upon the rocks. On impact, the masts snapped and only the mizzen held together, to which the men clung, but it later broke. The men, except the ship's carpenter, jumped clear. His legs were broken in a fall and he fell from the ship into the raging sea.

People of many nationalities were aboard the ship: English, Swedish, French, Russian, Irish and Finnish. Despite the barrier of language, the passengers on board the ship had but one thought in mind and that was to survive as best they knew how. On this trip Captain Hughes had brought his wife and three year old daughter and, with them, a young English girl who was a friend of the family. The Captain and some of the crew attempted to launch a lifeboat for their safety. While his wife, daughter, and the English girl waited for the boat to be lowered over the side, all three, along with other passengers who were standing close by, were washed over the side by a large wave. Panic stricken, the Captain tried to rescue his family and the girl but, in the darkness, they could not be found. The sea around the ship was a mass of white waters and it was impossible to do anything to save them. They were gone.

By daybreak the fog lifted a little and those who were fortunate to get into one of the lifeboats drifted around the ship. They could see people clinging to some of the wreckage and they rowed to their rescue. While they were pulling them into the boat, the boat began to sink under the weight. When the load became too great, the high waves capsized the boat. All but two failed to reach the lifeboat again. Three more survivors died while struggling to keep one of the boats, whose gunwhales were under water, upright.

The people clinging to the lifeboat could see the large Gannet Rock jutting up some sixty feet out of the water like a great spear-head. The survivors rowed away from the wreck with all eyes upon the 1,447 ton iron ship as she pounded against the rocks. Out of the twenty-seven aboard the *Peter Stuart*, fifteen lost their lives.

—OWASCO—

Owasco, a three mastered schooner of 299 tons register, was built in Detroit, Michigan, and was skippered by Alonzo Carter. In the year 1892, during the month of June, the schooner sailed out of Philadelphia and set her course for the port ot Montreal with a cargo of 500 tons of coal.

During his trip up the eastern seaboard of the United States, Captain Carter enjoyed fine weather all the way. Towards the latter part of June, the *Owasco* experienced high winds which soon developed into a gale when she was off the coast of Nova Scotia. On June 30th late in the afternoon, a dense fog set in and the schooner drifted off her course.

Under such conditions the captain and the crew kept a watchful eye. They pitched and rolled under the heavy sea. The men could hear the crashing of waves, off in the distance and it was not long before they could hear the breakers roaring much closer. In order to avoid the rocks, the captain and the crew tried to turn the schooner about, but the strong undercurrent became too much for them.

By then it was too late. The schooner struck the rocks at 5:00 p.m. that afternoon. The rocks like so many jagged knives, ripped the bottom open and she filled with water. With the rising of the tide, the sea washed over her decks. In this predicament Captain Carter knew the schooner would not last long and he ordered a large yawl to be lowered over the side. He, along with six other men and a women stewardess, climbed into the yawl.

After a great deal of struggle in the raging water, they finally reached deep water and drifted about until the fog lifted. By 7:00 p.m. the fog lifted enough to enable them to see the lighthouse at Betty's Island. They made for the light and reached it within a short time. They stayed there until the following morning when they were taken to Prospect. A schooner from Weymouth took them from there to Halifax. From there the steamer *Olevette* took them to Boston and then on to Philadelphia.

As for the schooner, *Owasco,* she went to pieces within a half hour of hitting the rocks, near the same spot the steamer *Atlantic* had gone down. Everything aboard the schooner now lies strewn over the ocean floor.

—DORCAS—

The steamer, *Dorcas,* anchored in Sydney Harbour, Cape Breton, during a storm. She was under the command of Captain Ferguson and for three days lay at anchor. Captain Ferguson waited until the storm subsided and when the weather looked favourable, sailed out of Sydney Harbour setting his course for

43

Halifax.

Under a good head of steam, the *Dorcas* made pretty good time cruising the eastern coast of Nova Scotia. It seemed as if the port of Halifax was within reach of the steamer, but on Monday morning a storm arose out of the south-east. Captain Ferguson quickly checked his charts and located his position. From his calculations he thought he could make it safely to Halifax by running before the wind. With an hour and a half cruising time away from Halifax, this placed him somewhere near Graham's Head at Lawrencetown.

By night fall the *Dorcas* was in the midst of the storm and the people of Lawrencetown could hear the sea breaking heavily on the shore. They dared not venture from their homes as the weather outside was furious. The following morning the weather had changed, but the sea was still rough.

A few of the inhabitants of that area went to the shore and found the shoreline strewn with fragments of splintered timber and wreckage from the steamer. Mr. C. Hudson was on his way back from a business trip to the eastern shore. He was told of the wreck which had occurred near Graham's Head, and when he returned to Halifax, he told the authorities of the disaster.

No one knew what vessel it was until bodies washed ashore and later were identified. Four bodies were recovered from the water and of these four, Captain Ferguson was identified by the watch which was found in his vest pocket. On the back of the watch was the inscription 'THE EMPIRE 1889'.

Upon examining the face of the watch, the authorities noticed that the hands were stopped at 2 o'clock. This may have been a clue as to the time the wreck occurred, possible in the early hours of the morning on Tuesday, August 24, 1893. What really happened to the steamer and its crew will never fully be known, for no one ever lived to tell the story.

—ANNIE M. PRIDE—

On November 5, 1894, Halifax experienced a bad storm. The people living along the coast witnessed large waves crashing heavily against the rugged shoreline. While the storm raged, with

44

hurricane force and torrential rains, a small schooner fought its way towards Halifax, with a barometer reading of 28-40 being registered at the Citadel.

A man by the name of William Johnston, who was a resident of Bear Cove, gave an eye witness account of the wreck of the schooner *Annie M. Pride,* which was lost at Bear Cove.

"Shortly before six o'clock this morning I saw a vessel off Herring Cove. She was double reefed on the southern tack, and the captain was evidently trying to bring her about to get her off the land. I saw the difficulty she was in and watched her. The vessel was drifting towards Bear Cove, and they were doing their utmost to bring her about but without avail. There was a strong breeze and heavy rain, but this was not the worst feature: it was the tremendous seas which dashed against the rocks. Slowly the vessel drifted toward the rocks, and those on board must have felt death staring them in the face, for if they were to strike the rocks in such a sea, only a miracle could save them. The vessel got to within about thirty feet of the shore, when she was lifted from the water and dashed against the rocks with such a force that she was broken in two. She immediately fell over on her side and sank. It was less that a couple of minutes from the time the vessel struck and went down. It happened so quickly that it was not possible to render any assistance.

"I saw nobody on board from the time the vessel was first sighted. I then went along the shore, directly opposite to where she struck. She was only a few feet away. I could see her bowsprit and anchor and her stern, but the remainder of the vessel was in pieces. I tried to see if there was any sign of life on board, but I did not see any. When the vessel struck, the men were likely all below, and I do not think they were drowned but were killed when the vessel dashed against the rocks. There were a number of empty casks that came ashore and also a few fish."

It was later learned that the wreck was that of the schooner *Annie M. Pride* of Mabou. She was a schooner of 48 tons with a cargo of 800 quintals of fish for Boak and Bennett of Halifax. Those men who lost their lives aboard the schooner were: Captain Jas. G. Pride of St. Mary's, Bernard Pride who was the Captain's son, Charles Young of England, and Joseph Morris of Newfoundland.

—ANNIE MAY—

The inhabitants along the coast of Nova Scotia experienced a terrible storm on November 7, 1894. With high winds and torrential rains, the sea was a mass of white water. Large waves crashed heavily upon the rocky coast and anything in their way fell under their tremendous force.

Caught in the midst of this fury was the schooner *Annie May*. She had been battling mountainous seas in the Bay of Fundy all that day, and towards evening her sails were ripped from the masts. In this condition, the schooner was unmanageable and she could not keep into the wind.

Captain Hatfield and the crew decided that, under such circumstances, it would be best to try to beach the schooner. Captain Hatfield, at the wheel, strained every muscle in his body to keep her from capsizing. By nightfall the schooner was close to shore when the main mast broke. A member of the crew was crushed under its weight and he died within minutes. Later the *Annie May* drifted on the rocks, where she lay helpless against the oncoming sea.

In that position, the sea broke over the deck and at one point the deckload was washed away, two men with it. Captain Hatfield stood by the wheel as long as possible with the sea washing over him. When he saw the last of his men washed away, he lashed himself to the main gaft and he, too, was swept ashore with severe injuries.

When he recovered sufficiently, and to keep from freezing to death, he got to his feet and looked for the nearest house he could find. Sometime later he luckily reached the home of Joseph White of Victoria Beach, three miles away from the scene of the wreck. Clad in only a shirt and pants, he walked barefoot over rocks and through snow drifts waist high. When he reached Mr. White's home, he was more dead than alive. Captain Hatfield escaped the clutches of the sea, but he lost his schooner and his crew perished.

46

—CLARA F. FRIEND—

During the month of February, 1895, a lone schooner sailed out of Gloucester, Mass., and set its course for Nova Scotia. On the eighth day of the voyage the captain and crew of the schooner found themselves in a bad situation.

In the midst of a blinding snow storm, the captain lost his bearings. In the darkness of night, the high winds and mountainous seas tossed the schooner high out of the water and as she came crashing down, the deck was covered with icy water. Struggling to save their lives, the men kept the schooner into the wind and after many hours of battling the elements, the schooner drifted close to a place known as Eastern Head, located between Brooklyn and Coffins Island.

It was there that the ill fated schooner struck Neal's Ledges and began to break up upon the rocks. Knowing only too well what would happen if the men stayed with the schooner, the captain ordered all hands to abandon the schooner. Within a short time the men were in the dories, but under such weather conditions the small dories were no match against the sea. They rode high on the crest of the waves and came crashing down against the rocks.

Soon the dories became no more than a mass of splintered wood, and there was no escape for the men from the schooner. All perished upon the ledge. Seven of the crew members washed ashore at Brooklyn and the others were later found further along the coast. The place where the schooner went down is one of the most dangerous spots along the Western shore and is the scene of many a disaster. Today a monument stands in the town of Brooklyn to commemorate those men who lost their lives aboard the schooner *Clara F. Friend.*

—ARIADNE—

Nestled along the coast of Cape Breton lies a small inlet known as Neil's Harbour. Today, there is a fishing village in this little harbour appearing much as it did eighty years ago. Nothing much happens in the everyday occurrences of the inhabitants of this harbour. But if one were to visit the small cemetery of St. Andrew's, one would find a wooden cross among the marble headstones.

Upon closer examination, one will notice a picture of a full rigged ship in the centre of this cross. To the passer-by it may seem like any other cross, but to the people of Neil's Harbour this represents more than just a cross. It is a part of their past and a tragedy which took place not far from this harbour. To the seamen of this area it was a sad occasion.

What took place on that fatal night of October 7, 1896, will not be forgotten. Apparently the people of Neil's Harbour had experienced unusual weather conditions for that time of year. The air was cold with snow flurries and a lad, by the name of Jimmy, stood in the open doorway and remarked:

"Never have I seen such a stormy month for this time of year in all my born days."

For that brief moment, as he stood in the open doorway, the cool night air chilled the very marrow of his bones, and he quickly closed the door behind him and declared:

"Must be over two inches of snow down an blowin' a livin' gale right up from the eastern."

His friend, known as Skipper, had just returned from the wharf and was warming himself by the wood stove. He looked over at Jimmy and said:

"Sure is bad all right. Charles Payne an' me went down and hauled the dories up a bit higher. I brought up the net we got torn up last storm an' now we got to spread it out on the kitchen loft. We might be able to mend it tomorrow. It won't be a good day for fishin', that's for sure."

"Yeah, that's for certain," replied Jimmy, "There's a terrible sea in, an' the wind is enough to chill ya."

48

He paused for a moment and then looked over at Skipper and stated,

"Do you know a feller from the cove told me that there's a ship off Philip Hatcher's Point, and it seemed to be making poor headway. Suppose it be one of those foreign vessels on its way to Sydney or Halifax."

"That could be," said Skipper, "but it's kind of late for sailin' a craft an' to be 'round our shores."

There was an uneasiness that night, and Jimmy did not feel much like singing any of his old time songs. Skipper's wife had put the children to bed early because of the weather, while Skipper and Jimmy went down to the point to try to get a look at the ship. Upon their return, one of the villagers, by the name of Reuben Payne, came and told them that a man, by the name of Hinks, had come down from South Point to tell them that a ship was ashore near Green Cove.

Without hesitation the lunch box was filled, and all three men headed for the ship followed by other men of the village. By the time they reached the *Ariadne,* she was almost a total wreck and the heavy seas prevented the men from searching for any bodies that may have escaped the ship. Unable to do anything, the men returned to their homes wet to the skin, very cold and somewhat tired. The following day the wind subsided and three bodies were discovered and immediately taken to a warehouse along the shore. Two more were found the next day. It seemed that all they could find were five bodies which had washed ashore.

The people of Neil's Harbour and the fishermen of New Haven, which was commonly referred to as the Cove, together began the painful task of building caskets for these five men from Norway. A local merchant donated the material and the women made little white pillows to place under their heads. To help take away the barrenness of the plain wood, a cross, for each casket, was fashioned out of spruce boughs.

On the day of the burial the school was closed and in the homes the blinds were lowered as a token of respect to the dead seamen. Mr. Payne lit a fire in the little church to warm it up before the people gathered for the sermon. Reverend Robert Atkinson Smith looked somewhat tired as he watched from the doorway of the church the procession coming over the hill. The cold wind blew his hair back over his forehead and his robes ruffled with a sudden gust of wind. For the moment he looked bewildered and looked skyward as if searching for something that was not there. He again looked at the people coming his way and he went

49

to join them. Together they entered the little church and when all was quiet, Reverend Mr. Smith began:

" 'I am the resurrection and the life,' saith the Lord, 'He that believeth in me though he were dead, yet shall he live.' "

When the service was over everyone gathered in the small church yard and the burial service began. The captain's casket came first and then the other four were placed next to his, two on either side. The fishermen stood next to the open graves, heads slightly lowered, and clasping their wool caps in front of them. A short talk on the dangers of the sea was given by Reverend Mr. Smith, and in the background the white flag bearing the red cross of St. Andrew flew at half mast. As the caskets were being lowered into the dark brown earth, every so often the wind would send swirls of snow into the air. Slowly the people turned away and walked from the church yard, leaving behind five men unknown to them and yet tears of sorrow were shed that day.

That night the storm took its revenge upon the *Ariadne* and by morning it was gone, the only reminder of the ship was the five snow covered graves in the church yard. Months later Reverend Mr. Smith received a small parcel in the mail and upon opening it, he found a communion chalice which had been sent to him by the Norwegian Government. A letter accompanied the chalice giving thanks to the fishermen for giving the seamen of Norway a Christian burial. At the next church service Reverend Mr. Smith read the letter aloud for all those to hear and he expressed how proud he was of the congregation.

Today Reverend Mr. Smith and the men who took part in the burying of the Norwegians are gone, but a reminder of their deed lies in a small church yard at Neil's Harbour.

—ASSAYE—

In the year 1891 a firm, by the name of Elder Dempston and Company of Liverpool, England, commissioned a four mastered steamer to be built. When it was finished, they christened it the *Assaye*. The steamer registered in at 3,981 tons with a capacity for carrying large cargoes.

For six years the steamer operated between London and

Montreal without much difficulty. On March 23, 1897, the *Assaye* left Liverpool, England, with 2,000 tons of valuable cargo. The steamer at that time was under the command of Captain R. Corruthers.

Moderate winds prevailed for the first part of the trip but as fate would have it, the winds developed into a gale. Captain Corruthers logged the winds to be S.W. and W. on the 28th day of March. The following day the captain and crew experienced the full brunt of the storm. By the 30th of the month the winds had shifted to the S.E. and, without warning, they again shifted to the W.N.W., which brought extremely high seas.

Under such conditions there was very little the men could do but keep the steamer well into the wind as best they could, without capsizing it. During the height of the storm two of the starboard boats were lost, the upper tower bridge was badly damaged, and the deck fittings were washed away.

By the 31st of the month the weather moderated and fine weather followed with a strong breeze. The following day the steamer struck a field of drift ice. Captain Corruthers noted in his log book that their position on the 2nd of April was Lat. 42° 45' and Long. 39° 10'. Icebergs were sighted at the same parallel and later that day they cleared the ice.

The fourth of April brought slight breezes with a moderate sea running. It was not until the fifth that the weather changed and visibility became very poor with a blanket of haze surrounding them. Captain Corruthers took bearings and thought they had passed Cape Sable. Around noon that same day while all hands were on deck, keeping a sharp lookout for any sight of land, the steamer came to a grinding halt.

Immediately upon contact with the reef, the captain ordered the foreholds to be examined. The crew found that the plates had given way and the rest were badly cracked. What Captain Corruthers did not know was that he had struck the ill fated Blonde Rock, which is located three miles from Seal Island. The chief engineer reported to the captain that water was filling the boiler room. It was only a matter of time before the steamer would sink.

The first officer fired a disaster signal before leaving the steamer. With only three life boats remaining, the men crowded in as best they could and cleared the steamer. Due to the strong currents, the steamer swung around and pounded broadside against the rock. With the use of a long rope, the men managed to get a line to each other in order that they might stay together. A boat from Seal Island was well under way manned by six men of

51

the Seal Island life saving crew. Coxswain Crowell, a brother of the lighthouse keeper, guided the oarsmen to the ill fated steamer. Because of rough water and strong tides, it was slow going for the men of Seal Island. When they finally reached the *Assaye,* they found the remaining crew members of the steamer crowded at the bow to keep from being washed overboard. The seamen lowered themselves over the side of the steamer with the help of ropes and they were taken into the large life boat from the Island.

It was close to 5:00 p.m. that day before the rescued men left the scene of the shipwreck. They looked over their shoulders at the steamer and watched her being pounded against the rock. They were very thankful to be in the life boats and not on the steamer. Once on land the captain and crew were cared for, and later they were transported to the mainland by the steamer *Wauda* owned by H.D. Cann and Sons, Yarmouth.

—JOHN McLEOD—

Captain Stewart left his wife and family at Delaware, so they could get another vessel to take them back home to Newfoundland. He, in turn would sail the *John McLeod* with a crew of twenty-one men to Halifax. During his run, Captain Stewart encountered westward winds of gale force. He also experienced strong currents which caused drifting.

On the 7th of November, 1897, the *John McLeod* neared the approaches to Halifax Harbour. It was early morning and the sea was a rage of white water, causing much difficulty for the men aboard the ship. Unable to man their positions, the men stayed below in order to keep from being washed overboard. The captain stayed in the wheel house, so he could try to keep his ship on course. In the darkness of early morning, the ship was sixteen miles S.S.E. of Devil's Island and labouring heavily.

Near the dreaded Sambro Ledges, the *John McLeod* came crashing down at a place known as Black Rock. Immediately, upon contact with the jagged rocks, the ship's bottom was ripped open, forcing tons of water through the gaping hole. With water rising in the hold, the men scrambled to the top deck. They were faced with the choice of staying aboard the ship in the hope that she

52

would not slip into deeper water, or lower the life boats and take their chances in an open boat.

The sea pounded heavily against the ship and the men could feel it move. The shifting of the cargo created further problems.

Captain Stewart assessed the situation and ordered his men to abandon ship. He, along with his men, managed to get into the life boats without loss of life, and they fought their way from the sinking ship towards land.

The *John McLeod* had been built at Black River in New Brunswick in the year 1885. She registered in at 591 tons, with an overall length of 225 ft. and 4". Her beam was 41 ft. and 1" with the hold being 24 ft. and 3". She was double decked, built of spruce and birch. Later, in 1891 she had been dry docked and completly overhauled. The ship was owned by J.W. Pendy of Saint John, New Brunswick, and now she lies in some 30 fathoms of water with a cargo valued at $90,000.

—SUCCESS—

The discovery of a male nude body washed up on shore, just a short distance from Halifax Harbour, raised many questions. This find was a mystery to the people of the area, except for one man who had witnessed a tragedy at sea. When this man came forward and gave testimony as to what he had seen, the authorities of Halifax put together the puzzle as to what had taken place, and why the body was washed ashore along with another found nearby.

The gentleman, by the name of J. Bates, claimed one of the bodies to be a relative of his from the schooner *Success*. He stated that the schooner had sailed from Main-a-Dieu, Cape Breton, and was returning to Halifax during the month of November in the year 1898. While off the mouth of the harbour the schooner ran into rough weather.

There was a heavy sea running and, while off Herring Cove, the schooner laboured heavily. With darkness moving in, the schooner disappeared from sight. The following morning the men of Ferguson's Cove went out in boats to the scene of the wreck. They found the top masts, which were fore and aft rigged, protruding out of the water. It was apparent that all hands had vanished and the bodies found washed ashore were those of Captain O'Neil and his brother.

—CASTILIAN—

The steamer *Castilian* sailed out of Portland, Maine, bound for Liverpool in March, 1899. She set a course for Tusket Island

53

and had to pass through hundreds of reefs and ledges. Without knowing it, Captain Barrett was thirty miles off his course and fifty miles too far to the west. The navigator thought they were at least twenty miles clear of Brazil Rock which marked the danger limit.

During the night a south east gale with heavy rains suddenly sprang up. Visibility was poor as the 8,000 ton steamer moved slowly through the blackness of night. Early the following morning around 3:30 a.m., a thick blanket of fog set in. An hour later breakers were heard off the port beam and immediately the captain gave the order to reverse engines, but it was already too late.

The steamer hit lightly with very little shock which did not waken the passengers. With the engines in full reverse, she still could not free herself from the rocks. She held fast while the front end swung around with the changing of the tide. When visibility was a little better, they could see before them the mighty Gannet Rock about two miles astern of them. It was not long before water was reported entering one and two compartments. The engine room was flooded to a depth of six feet of water.

A crew was lowered over the side at five o'clock. The captain ordered the chief officer, McAffeer and the pursuer, Stewart, to get help at Little River. When they reached the settlement, they were taken to Tusket Wedge, where the nearest telephone operator was located. They managed to get a message off to Yarmouth and three steam tugs were sent out at 9:00 a.m. that same morning. That night a tug brought back fifty passengers to Halifax and gave the position of the steamer. It was located in one of the worst spots on the coast, which consisted of reefs, shoals, ledges and mud flats. The Bay of Fundy tides rip up this coast like a mighty river, and to be in such a position as this is disastrous.

The *Castilian* at that time was carrying 160,000 bushels of wheat, four thousand tons of cheese, eighteen horses, 782 cattle and sheep and miscellaneous goods. Her list of officers was as follows: Captain R. Barrett, R.N.R., Chief Officer D. McAffeer, Pursuer John Stewart, Surgeon Dr. Neville, Chief Engineer Daniel Colen, Stewart Edward Hurtnell and Stewardess Ada Ames.

—PORTIA—

The Red Cross steamer, *Portia,* left New York bound for Halifax and St. John's, Newfoundland, with a full list of passengers, most of whom were tourists. It was July, 1899, when the steamer ran into a thick blanket of fog west of Halifax near Sambro. Captain Farrell could not see land nor the light. He knew that the steamer was off course, but there was no way of knowing his proper location without the aid of the light off Sambro and the horn. Slowly she moved through the water in the dense fog. The chief officer at 6 o'clock put out the lead line to check the depth of water and found the vessel to be in fifty fathoms of water.

Forty-five minutes later the *Portia* struck heavily upon Big Fish Shoal in less than twelve feet of water. At that time with a light wind blowing, a considerable swell rolled heavily over the shoal. The engineer and firemen reported water rising rapidly below deck and the order was given to take to the life boats. The crew and passengers left the steamer with nothing but the clothes on their backs. Luckily the wireless operator managed to send a distress signal to the nearest telephone which was located at York Redoubt. The signal was picked up and forwarded to the steamer's agent, F.D. Corbett and Co. Immediately the tug *A.C. Whitney* was dispatched to the scene of the wreck and proceeded to the aid of the *Portia.*

A fisherman from the inner Sambro Island, located a half mile away, heard the noise from the steamer. He got into his boat and went out to see what had taken place.

120 persons had perished by the time the tug reached the steamer. A small Italian boy, on his way to join relatives in St. John's, Newfoundland, could not be saved and was lost from view in the heavy sea. Those who were fortunate enough to make it were taken to Halifax by the tug. The *Portia* was left to the mercy of the sea.

The fisherman found the steamer and stayed for forty-five minutes and then left for home. He watched as the steamer drifted from the shoal, with only its upper masts showing. She drifted for about a half mile to the eastward and sank in eight fathoms of water. She now lies midway between Inner and Outer Sambro Islands.

The theory behind the wreck was as recorded: Captain Farrell was steering a course of E.N.E. and heard the Sambro gun, but he thought it was off the port bow in which case it would have brought him safely to port. But it was also thought to be off his starboard and accordingly he ran onto the Big Fish Shoal, which lies about three-quarters of a mile from Sambro Light. The fog horn had just recently been changed from Sambro Light to Chebucto Head and this could have caused the wreck of the *Portia*.

The *Portia* was an iron schooner rigged, screw steamer of 732 tons register, she was 220 feet in length, 31 feet wide and 23½ feet deep. She was built at Newcastle in 1884 and was owned by C.T. Browning and Co. of New York.

—CITY OF MONTICELLO—

The *City of Monticello*, which was originally the *City of Norfolk*, made her first voyage to Saint John Harbour on March 19, 1889. She was built by Hartland and Hollingsworth of Welmington, Deleware, in 1866 and, later overhauled with new boilers in 1886, by Quintard Iron Works of New York. The *City of Monticello*, as it was now called, was an iron steamer with side paddles and schooner rigged. She was 232 ft. in length and a beam of 32 ft., her depth of hold was 10.9 ft. and weight was 478 tons gross. She had a cruising speed of twelve knots and drew eight feet of water.

After the steamer finished her operation in southern waters, she was purchased by the Bay of Fundy Steamship Co. in 1889. When the company took the steamer over, they decided to cement the bottom of the hull and use her between Digby and Saint John, New Brunswick.

Unfortunately the steamer's career was short lived in our waters. While under the command of Captain Harding, on one of her usual trips between Digby and Saint John, during the month of November in the year 1900, she encountered gale winds of up to sixty miles an hour. At the peak of the storm she drifted off course. Sometime later she struck Bull Reef which is just off

56

City of Monticello

Chebogue Point, and south east of Yarmouth Cape. It was not long afterwards that she broke in two and foundered with thirty-nine people on board. An inquiry concerning the wreck of the steamer was held later at the Grand Hotel in Yarmouth.

Captain Murphy gave an account of a record which he kept during the gale of November 9th which went as follows: at 9:00 a.m. the wind was south east at nine miles per hour; at 4:00 p.m. it was south west at 28 m.p.h.; again at 9:00 p.m. the wind was 40 m.p.h.; by 5:00 a.m. it dropped to 24m.p.h. and was blowing south west; by 9:00 a.m. the following morning it was westerly; and at 11:00 a.m. it dropped to 25 m.p.h. Then Captain Murphy went on to say that he had recorded winds of up to 60 m.p.h., but on the day before the wreck took place the wind was not harsh.

It was later discovered that the cause of the wreck was due to carrying too much cargo. Captain Harding, who was in command of the steamer, lost his life along with thirty-six others. One of the sad stories of that trip was the loss of a pretty young girl of sixteen years. Her name was Elsie McDonald. Her home was in Yarmouth and she had been visiting a friend, Mrs. Lowrey, at 202 Rockland Road, Saint John. This was her first visit to Saint John and before Christmas she was returning home to be with her parents. She, along with other passengers, perished when the steamer struck upon the rocks.

—ST. THOMAS AND JUVENTA—

During the month of June in the year 1899, the little town of Guysborough was mentioned in the front pages of the *Halifax Herald.* All through the county as well as in the city itself, people were talking of the scandal and of the court case which was to take place at Guysborough. The case involved two sea captains and several men, who tried to defraud an insurance company.

According to the court proceedings and the information taken at the trial, the story went something like this: in the month of June, 1899, John S. Weil of Whitehead had shipped eighty-one cases of lobsters aboard the schooner *Juventa* which was bound for Halifax. Unknown to Mr. Weil, the *Juventa* did not sail for Halifax, but instead she set sail for Isaac's Harbour where she rendezvoused with the schooner *St. Thomas.* It was there that the cargo from the *Juventa* was transferred over to the *St. Thomas.* When all the cargo was aboard the *St. Thomas,* she set sail for St. Pierre under a new name. The *Juventa* meantime sailed off Liscombe where she was scuttled and went to the bottom.

Upon the arrival of the *St. Thomas* (under the name of *Mary A. Abner*), she was met by Otto H. Feltmate who was using the name of John Ross. He took care to see that the cargo was landed and once this was done, the schooner was taken out of port and scuttled also. Both captains and crew members returned to their homes and waited to hear from the insurance company. When the day came to settle the insurance on these schooners and their supposed cargoes, the captains received only a portion of the money. Because of this the men became angry and somehow the cat was let out of the bag. The insurance company became suspicious about the whole set up. They in turn did a little investigating on their own and came up with a case of swindle. At once the local authorities were notified and Deputy Sheriff E.C. Peart, along with a few constables, set out for a place called Whitehead. There they found five of the men involved in the conspiracy.

Warrants were issued against them, and they were brought back to Guysborough and placed in the county jail until their trial date. On the day of their trial, in the warm sunlight of a September day, the court house was crowded with spectators. Everyone came

58

to get a glimpse of the men who were brought before Judge M.H. Davison to give their testimony. Captain Duncan and Captain Abner Munroe, along with his two sons Wallace and Perry, Morgan Dicks, and Otto N. Feitmate and a few others testified. They were asked to give their statements as to what had taken place and for what reason they attempted to defraud the insurance comany.

When the trial was finally over and all the evidence was weighed, the court had no alternative but to sentence these men for a crime not befitting a captain and the men who served under him. As it was in those times, as well as today, they were not beyond the law.

Grecian

—GRECIAN—

During the month of February, 1902, a steamer, by the name of *Grecian*, was making her way towards Halifax Harbour when she encountered a sudden snow squall. Captain Harrison and the pilot, William Flemming, were on the bridge at the time of the squall. They examined the compass and found it to be all right and on course. Before long the steamer came to a grinding halt upon Martin's Rock at Sandwich Point, between York Redoubt and Herring Cove. Shortly, about twenty feet of water was reported in her fore and aft sections and rising with the tide. On Sunday around 2:40 a.m. the steamer was sighted by the look out at Camperdown and immediately she was reported to the Citadel. A life boat from Herring Cove set out for the stricken vessel and removed the only passenger aboard, Henry Blair, a merchant from St. John's, Newfoundland. Later W.S. Davison of G.S. Campbell and Company, who was the agent of the steamer, sent a gang of stevedores to unload the vessel.

When Captain Harrison was questioned about the wreck he stated as follows: "It is a mystery how the steamer ended upon the rocks. We had taken every precaution to insure the safety of the steamer during the snow squall. The first buoy was sighted, but the second was nowhere in sight. As we moved slowly ahead, a cry from the look out shouted, 'Land ahead'. When she struck, I had no idea where we were and ordered the engines in full reverse. We were free for the moment and then struck another rock and bounded forward in the blackness of night. It seemed that ledges were everywhere and we swung broadside and held fast. When daylight came, we found ourselves ashore on Sandwich Point, just north of Herring Cove. Ahead of us was Martin's Rock on which the steamer first hit, and aft was the Holy Stone from which she rebounded after the engines reversed. Not more than fifty yards away was the bold precipitous western shore of the Arm."

—ONORA—

The schooner, *Onora,* was built in Bridgetown by J.E. Shaffner in 1890. She was a sleek schooner 96 feet in length and registered in at 137 tons. Mr. C.B. Whidden of Antigonish was the first owner, and later C.F. Longley and Company who in turn sold her to a firm in St. Pierre by the name of G.P. Mitchell and Sons. On April 9, 1904, the schooner under Captain John Atkinson left Fejardo, Peurto Rico, and sailed for Halifax. She had a cargo of molasses aboard when the schooner reached the coast of Nova Scotia of May 6th. The weather turned sour and while trying to make the port of Halifax, on a Friday night, the schooner hit upon Duncan's Ledges. Before long the six men on her perished while attempting to reach shore in a small boat. Had they stayed with the schooner until the steamer tug *A.C.Whitney* arrived, they might have lived as the schooner held together until Sunday. Apparently while off Sambro on that Friday around 2 o'clock in

60

the afternoon she did not signal for a pilot as the wind was light. It was thought that because of the heavy sea, the schooner was carried closer to shore than Captain Atkinson realized. The Schooner was well inside Duncan's reef spar buoy not too far from shore, when she hit. On Saturday morning when the *Whitney* arrived on the scene, under Captain Landry, the schooner was slowly sinking. The crew, all of whom was lost, was made up of: Captain John Atkinson of New Brunswick; John F. Bowden, the cook, from Guysboro; Archibald Baird of St. John's, Newfoundland; Jno Long of Richibucto, New Brunswick; and H. Haivista of Finland. Only one body, which was identified as Archibald Baird, was found by Daniel Connors of Duncan's Cove.

—DEMARA—

Demara was a coastal steamer owned and operated by the Furness Lines of Halifax. She frequented the Eastern coast line of Nova Scotia. On February 8, 1905, the steamer turned her bow eastward under the command of Captain Gorst. Aboard the *Demara* at that time were thirty-four persons consisting of crew and passengers. Just a short distance from Halifax the steamer ran into snow flurries. For this time of year it is not uncommon to experience snow or a slight gale. In the darkness of night, Captain Gorst kept a watchful eye on the compass to make sure that his course was in line with the charts.

As the evening wore on, the snow became increasingly heavy until it was almost impossible to see a few feet in front of the steamer. Concerned for the safety of his passengers and crew, the captain ordered his steamer to half steam and later to dead slow ahead. Because of the snow and continuing high winds, Captain Gorst was very worried over the chance of drift and had his mate check the charts in conjunction with the compass and their running time. The mate informed him that all was well and speed was increased. Around 2:30 a.m. on a Tuesday the steamer was off Jeddore when a sudden crashing noise awoke those who were asleep.

Without hesitation the alarm was given and everyone rushed on deck. In the blinding snow storm it was hard to see and most groped around looking for something solid to cling to. Upon impact the engine room filled with water and the *Demara* began to sink. The crew members lowered the life boats and did their best to calm the passengers, but, in a state of shock, some of the passengers lost control and tried to get into the life boats by jumping from the deck of the steamer, but their attempt proved to be fatal. In only a matter of minutes the icy water claimed its victims in the darkness.

Those who were fortunate enough to reach the life boats safely managed to row twelve miles through high winds, freezing snow, and ice floes. By morning they neared the shore where a group of local fishermen waited to help them up on the beach. A report of the wreck was turned over to the owners of the steamer, it stated that out of the 34 aboard, 15 had perished. The unfortunate were: Captain J.B. Gorst of Norway, Mrs. Algernoon Prowse of St. John's, Newfoundland, and thirteen others.

The steamer now lies at the bottom of a reef just five miles of Jeddore. She was a steamer of 1,145 tons; length, 275 ft.; 35 ft. breath; and a depth of 25 ft. in the hold.

—SALERNO—

The *Salerno* left Barcelona on June 2, 1905, enroute to Cadiz and later bound for Halifax under the command of Captain Olsen. Aboard the ship was a carog of salt for A.N. Whitman of Halifax. The ship was to proceed to Labrador, after she made the delivery. This, however, was a port she would never see. Her career came to a close upon the rocks off the coast of Nova Scotia. On the morning of July 2nd of that year, a pilot, by the name of William Flemming, boarded the Salerno to guide her safely into Halifax Harbour.

In the cover of dense fog at about 5 o'clock in the morning, the *Salerno* came to a resting place upon the Litchfield Shoals, just below the Thrum Cap Shoal. When word reached the city that the *Salerno* was aground on the shoal, the tugs *A.C. Whitney* and *Togo* were sent to aid her. Within a few hours the tugs returned to Halifax in order to take out a crew of men to help remove the cargo. Hopes of getting her off the shoal ran high until later that afternoon when two Beazely brothers, who were divers, discovered

62

that the No. 1 and No. 2 holds were leaking. Later they filled with water.

Because she struck the outer edge of the shoal, attempts were made to try to get her into deeper water. The tugs worked all day in hopes of pulling her off the edge and into deeper water, but her bow rested too far on the rocks, even though her stern was far enough into the deeper water. The men gave up when it became evident that attempts to try to keep the water from rising any further in the holds proved fruitless. They stood by and watched as the ship rolled and pounded on the rocks as the sea rose with a swell and fell again. Even with the help of the dockyard steamers, *Highland Mary* and the *Shannon,* they could not budge her from the rock which now pierced her bottom.

Men in the area, who lived by the sea all their lives, knew her ways, and they were convinced that the *Salerno* was there for good, and any efforts to try and refloat her would be useless.

The *Salerno* was a vessel of 2,723 tons and was built at West Hartlepool in 1834. She was owned by McBeth and Gray of Glasgow, and at the time she struck the shoal, she was chartered to the Grand River Pulp and Lumber Company.

—STRATHCONA—

The *Strathcona* sailed out of Halifax harbour in December of 1906. Her scheduled course was for the eastern shore. At that time of year the roads along the coast were impassable and travel by sea was much easier. She carried a group of Dalhousie and Acadia students on their way home for the holidays, along with other passengers.

The vessel had just passed Thrum Cap, when bad weather with strong winds from the south-east struck. The *Dufferin,* a steamer heading west, passed her, as the *Strathcona* sailed eastward at a slow speed, taking soundings as she approached the Beaver Light. A close watch was kept for Red Pole light, and they were unable to see it. The second mate and the quarter master watched from the wheelhouse. The captain was on the bridge, while the first mate was forward with the men taking soundings. They would stop every hundred yards or so and take another sounding. Mr. C.F. Andrews, who was a mining engineer from

63

Isaac's Harbour at the time, was asked if he would help the captain with the soundings so that, in conjunction with the charts, they might obtain their proper location.

Just as they were about to anchor for safety reasons, they discovered that smoke was filling the saloon and gangway. Soon flames burst overhead as high as the top of the stack. They could also see flames shooting out from around the stack, and the boiler room was engulfed with flames. Shortly the lights went out aboard the vessel. The second engineer, Byron Irwin, reached the upper deck through the smoke and fire and passed out once topside.

It was now evident that they could not anchor and it was necessary for the captain to risk placing the vessel under full steam ahead in hopes of reaching land in the blinding fog. As she moved swiftly through the grey waters, the fire burned from rail to rail amidship, cutting off a small party which was aft from the main body of officers. The captain remained on the bridge directing the course to follow, so he could beach her as soon as possible. Mr. Kaiser remained at the wheel, watching the compass as the orders were given, so he could steer her on course. He turned the vessel slightly to the east and within minutes they saw a shoreline and headed directly for it. She was run as close to the shore as possible, with the engines still running. Immediately the boats were lowered and the women were brought forward from their cabins and placed on the main deck. There were some sixty casks of kerosene oil on the deck in the same area as the passengers, but at the time the captain deemed it necessary for them to be lowered into the boats at that position. The boats on the starboard quarter were burning but, with the use of what life boats were left, the passengers and crew made it safely to shore. It took only a total of twelve minutes from the time they beached. Shortly thereafter the 60 casks caught fire and exploded, sending a large sheet of flames upon the water surrounding the *Strathcona*. Most of the personal belongings of the crew and passengers were lost, but, during the whole operation of getting the passengers ashore, only one boat upset and that without loss of life.

—HESTIA—

On April 28, 1906, the steamer *Hestia* sailed from Glasgow, Scotland, under Captain Ferguson. He had a crew of thirty-nine and there was one passenger. The steamer was bound for the port of Saint John, New Brunswick, on a business venture. She was owned and operated by the Donaldsons of Glasgow and was approximately fifteen years old, steel constructed, with a length of 365 feet and a weight of 3,424 tons.

The *Hastie* had very little trouble in making the trans-Atlantic crossing until she was approximately three miles off Cape Sable Island. Then she struck a submerged object around 10:30 in the morning on May 12th. Within a short time the steamer began taking in water and soon the fires in the engine room were out. She was now helpless to do anything, as she lay fixed upon the submerged object.

It seemed at the time that lady luck was with the *Hestia,* for not far off was the *Lady Laurier* who picked up her distress signal. Within a short time the *Laurier* was alongside and, with the use of strong ropes, the *Laurier* managed to pull the *Hestia* free. Together they made their way for Shelburne, the *Hestia* being towed by the other vessel. When they were entering the harbour, the tow lines snapped. The *Hestia* swung about and within minutes was aground on the north side of McNutt's Island.

She lay in a fairly well protected spot some nine miles from the town of Shelburne. When the captain was later questioned as to what had happened, his only comment was:

"Judging from our position at the time, it is possible that we struck an unknown wreck, which is likely low enough to go unnoticed by other vessels."

Most of the steamer's cargo consisted of coal and piping which was to be unloaded at Saint John. The water was nearing the upper deck of the steamer while she lay aground. The crew remained aboard until they were removed with the help of vessels in the area. When the message was received by the wireless at Camperdown, the word was passed on to Pickford and Black who were the agents for the Donaldson lines.

Divers and equipment were sent to the area by way of the *Highland Mary*. The owner of the salvage company, Mr. William Beageley, accompanied the crew of divers along with the tug *Togo*. Later G.W. Hensley left Halifax for Shelburne to supervise the salvage operations.

—HAVANA—

Upon returning home from a Seal hunt along the coast of Newfoundland, Captain J.A. Farquhar, owner and operator of the schooner *Havana,* was told of the schooner *Alexander R.* which had sunk off Point Pleasant. This unfortunate accident had occurred three weeks prior to their arrival. She had been sunk by the steamer *Afranmore* in the early hours of the morning.

Anxious to try to salvage any cargo that the *Alexander R.* may have carried, Captain Farquhar and his crew set out for the spot where the schooner went down. As well as being a Seal hunting schooner, the *Havana* was also equipped for salvage work. Just off Point Pleasant, the *Havana's* anchor was lowered over the side and when it was set, she was tested for drift.

Positioned well, the men of the *Havana* worked diligently through the day with hopes of recovering whatever the *Alexander R.* had been carrying. During the darkness of night, Captain Farquhar made sure that the signal light on the main mast was always showing. But on April 26, 1906, the currents changed off Point Pleasant and swung the schooner broad side towards the Harbour's entrance.

Since the schooner had shifted into this position, it was apparently difficult for an inbound steamer, called the *Strathcona,* to see the light on the mast. The men on the bridge of the steamer, as stated by Captain Reid, could not see the schooner which lay directly in their path. By the time they saw what lay ahead of them it was too late.

The *Strathcona* tried to veer off from the *Havana,* but because of the schooner's position, she caught the *Havana* broadside. Under such force, the steel constructed steamer cut deeply into the wooden hull of the *Havana.* Upon impact, the water began to fill the lower section of the schooner. Had the steamer backed off, the *Havana* would have sunk immediately with the possibility of loss of life occurring. Captain Reid held the schooner above water long enough for the men of the *Havana* to reach the steamer safely.

When they were all aboard the *Strathcona,* the steamer backed off and everyone watched the schooner sink out of sight within minutes. She now lies close to where the *Alexander R.* went down. The twelve passengers who were aboard the steamer at the time experienced their first sea accident and they were only too

66

anxious to tell anyone who would listen about the episode. As for Captain Farquhar, he had lost a comparatively old schooner while trying to earn extra money.

But this story has an ironic ending: it happened during the month of December of that same year that the *Strathcona*, while on a routine run along the Eastern Shore, caught fire and sank at a place known as Port Dufferin.

—SHAFFNER BROTHERS—

Just three and a half miles south east of Brier island lies a bar at Gull Rock, and it was here on January 10, 1906, that the schooner *Shaffner Brothers* struck heavily. The schooner was later discovered by Frank Morrell, a signal agent located at Westport. The schooner was returning from Gloucester under Captain McDonald and was bound for Sydney, Cape Breton. When the schooner struck the bar, the captain signaled for assistance and one of the tugboats belonging to the Cann's left Yarmouth at night for the scene of the disaster.

The wind had changed to the south east and lighter boats in the area managed to get the crew off the schooner. If the weather changed, the schooner would become a total wreck as she was lying in a dangerous position. The schooner was built at Clementsport in the year 1894 and is registered at 148 tons. She was owned by Thos Townsend of Louisbourg, and at the time she struck the bar, Mr. J.F.L. Parsons, who was the agent of the Marine and Fisheries Department, received a telegram from Harbour Master Anderson at Digby explaining the particulars of the situation and giving the assurance that everything possible was being done to save the schooner.

—KILDONA—

In the year 1888 a steamer, christened the *Indra,* slipped from its cradle into the Mersey River. She was built in the dockyards of Liverpool, Great Britain. Her overall length was 361.8 feet with a breath of 44.3 feet and a depth of 27.1 feet. She registered in at 2,349 tons.

After nineteen years of continuous service in European waters, the *Indra,* under the name of *Kildona,* was commissioned to serve in North America. On November 27, 1907, she sailed from Shields, Great Britain, under the command of Captain Roberts. Her first port of call was Portland, Maine. The *Kildona's* first trip across the Atlantic was an uneventful one, until she approached the coast line of Nova Scotia.

It was now the month of December and weather conditions at that time of year were very unpredictable. Captain Roberts encountered snow flurries which soon developed into strong gale force winds from the north east. In the darkness of night the steamer pushed its way through the blinding snow storm, unaware that she was on a collision course with the dreaded Brazil Rock. With each rise of the bow and stroke of her great pistons, the steamer pushed forward in the hopes of riding out the storm without any mishap.

In the midst of the storm Brazil Rock was seen just in front of the steamer. Unable to alter course in time, the *Kildona* rose high out of the water as if pushed up by a giant hand and, with a tremendous crashing noise, she fell upon the rock, ripping her hull open. Within minutes the steamer began filling with water and those aboard her scrambled to the upper deck. Captain Roberts gave the order for distress signals which were picked up by the passing steamer the *Louisbourg.* In a very short ime, the *Louisbourg* was along side the striken steamer and emergency measures were skillfully carried out. When last sighted, the aft section of the *Kildona* was submerged and she had a bad starboard list. The nearest point of land was Baccaro, which is six miles away and seven miles for Cape Sable Island.

Mount Temple

—MOUNT TEMPLE—

The *Mount Temple* of the C.P.R. lines left Antwerp and set her course for Saint John, New Brunswick, in the month of November, 1907. She was a liner 485 ft. in length, 59 ft. in width, 30.4 ft. deep and had a weight of 4,989 net tons. Her engines were 694 h.p. and at the time she carried a cargo of German goods, axles and other iron works, with a weight capacity of 3,500 tons.

The Canadian Pacific steamship was under the command of Captain Boothby, with a crew of a hundred men and a passenger list of 630. As the ship neared the coast of Nova Scotia, the captain gave orders to keep well north of Sable Island, but somehow they were too far north by some fifty miles. Following such a course the ship was nearing the coastal waters of Nova Scotia and, under the cover of darkness, it was difficult to tell exactly where they were. On Sunday afternoon of December 1, 1907, Captain Boothby stayed close to the bridge until midnight and, because the weather was clear, he felt sure everything would be all right. He left orders that if the weather should change he was to be awakened. While he slept the weather changed and a sudden snow squall hit the ship, blinding the view of those on the bridge.

Around three o'clock in the morning the captain was awakened by the sound of a heavy crashing noise. He knew that

69

they had hit a reef or run aground. His first reaction was to get to the bridge and question the men as to what had happened and to locate their position. Because of the strong currents, high winds, and darkness, it was almost impossible to reach a conclusion as to where they were. It was not until the morning of the 2nd that the crew and passengers looked down at the rocks of Ironbound.

While the ship sat firmly fixed upon the rocks, the sea began washing over her decks, smashing the life boats and leaving only half of them fit for service. In the midst of darkness, guns and rockets were fired in the hope of attracting someone. The few inhabitants on the Island heard the distress signals but could do nothing until daylight. When daylight finally came, the crew and passengers looked up at the barren island and saw that they were no more than 75 feet from the shore. When the captain checked the charts, he found that he was aground at Ironbound which is an island at the mouth of the LaHave River.

Apparently there were only two families living on the island at that time and, with the sea running heavily and strengthened by high winds, it was impossible to launch the life boats. The thought of trying to reach the rocky shoreline and climbing the steep cliffs of this island terrified the passengers. Because of the danger involved, Captain Boothby thought it best to try to secure a cable line from the ship to the top of the cliff. Two of the crew members got one of the life boats to shore safely under the watchful eyes of the passengers and the rest of the crew. The sea broke heavily all around them and, with one wrong move, those two men would be smashed against the cliff. But as luck would have it, they managed to secure the cable to the base of the cliff and cheers of joy echoed between the cliffs and the ship.

A basket was suspended from the cable and was used as a means of getting the children from the ship to the island. At first the passengers did not understand what the captain was trying to do as they could not speak English. They were mostly immigrants, Hungarians and Russian Jews. It was not until Miss Demeester, the ship's stewardess, made the first crossing in the life basket with a three year old motherless child, that the rest followed in the same way.

Shortly afterwards the exodus began, with the women and children using the basket, while the men got to the island by means of the life boats. It took the crew and officers from ten o'clock until five in the afternoon to land the passengers safely on the island.

Once the passengers were on the island, they were faced

with hunger and cold weather as there was very little protection from the high winds. Many of them were poorly dressed and some of the children were barefooted in the snow and slush. Blankets and what food was aboard the ship were sent over by the cable and by the life boats.

The people of the light did their best to comfort the passengers by building large fires and helping to prepare food which they received. That night many of the men spent the night on the snow covered ground, wrapped in blankets, close to the large bon fires. Others stayed aboard the schooners *Hazel* and *Guide,* which had come to their aid. Most of the women and children huddled together in an old warehouse a mile from the wreck. They also crowded into the lighthouse and the two dwellings which were owned by fishermen. The infants and babies rested in the arms of their mothers protected from the harshness of the wind and cold. Most of the crew and officers stayed aboard the ship. They kept an eye on the water which was in the forward hold, the engine room, and the rest of the ship except number seven hold.

The following morning the steamer, *Trusty,* came down the river for the passengers, but she could not get within a hundred feet of the island and it was slow work getting some of the people off the island by means of small boats. The water was calmer, but getting the passengers to the *Trusty* was difficult. By four o'clock that afternoon the *Trusty* started back up the river with 150 passengers on board, leaving the rest to the steamer *Lady Laurier* and the coastal steamer *Canada* both from Halifax. Two divers from the *Canada* were sent down to examine the ship's bottom and by nightfall the steamer *Lady Laurier* returned from Ironbound with the remaining passengers. They were all looked after at Halifax until arrangements were made to send them west by means of trains. The *Lady Laurier,* with wrecking appliances, returned to the wreck that same night accompanied by Captain J.A. Farquhar who was a representative of the London Salvage Association.

Because of the many wrecks which have occurred around that area, I thought it would be justifiable to give a brief account of the history of the area and of the island.

The Ironbound island, more definitely designated as LaHave Ironbound, lies at the mouth of the LaHave River. Its rock bound shores have a most forbidding appearance and the lighthouse was placed there to warn ships to keep away from the area. The island has a desolate appearance and very few trees are found there, which is a striking contrast to the nearby islands. About twelve miles from Ironbound is Fort Point and every inch of

71

ground in this vicinity is steeped in 17th century romance and the latter day romance of the German and English settlements. Such names as Marc L'Escarbot, the French poet, and lawyer M. de Saussaye, Issac de Razilly, D'Aulnay Charnise, La Tour, Le Borgne, Perrot and de Broulliah are among the noted Frenchmen whose names are closely connected with this pioneer outpost of France. The ruins of the Fort and Chapel may yet be found by those wishing to seek a little glimpse of the past.

The island of Ironbound itself lies about fifteen miles from Bridgewater and about fifteen miles away from Lunenburg, but in spite of the many lighthouses in the area, many wrecks have occurred on this coast. Some fifty years ago the schooner *Jack Hilton* of Liverpool was totally wrecked on Ironbound Island. The schooners *Amanda, Isabella* and *Lillian* were wrecked near this island in the year 1893. The steamers *M.A. Starr* and *Scud* ended their careers less than ten miles from this island and the brigantine *Diadem* also was lost in this area.

—AURORA—

On November 27, 1908, the barque *Aurora* with a crew of twenty men sailed out of Digby Harbour under the command of Captain Saarum. Her destination at that time was the port of Buenos Ayres. She was carrying a cargo of lumber.

About an hour from port, the *Aurora* ran into rough weather. It was early morning with a thick blanket of fog prevailing. As Captain Saarum steered his vessel according to the compass, the weather seemed to change for the worst. A strong wind of gale force sprang up, forcing the *Aurora* off her course by five miles.

Because of the change in course, Captain Saarum had no idea of his position and, to make matters worse, the fog enshrouded the barque and obscured their vision. The men of the *Aurora* kept a watchful eye as well as a close ear for the sound of crashing waves. The barque was almost three hours from Digby, and the weather had not changed. Now, just a mile north of Brier Island Light, the crew of the barque *Aurora* found themselves high out of the water and tossed about like rag dolls.

They were hard ashore with a gaping hole in the bottom, with the sea washing in. Although she struck within twenty yards of shore, the sea was running high. It seemed that with each crashing blow, the barque would fall apart. Soon the main mast broke and it fell into the foaming water. The scene was a wall of crashing waves, with fragments of splintered wood everywhere. It was a daring struggle for the men of the *Aurora* to try to reach shore safely. Seated in their life boats, the men were tossed about like corks. The wind increased and, with each thrust of the tremendous waves, the barque was forced higher onto the rocks.

After all hands reached shore safely, attempts to try to save the barque proved fruitless. The weather continued with all its fury and this hampered other vessels from approaching the *Aurora* in attempts to free her. The owner who lived in Norway was later notified that his vessel was a total loss on the rocks near Brier Island Light.

—JOHN BENNETT—

The barquentine *John Bennett* out of New York and bound for Halifax during the month of November, 1909, ran a collision course with the four mastered schooner *Merrill C. Hart* off Black Island. The schooner *William Jones,* commanded by Captain Bullock, picked up two Filipino sailors who were off the barquentine *John Bennett.*

Captain Bullock later stated that on Monday morning, about one o'clock, his vessel was approaching Black Island when he spotted lights from another vessel. He approached the vessel and called out to it. The captain from the *John Bennett* answered and requested help. Immediately Captain Bullock came about and made ready a life boat to rescue the men of the barquentine. Before he could lower a boat the vessel vanished from sight. Captain Bullock then made for the spot where he last saw the *John Bennett.* All he found were bits of the wreckage and the two sailors. He could not learn anything from them because he did not speak their tongue. The schooner *William Jones,* which was bound from Stockton Springs, Maine, for New York with a cargo of lumber, made a quick trip to New York to let the Filipinos off. An interpreter talked with them and found out they had worked

73

aboard the *John Bennett* and that the vessel had been hit by a four masted schooner and, out of a crew of eight, they were the only ones left. It was also learned that the crew of the schooner *Merrill C. Hart* had perished. Aboard the *John Bennett* were Captain Jones Firth of Lockeport, first mate Hadley, second mate Aubrey Gelbert both of Lockeport, Daniel Stoutley, and two seamen.

The barquentine was owned by A.W. Henry and Son of Liverpool, Nova Scotia. She was thought to have gone down about the middle of the sound between Point Judith and Sandy Point on Black Island. The schooner *Merrill C. Hart* was built in Bristol, Maine, in 1866 and its registered weight was 182 tons, with a length of 97.9 feet, 26.7 feet in width and 12 feet in depth. Her owners were Dun and Elliot of Thomosston. The barquentine was built in Liverpool and owned by A.W. Hendry. She was copper sheathed and had a weight of 299 tons net.

—RENWICK—

Many of the circumstances surrounding shipwrecks are directly attributable to adverse weather conditions, unknown shoals, reefs, or sailing under the cover of darkness in unfamiliar waters. Such was not the case in the loss of the steamer *Renwick*. Her misfortune was caused by the element of human error. According to the records, the steamer *St. Pierre Miquelon* sailed out of Halifax Harbour bound for her home port by way of North Sydney. The steamer cruised along the eastern coast of Nova Scotia at a moderate speed, under fine weather conditions.

Meanwhile another steamer, the *Renwick,* under the command of Captain Chapman left Port Hastings bound for Bridgewater. She carried in her hold a full cargo of coal. Both vessels, unaware of each other's position, pursued their course without hesitation. The sea was relatively calm with blue sky overhead and visibility extremely clear. This weather prevailed for some time.

In the early morning light on December 28, 1911, first mate Bichet of the *St. Pierre Miquelon* was on watch. Their position was somewhere off County Harbour and, to the surprise of Bichet, he saw the *Renwick* looming up under their bow. Upon his command, the engine room placed the engines in full reverse, but

74

the *Renwick* which was the smaller of the two collided with the French steamer. Immediately upon contact the *Renwick* took in water and the men in the engine room were trapped.

There was nothing that could be done to save the *Renwick*, it all happened so fast. Within minutes the steamer went to the bottom because of the heavy cargo she was carrying. As the steamer was sinking, Captain Chapman and eleven of his crew managed to escape by leaping into the icy waters. They were quickly picked up by the men of the French steamer, brought safely aboard, and taken below to warm quarters. The damages sustained to the French steamer were slight and once the *Renwick* was lost from view, the French captain ordered his steamer to proceed to Sydney.

When questioned about the loss of some of his men, Captain Chapman as best he could remember gave the names as follows:

Hahn of Port Hastings, William Wiggenton from Birmingham, England, and a third man who was unknown.

The *Renwick* was owned by the Inverness Railway and Coal Company. It registered in at 402 tons and was built in 1890.

Bruce

—BRUCE—

The 313 ton *Bruce,* which was both a passenger ship and a freighter, and which operated between Port Aux Basques and North Sydney for fourteen years, came to an end at Port Nova just eight miles from Louisbourg on March 24, 1911. She was of the Reid Newfoundland steamship lines and sailed under Captain R. Drake with a crew of twenty-seven and carried a list of 128 passengers at the time she went aground.

As the story went: the *Bruce* left Port Aux Basques at 11 o'clock on March 24th and encountered heavy drift ice. She was making for Louisbourg on that trip and took the inside course at Scattarie Island which was unusual for a vessel to do. It was close to four o'clock in the morning when one of the passengers heard the steward tell the captain that there was land ahead. The captain told him that he must have spotted ice not land.

The truth was that Captain Drake was ten miles off his course and he was not aware of his position in the cover of darkness. He was on the bridge and had just relieved the first officer Taylor. He knew the steamer was taking on water but kept it from the passengers as he did not want to alarm them. He altered course for Port Nova to beach the steamer before she sank due to the full load and taking on water fast.

At four o'clock the steamer struck on the rocks and immediately the passengers were awakened. They rushed to the upper deck with only the clothes on their backs. The water was rushing in through the gaping hole. Because of the speed at which the steamer was travelling, it carried itself over the ledge and piled up on the large rocks, just a few hundred yards from shore, almost within a half mile of the wreck of the *Ben Carachan* which had occurred the year before.

Chaos developed on the upper deck as screams of terror rose above the sound of crashing waves below. Several of the women passengers were holding their babies in their arms and were very much concerned for their safety. Some of the men lost control of themselves and broke down, and this did not help matters where the safety of the other passengers were concerned.

The captain ordered the life boats over the side and the women and children to go in first. While the launching of the life boats was taking place, a man by the name of Shea lost his footing and fell over the side into the raging sea and was never seen again.

76

Fifteen minutes later another man, by the name of Pike, was drowned as he was about to step into one of the life boats. A large wave hit him and washed him over the side.

Apparently the life boats were in bad condition, for, while rowing ashore, most of the passengers were kept busy bailing the water from the bottom of the life boats. Because of the steamer's position, the passengers and crew had to row around her, in order to clear the rocks. It was 8 o'clock before the last boat load reached the shore safely. Many of the passengers suffered from cold and one passenger, by the name of A. W. Crawford of Boston, suffered with frozen feet. While Captain Drake and the first officer remained on board the steamer, the rest of the crew and passengers found shelter in a few small fishing huts. They managed to build a large bonfire which helped to keep them from freezing.

It was not long after they reached shore, that a rescue team reached them and those who wished to drive to Louisbourg did so. The others were taken off by the Dominion Coal Company's steamer *Louisbourg* and the tug *D. H. Thomas* and brought to the town of Louisbourg.

The passengers were expected to go to Sydney by the evening express, but the majority refused to leave until they could find out what was going to happen to their luggage which was still on the *Bruce*. Later they learned that the *Bruce* was being pounded to pieces on the rocks and it was almost impossible to save any of the mail bags or freight.

On the evening of the wreck a telephone call to Halifax from Louisbourg stated that the *Bruce* had parted in the center and efforts to save most of the mail and cargo was given up. Because of the relentless crashing of heavy waves and ripping tides, the once noted *Bruce,* which was built in 1897, met its fate upon the rocks at Port Nova.

—ISLEWORTH—

Captain Redding, in command of the steamer *Isleworth*, sailed out of Boston Harbour and set his course for the Port of Louisbourg. The steamer followed the eastern sea board and then turned her bow towards Nova Scotia. Her trip along the western

77

shore was uninterrupted until she was some twenty miles off Halifax.

The steamer's propeller began to develop trouble and Captain Redding would not push on. He decided to put into the port of Halifax and have the propeller checked. Unable to maintain a constant speed, the engines were ordered dead slow ahead.

Weather conditions on the 12th of March, 1912, were not the best for navigation. Dense fog closed in around the steamer and visibility was almost nil. Strong currents prevailed and Captain Redding found it difficult to keep his vessel on course. There was very little he could do but to push on in the hope of reaching Halifax before the steamer broke down.

The men were ordered to keep a sharp ear and a close eye in all directions. With a southwest wind blowing, Captain Redding was unable to hear the whistle from Chebucto Head. By 5:00 a.m. in the morning the jagged rocks of Chebucto Head loomed up out of the water in front of the *Isleworth*. Immediate orders were given to reverse engines, but due to the steamer's faulty propeller she could not bring herself to a complete stop. Because of the weight and momentum of the steamer, she came crashing upon the rocks. Striking side on, the *Isleworth* fetched hard up against the cliffs.

It was only a matter of time before the sea began to break over the steamer. Because of its location, she was vulnerable to all the elements and, in this predicament, the captain and his men abandoned the steamer. Their only escape was by way of climbing the granite cliffs in the early morning darkness.

All thirty-nine reached safe ground and found themselves just 100 yards from the Chebucto Head Lighthouse. At the time of the shipwreck, the *Isleworth* was under charter to the Dominion Coal Company. She was owned by Watts, Watts and Company of London, England. When launched at Stockton-on-Tees, the steamer registered in at 2,988 tons and now, eight months later, she lay helpless upon the rocks just off Halifax.

—MINA GERMAN—

On the evening of February 8, 1912, a blinding snow storm swept across the Atlantic seaboard. The schooner *Mina German* was caught in the midst of this. With mountainous seas breaking over her decks, the schooner made very little head way. Under the command of an experienced skipper, the schooner had sailed from Weymouth bound for Peurto Rico with a full cargo of lumber.

Unable to maintain a steady course under such conditions, the skipper attempted to round Southern Point. Once around the point, the schooner made its way into St. Mary's Bay and it was here, at a place called Grand Passage, that the *Mina German* came to a grinding halt upon the rocks. A steamer by the name of *Wesport* was in the area and picked up the S.O.S. from the schooner. Sometime later, the steamer came alongside and, with the aid of strong ropes, tried to free the *Mina German* from the rocks.

After several attempts to free her, the captain of the steamer signalled to the men of the schooner that it was useless. Shortly afterwards the men were taken aboard the steamer and brought safely back to port. While at Annapolis Captain Thomas German, who was the owner of the schooner, was notified of the loss of his schooner. Because of her position, the heavy seas and high winds beat the *Mina German* into a mass of broken timbers. She had been built at Meteghan and registered in at 148 tons.

—PATRICIAN—

The schooner *Patrician* sailed from Gloucester in the month of March and reached the Port of Shelburne on Thursday, March 16, 1912, at 5 o'clock in the morning. After taking on supplies, she set sail for the fishing grounds and spent most of the day gearing up for the fish.

Towards evening the sea became rough and the winds began to blow and it soon became evident that a storm was brewing. The schooner was some 23 miles off the coast of Shelburne and, under the heavy rain, Captain Harding gave the order to head the schooner for Shelburne.

By the time they reached the coastline, the south westerly winds were fierce and the torrential rains, mixed with fog, blinded their view. Under the cover of darkness, Captain Harding misjudged his bearings and mistook Bull Rock Light for the Shelburne gas buoy. This placed his schooner in danger.

When he realized his mistake, it was too late. The schooner's bow rose high in the air and came down with a crash upon the Black Rock ledges, just a half mile inside Gull Rock, some two miles from Jordan Bay. Minutes after the crash, the schooner broke up under the pounding of high waves. The impact upon the rocks opened her bottom, allowing the water to surge through the schooner, ripping her to pieces.

Captain Harding and nine crew members tried to reach the dories but were swept over the side into the cold black water. They were never seen again by the remaining ten aboard the schooner. Those men who were left on the sinking schooner managed to get four of the dories into the water. They were tossed about in the raging sea and one dory was without oars. The fishermen in the dories made their way for shore as best they could in the darkness.

While making for shore, one of the dories upset and the men were thrown into the sea. After a great deal of difficulty, they got hold of the dory. They clung to the boat and drifted with the tide in the wake of white caps. By midnight the ten men reached shore and made their way along the shore until they came to the house of Captain McAlphin at Jordan Bay. The men were well looked after by Mr. McAlphin, and later they were taken to Yarmouth where they caught a boat for Gloucester.

The neighbouring boats in the area searched the wreckage for the bodies of Captain William Harding, John Goodwin, Albert Goodwin, Holman Hopkin, James Nickerson, Clarence Terry, Michael Jenning, William Gill, Joseph Robicheau, and George Sharpe.

—URANIUM—

The 3,315 ton steamer *Uranium,* under Captain Eustace, sailed out of Rotterdam bound for Halifax with nine hundred passengers aboard. While entering the approaches to Halifax

Harbour, she was enshrouded with thick fog and cruised at a slow speed. She was approximately 1000 yards north of the lighthouse at Chebucto Head, and within 300 yards from shore, when the steamer hit upon the rocks at 10:45 on a Sunday morning in January, 1913.

The place where she went aground is known as Shoal Point, one of the roughest points on the rocky coastline. The bow of the steamer was out of the water by eight feet and, if the wind had been blowing from the south east instead of the south west, things might not have turned out so well for those on board the *Uranium*.

At the time she hit, the keeper could not see the steamer from the lighthouse. However, a message was received by the wireless at Camperdown and immediately relayed to the lighthouse keeper, Mr. Holldan, who in turn sent the news of the stranded vessel to agent C.H. Harvey of the Marine and Fisheries Department, and to P. Mooney, the Canadian Northern agent. The *Lady Laurier* was quickly dispatched to the scene of the disaster.

Mr. Mooney meanwhile arranged for the tug boats, *Scotsman* and *Togo,* and the steamer *Bridgewater* to leave at once to aid the stranded *Uranium.* Although the captain thought the steamer to be in no danger, he ordered the passengers transferred to the *Lady Laurier,* the *Bridgewater* and the *Scotsman,* and they were brought to Halifax.

The bow was considerably smashed upon impact and where she lay were sixteen fathoms of water at the stern and eight fathoms of water amidships. The local fishermen of the area could not understand why the steamer did not hear the fog whistle, which is five seconds silent, three seconds on, five seconds silent and then on forty-seven seconds. Apparently there was no pilot on board at the time she struck, as the pilot was ashore at Portuguese Cove. Mr. Holland was at the fog station and heard the steamer blowing before she hit. The captain later stated that he missed Egg Island Buoy in the dense fog, but from the wireless of the C.P.R. lines *Empress of Britain,* which had just sailed from Halifax for Liverpool, England, he learned of his position. With the message he received, he proceeded towards Chebucto Head and when he picked up the fog alarm from the station there, he set his course for the pilot. When he spotted the coast dead ahead, he ordered the helm hard to port. This should have swung the steamer to the starboard and northwest, but it was not soon enough, because of the tides and currents which were running strong against the starboard bow. This left only one alternative for the captain and that was to reverse engines full speed astern. It was already too late. She hit the shoal in three successive bumps.

The men of the Duncan Cove life boat crew, and the Herring Cove life boat crew, who arrived at the scene to aid the removal of the passengers after a hard five mile row against a stiff head wind, must be congratulated for their fine efforts as seamen helping those in distress along this coast. After attempts were made to try to refloat the steamer, it was given up, and she was left to the mercy of the sea.

Scene of a wreck of unknown schooner in Bay of Fundy

—CITY OF SYDNEY—

During the early hours of the morning of March 17, 1914, the rugged coastline around Halifax lay in a blanket of fog and total darkness. The only sound from outside the wireless station at Camperdown was that of the waves, as they crashed against the great granite wall which rose up from the waters' edge.

The men at the station were waiting patiently to be relieved after a long lonely night. While they sat within the confines of the station engaged in low conversation, they were interrupted by the sharp sound of the wireless, as it sounded its dots and dashes. In the silence of the early morning, a distress signal carried across the open water to Camperdown.

The dreaded sound of S.O.S. sounded over and over again throughout the station. The signal gave the ship's approximate location, which was somewhere near the south west ledges off Sambro. Once the message was copied for the records, the men by phone notified the marine and fisheries department of the mishap. Now that the message had been passed to them, they immediately put the wheels of motion into play.

The rescue station at Duncan's Cove was notified and they put together a lifeboat crew. Word was relayed from Duncan's Cove to Sambro, which was some seven miles south. At that time the forty ton lobster boat *Rosemary* under Captain McPhee was lying at anchor. The captain and his crew, upon notification, put out to sea in search of the *City of Sydney*.

The steamer *Montmagney* was lying at anchor in the dockyard at Halifax. Captain Robson was instructed to weigh anchor and proceed immediately to the scene of the wreck. Before the vessels left in aid of the *City of Sydney*, a message came from her saying that they needed help as soon as possible. Again around 6:00 a.m. another call was received over the wireless that the stokehold was filling with water.

W.S. Davidson, of G.S. Campbell and Company, who was the ship's agent, was informed of the wreck. The company sent out the tugs, *Togo* and *Scotsman*, to assist the other rescue vessels. Meanwhile the owners of the ship, the Dominion Coal Company, had dispatched their own steamer *Cabot*. The *Cabot* was scheduled to sail for Louisbourg that same morning.

The government boats, *J.R. Nelson* and the *Capton Wrayton*, were sent out, along with any other available craft in the

83

area, to try to help the distressed ship. By daylight the water was fairly calm but the fog hung over the area like a great mass of grey. Visibility was so poor that most of the vessels groped around trying to find the ship without colliding with other vessels doing the same thing. Captain Robson of the *Montmagny* reported to the Marine and Fisheries Department that he had fixed his position as a mile and a quarter south west off Sambro Island, near the Southwest Ledges. The fog was still heavy.

Upon receipt of this message, the Department notified the *City of Sydney* and informed Captain MacDonald to tansfer his passengers to the *Montmagny* upon arrival. As it turned out, the *Montmagny* and *Cabot* were unable to locate the *Sydney's* position because of the dense fog. By 8:30 that morning, the *Rosemary* had located the wreck and pulled alongside. Captain MacDonald had already given the order to abandon ship and ordered the lifeboats swung out on the davits. He knew, upon close examination of the ship, that she was finished.

All the passengers, and most of the crew, were placed aboard the *Rosemary* and taken to Halifax. Meanwhile, after a long strenuous row of some six miles through dense fog and rolling sea, the men of Duncan's Cove arrived upon the scene. The tugs *Togo, Scotsman,* and the *J.L. Nelson,* pulled alongside shortly afterwards. These vessels, along with Captain MacDonald, a few officers and engineers, remained close at hand for the next nine hours.

When it was finally decided what to do, Captain MacDonald and the men with him left the *City of Sydney* and boarded the tug *Togo* around 4:00 p.m. that afternoon. Upon his arrival at Halifax, the effects and strain of this experience were begining to show on Captain MacDonald's face. He had no comment when confronted by reporters. He was disheartened over the loss of his ship and, pending a formal inquiry, he would say nothing of the circumstances before the wreck occurred.

It was later learned from one of the passengers, by the name of Albert Blumiein, that from the time the ship sailed from New York, they had encountered heavy fog. "It was so thick at times, that the forecastle head was shrouded from sight."

The ship, with its crew of fifty or so and eleven passengers, had sailed a course almost by dead reckoning most of the time. It was not until the ship made the approaches to Halifax Harbour, that they encountered extreme heavy fog. Checking and rechecking his charts, Captain MacDonald decided that they were

84

in dangerous waters and too far inside the buoys. This brought him well off his course. He ordered the ship to alter course in order to swing off from the land, but it was too late and, before she could be brought around, the ship struck upon the dreaded Shag Rock around 3:15 a.m. Upon contact, most of the passengers were awakened by the deep thumping sound and a sudden lurch of the ship.

When they reached the upper deck, it was almost total darkness and due to the fog, they could not see very far ahead of them. The ship was heaving heavily, with each swell of the sea, and the grinding sound of metal against the rocks sent a cold sweat over the bodies of those aboard the ship. They had no idea that the ship which they had sailed on was doomed to destruction by the open sea.

The following is a brief history of the ship. For a period of fifteen years the *City of Sydney* visited the port of Halifax under various owners. She was built at Wallsendon-Tyne in 1890, at a length of 300 feet and registered in at 3,500 tons. Her cruising spped was around 13 knots and was first used for the German West African trade. The ship was first christened the *Admiral* and, after serving her time as a trade ship, she was then purchased by the Red Cross line to replace the *Portia*. During a twelve year period as the *Rosalind* she ran between New York, Halifax and St. John's, Newfoundland.

While under this name, she spent her time in the St. Lawrence and around Newfoundland under the Dominion Coal Company. On a few of her maiden voyages she had close calls with other vessels. On July 1, 1907, she collided with the steamer *Seniac* and sank her in dense fog off George's Island. Again in the month of November on the 13th, 1912, she collided with the tug *Douglas H. Thomas* in Sydney Harbour. At that time, four of the tug's crew were lost, and now just two years later she had come to her final end.

—COBEQUID—

On January 13, 1914, the steamer *Cobequid,* under Captain John Howson, struck upon Trinity Ledge. It was later stated that the captain said that the buoy was not lighted, and that it was

85

approximately a mile out of its original position. This was claimed to be the reason why the steamer struck the ledge and tore a hole in the bottom of the steamer.

At the time the *Cobequid* hit on the ledge, the tide was almost low and, upon the return of the tide, the steamer began to flood. In order to prevent an explosion, it became necessary to close down the boilers. Before the boilers were shut down the wireless managed to get an S.O.S signal off, giving the steamer's location which was then thought to be Brier Island. As the water rose slowly into the lower section of the steamer, the passengers were forced to seek shelter on the upper level.

Because of the circumstances and the waiting period before help came, the passengers and crew were reduced to eating dried biscuits, washing them down with water which had to be melted from ice. They used an iron pot as a make-shift stove, kindled with the furniture from the smoking room.

When the sea was at its highest peak, the waves broke over the deck, smashing the life boats on the weather side. The crew made ready the life boats that were not damaged, in case it became necessary to leave the steamer before help came.

When help finally did come, the steamers, *Westport 111* and *John N. Cann,* saw a sight for sore eyes. The men who helped to preserve life and make it as tolerable as possible were as follows: the steamer's surgeon Dr. Lister, the fifth engineer, H.H. Gladwin, the wireless officer, E.T. Gladwin Jr., the boatswain, E.W. Grinter who had been through three ship wrecks, boatswain's mate, Peter Pollock, the chef Haupe, storekeeper Caw, Prognell, Warner Jr., Fisher, Booth and one of the crew by the name of Vacey, who in the process had both his feet frozen.

—LETITIA—

Once a great modern ship of her time, the *Letitia* made her run from Montreal to Glasgow and was considered one of the finest of the Donaldson line. She was built on the Clyde in the year 1912, and her brief career as a liner came to an abrupt end when the first world war broke out.

Because of her speed and equipment that was modern at

Letitia

that time, she was immediately requisitioned for hospital service. When she arrived from Montreal and sailed into Glasgow, Captain McNeill was requested to take the *Letitia* to London where she was to undergo a complete paint job and slight alterations, according to the regulations of the Hague convention.

Once equipped with the necessary items and with a staff of medical officers, nurses and orderlies, her first assignment was the Mediterranean Sea, where she carried Sikhs and Ghurkas from Marseilles during the Gallipoli campaign. She also acted as a ferry between Suvla Bay and Malta, a distance of about seven hundred miles.

During her trips as a hospital ship, she witnessed the sinking of other ships around her and passed through many a mine field, barely escaping sudden death. On one occasion, while the Anzacs were trying to drive back the Turks from their stronghold at the gate of the Dardanelles, the *Letitia* received orders to move in as close as possible to shore. The intrenchments were not far from the water's edge and there was no land left to set up a hospital for the wounded.

While the battle raged, with the English battleships just off shore and the enemy on the mainland, the *Letitia* was caught in the cross fire. The heavy fire from both sides caused much concern to those aboard the hospital ship. But through it all, not one shell hit any part of the ship. The Turkish army made no attempts to shell the *Letitia* and, under the smoke of battle, small boats made their way to and from the *Letitia*.

Within thirty minutes from the time the British soldiers who were wounded left the trenches, they were in the hands of skilful doctors. The operating rooms were filled, emptied and refilled again. For many hours the ship lay at anchor while the battle continued and not once did the Turks lose their respect for the Red Cross ensign.

Another incident in her short career occurred when she was carrying two hundred wounded men from Suvia Bay to Malta. She was approximately midway on her voyage when she received a wireless message that the steamship *City of Birmingham* had been torpedoed not more than twenty-four miles from where she was. Immediately the captain turned the ship around and set a new course for the distressed steamship. The order was given to proceed with all speed and the engine room pushed to a record of 15½ knots, with the pressure considerably over the two hundred mark. By the time they reached the area, the *City of Birmingham* was lost from view. The only thing visible was the life boats, carrying the survivors, scattered over the pale green water of the Mediterranean. Just lying off from the life boats were two Austrian submarines watching the *Letitia* as she rescued the three hundred and fifty persons.

While the last of the survivors were being picked up, Captain McNeill was scanning the horizon with his binoculars when he zeroed in on a dog afloat on a piece of the wreckage about a mile away. Because of his love for animals, he could not let the sea have this dog and he ordered his chief officer to take one of the ship's small boats and rescue the dog. While the boat was being lowered into the water, it was impossible for the officer to see the dog, but , with the help of the captain on the bridge, by means of signals, they were able to locate the dog. Shortly the Airedale was brought safely aboard the ship and, to show his appreciation, he was affectionate to everyone and went around licking their hands. He was very fond of the chief officer and showed him his love by licking his face and hands.

The ship once again started for Malta, when she received word that a French passenger steamer had been hit by a torpedo and its location showed that they were not more than two hours away from the sinking steamer. With some 790 passengers aboard, the hospital ship moved out at top speed. This time she arrived in time to see the steamer go to the bottom, the French captain was still on the bridge when she went down. He was wearing a pneumatic vest at the time and although he was drawn down with the ship, he came to the surface with such speed that he was thrown clear of the water. The French captain was quickly rescued by one of the boats, along with 210 from his steamer. When the old French captain came on board the *Letitia,* he quickly expressed his gratitude by kissing Captain McNeill on both cheeks. Soaking wet and with his long beard dripping wet down to his waist, he must have given Captain McNeill the feeling that he had just met with Nemo himself for the first time. Among the survivors of the French steamer were many young, pretty French girls, whom Captain McNeill would much rather have received a kiss from than from the old skipper.

Just before the withdrawal from the Gallipoli campaign, Captain McNeill was in the company of fourteen other hospital ships at a place called Mudros. They were all gathered there for the purpose of removing heavy casualties during the withdrawal from the peninsula. Apparently only two ships were sent up to the embarking point and one of these ships was the *Letitia.* She had taken on only forty of the wounded soldiers and then embarked to another place where she was required.

These events were only a few in the career of the hospital ship *Letitia.* She had had a number of close escapes and all those assigned to her believed that she was one of the ships with a charmed life. Now that she had survived the war, she turned her bow once more to the open waters of the Atlantic, with a load of Canadian soldiers bound for Halifax for disembarking. While nearing the approaches to Halifax harbour, the captain took on a pilot and turned the command of his ship over to him. It was only ten minutes from the time that the pilot took command, that she piled up on the rocks at Portuguese Cove during the month of August, 1917. There her brief life came to an end. The career of one of the finest ships had closed in the log book. Captain McNeill was later given command of another ship and with him went the chief engineer Thompson to serve under his command.

Halifax Explosion

—THE MONT BLANC AND IMO—

There are many people living who can remember the 'Great Explosion of 1917.' These people, mostly children at the time, today, as adults, still vividly remember that dreadful day.

Once a year on December 6th, most of the population of the Halifax area looks back and remembers.

The explosion was one of the largest in the history of North America. In many ways it resembled a small atomic bomb without the effects of radiation. For a city the size of Halifax at that time, the results were devastating. The entire North End of the city was wiped out and, in the wake of this tremendous explosion, hundreds of buildings lay strewn over many acres of wasted land.

There are many theories as to the actual cause of the explosion. One theory is that, being at the time of World War I, there was thought of sabotage involved and the explosion deliberate. Another theory claims it was an insurance trick, and then again many claim it was must plain carelessness on the part of both captains.

The weather was beautiful on that winter's morning and the water clear and calm. Conditions could not have been better for the captain of the French ship *Mont Blanc,* as she made her way up the harbour of Halifax towards Bedford Basin. The *Mont Blanc* was carrying a cargo of Benzine on her upper deck and some three thousand tons of Nitro Glycerine (T.N.T.) below her decks.

As the French ship moved slowly towards the narrows, another ship was coming from the Basin and into the narrows also. The Norwegian ship *Imo* was leaving the Basin with a cargo of relief supplies for the war victims of Belgium. The 'Narrows' spans nearly a quarter of a mile from the Halifax to the Dartmouth shore and is of considerable depth. It is a good area in which to manoeuver two ships, and therefore gives rise to the theories regarding the cause.

Records show that the two vessels collided and almost immediately the cargo of Benzine on the *Mont Blanc* caught fire. About twenty minutes later, at five after nine, the three thousand tons of T.N.T. exploded sending up a huge cloud of yellow smoke. The roar of the blast defies description. Chaos reigned throughout the city. Richmond in the north end, almost two square miles, was a smoking ruin. Most of the waterfront area was devastated, with few windows in any building, private or public, remaining intact. Many homes and residences were lost.

Windows were broken in homes miles from the Halifax area and it is said that the ground and windows trembled as much as eighty miles from the disaster area. Fragments from both ships were blown for miles around, embedding themselves upon impact, later to be found and marvelled at. A gun from the *Mont Blanc* came to rest in a Dartmouth lake miles from the explosion.

The estimates of damage to homes, properties, and businesses came to sixty or seventy million dollars. Those killed or maimed took a toll that can never be estimated by any monetary scale, with some 1,400 killed, 2,000 wounded and 6,000 homeless.

The people who were, at the time of the explosion, living in the south end of the city, had no idea of what had taken place. Even there, windows shattered around them and doors blew out, causing cuts and abrasions. It was thought that an enemy bomb

Scene — Halifax Explosion

had hit the ammunition magazine. They only realized the full extent of the disaster when crowds of injured people came to the hospitals in the area, crying for help. The injured were in shock, covered in blood, their own and mixed with others'. Limbs were lost, eyes missing and, in some cases, people were blinded for life. Such was the case of Mr. Eric Davidson, who still resides in Halifax. At the time of the explosion he was about three years old and, as time went on, he overcame his injury. He learned by trial and error to become one of the better mechanics now employed with the city of Halifax. His hobby is working on antique cars and, as I understand it, he was the only mechanic in the area who could work on the famous Rolls Royce.

Many of the injured were carred in by others in all manner of vehicles, or managed to stagger in by themselves. The hospitals were soon filled to capacity. Mattresses were put on every available floor space. Nurses and doctors worked hour after hour and women from the St. John's Ambulance Brigade and many volunteers worked steadily. The injured had every sort of wound imaginable and there seemed to be no end to them.

Soldiers and civilians formed groups to search the ruins. Most of those they found were dead but there were times when they dug out a living person, usually badly injured but still living and so the search continued.

A United States ship, the *Old Colony,* served as a floating hospital. Hundreds were cared for there. The naval hospital was destroyed and the military hospital was also wrecked, but still people were brought for aid and received it. As news of the disaster went out across Canada and the United States, doctors and nurses from the Eastern States and Eastern Canada were soon to start arriving by train to help the stricken city.

The first outside help received arrived in Halifax from Boston on Saturday afternoon. The medical aid was under the direction of the Hon. A.C. Ratschesky, who was the personal representative of Governor McCall of Massachusetts. A temporary hospital was immediately established at St. Mary's College by the American Red Cross with the help of the military forces stationed in the city.

While help started arriving to the stricken city there also came unexpected trouble. A heavy snowstorm started on Saturday, with heavy drifts and low temperatures. This hampered the trainloads of food, clothing and other essentials from getting into the area. Every man and woman able to help pitched in without protest and all were heroes in their own way.

The will and courage of these people soon won out over the hardship. Temporary houses were put up on the Commons and Exhibition Grounds. The government appointed Mr. T.S. Rogers, K.C., as chairman of the committee in the handling of two million dollars for this undertaking.

Most of the industrial buildings: the Hollis Foundry, Dominion Textile on Robie St., Richmond Sugar Refinery, Emmets Ltd., the Provincial Exhibition building, Richmond School, Halifax Graving Docks, and Richmond Piers were destroyed . A few of the larger churches were destroyed: St. Joseph's and its Hall on Gottingen St., the Grove Presbyterian Church, the Methodist Church on Kaye St., Trinity Church, and St. Mark's Church.

The following is a partial list of those who were killed and not identified. It was included so as to give some grounds for recognition on the part of the reader and therefore possible identification. The list is taken from the book *A Romance of the Halifax Disaster* by Lt. Col. F. McKelvey Bell, A.D.M.S., and was published in 1918 by the Royal Print and Litho Limited, Halifax. The list itself was compiled by A.S. Barnstead, chairman of the mortuary committee:

A young girl between the age of 10 or 12 years, long brown hair with light complexion. She has one tooth missing in front, otherwise good. Her body thin and she was wearing black bloomers, grey underwear, black garters, stockings and one black buttoned boot.

A girl about ten years old, long light brown hair with light complexion. She had one upper tooth missing, a mole below elbow and vaccination marks on left arm. She wore a blue and brown plaid coat, corsets, white calico apron, tan stockings with light Stanfields underwear.

A girl about 9 or 10 years old, with light brown hair. Some people who viewed her body thought she might be Lina Parslow of the Protestant Orphanage. She was wearing a grey and black checked bodice with blue trimmings around the cuffs, also red buttons. She had a black and white checked skirt, black bloomers, ribbed underwear, black stockings, black buttoned boots, one gold necklace with a heart pendant.

An infant of about eight months, light brown hair, fair complexion with good teeth. She had on a flannel waist and skirt with pink flannel underskirt and was wrapped in a patch work

Devastation — Halifax Explosion

baby's blanket.

A young girl about 8 years old, with light brown hair and fair complexion. She wore a black and white coat with red linning, black skirt, white petticoat and fleece lined underwear. Inside her pocket was a note which said, 'from corner Barrington and Duffus street.' There was also a London Life Premium receipt book with the name Hyland.

A young girl about 5 years old, long brown hair with light complexion. She wore a blue sweater and a blue velvet dress. She was found under the Flynn Building.

A young boy about 6 years old, light hair with good teeth. He was wearing a grey sweater with red border and red belt and corduroy pants. He had a small signet ring with no name and was found due east of Hillis Foundry.

A boy of 12 years, brown hair and thin body. He wore a blue sweater, jersey style with white fleece lined underwear. He also had a black leather belt, black stockings, black laced boots and a brass ring with an oval piece containing the Union Jack. In the pockets were some papers with the name Albert Walsh and two envelopes containing various strips of paper with the following names in rubber stamp type; A. Walsh, D. Smith, W. Johnson, M. Elliot, Cecil Finlay, Dorothy Smith, P. Cash, N. Elliot, Wm. Hart along with others and an advertisment, 'Buy a Victoria Bond.'

A young boy about 10 years old, light brown hair with a disfigured face. He wore a black and white coat and vest, blue jersey with dark shirt and black garters.

An infant boy about nine months, no hair with light complexion and blue eyes. He had no clothing when brought to St. Mary's College Hospital on December 19th 11:10 a.m. and died on the following day.

A boy of 13 years old, with light brown hair and disfigured face. He had a bandage around his right heel, indicating that he had a sore heel. He was found north of the Canadian Government Railways Cattle Shed at Richmond, wearing dark blue pants, blue and white striped flannellette drawers, a pair of cashmere stockings with one extra black ribbed sock on right foot, and a pair of black laced boots.

A women with her head missing, one ring on her finger with two stones missing and a number of small pearls. She had a sum of money and two car tickets in her pocket.

A women of about 45 to 50, brown hair and fair complexion. She had decaying teeth and an injured right arm and head. She had very little clothing on except a piece of undershirt

95

Industrial building destroyed — Halifax Explosion

and blue stockings. On her third finger of her left hand was a ring of brass or gold with a red stone.

A women of about 60 years old, light complexion with long grey hair and no teeth. She wore corsets and light combination underwear, white muslin drawers, black stockings and a plain gold wedding ring.

A women of 34 years old, long dark hair and light complexion. She had a thin body and wore corsets, light undershirt and white petticoat. She had a gold signet ring on her second finger of her right hand, with a monogram 'EMCH'.

A women of about 35 years old, fair complexion with long light hair. She had a gold plate on her front teeth and wore a navy blue coat with fur collar. She also had a blue Norfolk jacket, brown knitted sweater, grey skirt with black braid, white flannel petticoat, a union suit underwear, linen chemise and black stockings. She also wore high heeled no. 4 boots, one ring on her third finger of left hand, like a wedding ring (Tiffany style) and a silver link chain around her neck.

A young girl about 20 years old, dark brown hair with fair complexion. She wore a striped underwaist and chemise, short corsets, light ribbed pink underwear, long black stockings and

96

patent leather no. 4 lace boots. On her hand she had a plain gold ring, one gilt brooch open bar pattern with heart at centre and blue stone in centre of heart. She was found at 14 Duffus Street.

A man of about 45 years of age, grey hair with sandy moustache. He had a stout body and small nose, a tatto mark on his left arm consisting an anchor surrounded by three flags folded and the words 'Windsor N.S.'. There was also a mark of an eagle with shield on its breast and a star underneath. He wore a dark vest, dark serge pants, heavy blue sweater, grey ribbed underwear, grey socks, black laced boots and a longshoreman's button, local 269. He also had a card in his pocket which said, Herbert Greenough, car inspector.

A man with his head missing. The body was dressed in a dark shirt, light grey, medium weight undershirt, black socks and black laced boots.

A male about age 40, dark hair with fair complexion. His face was disfigured and his body nude, except one sock and a shoe.

A man about 28 years old, light brown hair with gold filling in front tooth and one gold crown. There were tattoo marks on his right arm with a heart, Norwegian flag, a horse shoe and a female figure also a sailor's grave and the words 'Good Luck'. On his left arm was a figure of a sailor and a girl and the word 'Farewell'. He wore a dark coat and pants, blue overalls and brown overalls, a khaki shirt with a blue collar, heavy underwear, grey wollen socks, black low cut shoes, also an enamel button with the letters 'B.R.T.'. He might have been a Norwegian sailor from the steamer *Emery L. Ford*.

A male about 38 years old, dark hair with a sandy mustache. Two teeth out in front and on his left arm was a tattoo of a horseshoe, a heart and bunch of flowers with the word 'Amen' on right arm. He wore striped working shirt, dark pants, grey ribbed underwear with black heavy lace boots.

A male about 35 years old with black hair and a small mustache. This man is presumably a west Indian or negro with dark complexion and good teeth. He wore light blue overalls and one piece of army underwear, his body was wrapped in a heavy brown blanket.

A male about 30 years old, red hair and fair complexion. His body was thin and nude. It is said that he died on Sunday the 9th of December from the snow. Possible identification that of Johnston.

A man of about 25 years old, Negro with black hair and good teeth. He was without clothing and is said to be I. Turner of

106 Maitland St. or Charles Simmonds of Africville.
A male about 32 years old, dark hair and fair complexion. His body was nude and disfigured.

A male about 38 years old, with body disfigured beyond recognition except a heavy ring marked 'gold filled', with one light red stone and a place in same for another stone which was missing.

A man about 20 years old, with brown hair and fair complexion. He had some top teeth missing and a tattoo mark on left arm with the word 'Mother' and a scroll surrounded by a Rose and dagger. He wore dark grey heavy shirt, light brown wollen undershirt with the number 157721 written in indelible ink. He also had a 18K gold signet ring with plain shield marked E and W on the inside.

The list of dead goes on and on, and for those who were not found, their place of rest will remain concealled for all time. Even to this day, the mystery of how such a disaster was allowed to happen, has raised many questions in the minds of those who lived through that fatal day, on December 6th, 1917.

Street scene — Halifax Explosion

—CITY OF VIENNA—

The steamship *City of Vienna* was on a return trip from Europe, carrying with her some 700 Canadian soldiers back from the front. Unaware of the danger around her, the ship stayed on the general shipping route, cruising at a moderate speed.

As she neared the coast of Nova Scotia, a wall of greyness mixed with heavy mist confronted the *City of Vienna*. Within a very short time she was enshrouded by fog, making it almost impossible to see in any direction. To make matters worse, the wireless aboard ship had just received an urgent message, stating that all ships should be on the look out for German U-boats, as they were lurking within the shipping lane. The wireless operator brought the message to the bridge and when the captain read the note, he immediately ordered the engine room to cut speed and, for the safety of those soldiers aboard his ship, he altered course.

Under such poor weather conditions, the captain, in order to avoid any contact with the enemy, remained on the bridge and guided his ship as close as he dared to the shores of Nova Scotia. Steadily the ship moved up the coast line under the cover of a thick blanket of fog. The captain took chart readings every so often and, using his own judgement, he managed to bring his ship within the outer limits of Halifax harbour. He was not familiar with the approaches to the harbour and the fog did not help matters, but still the captain was determined to try to get his ship and the soldiers safely into the harbour.

In the early morning darkness on July 2, 1918, the ship struck hard upon the Black Rocks, just off Sambro Island Ledges. When the ship came to a grinding halt, the captain immediately ordered the engines in full reverse. But she held fast, unable to move from the grip of the rock ledge. The captain then ordered an S.O.S. to be sent out to all vessels in the area, as well as firing her signal guns.

Through the thick fog, her call for help was picked up by a patrol boat which was anchored in the harbour, waiting for the fog to lift. The wireless on the patrol boat replied to the distress signal and soon a search was underway. The only means of locating each other was by the use of horn signals. Long before the patrol boat had reached the ship, fishermen in the nearby area, with the use of small boats, risked their lives to try to save those

99

aboard the ship. Even with the sea running high and a strong current, the fishermen managed to get a large number of the troops off the ship and safely to shore. By the time the patrol boat arrived, the captain had ordered his men to lower all the life boats in order to assist in the rescue operation of the troops. He knew from his previous assessment of the situation that it was hopeless to try to save the ship.

Because of the heavy seas, it was impossible for the patrol boat to get close to the ship and she was settling fast. With the use of the lifeboats, the fishermen, after several hours of hard work, succeeded in making the rescue. Later during the day the sea began to take its toll and soon the ship began breaking up.

According to the records, the *City of Vienna* was captured by the English from the Austrians, after the war began, and was used as a troop carrying ship. She was built in Belfast in the year of 1914 and was owned by the Ellerman Lines Limited.

—MONTRA—

In the earlier years of her career, the *Montra* operated between San Francisco and Alaska. Later she worked the Williamette River in Oregon, and it was there that she ran aground and sank. She lay on the bottom for a period of two years until a salvage firm decided to raise her. After many repairs, the firm decided to use the *Montra* in overseas service. After the outbreak of World War I, all vessels that could float were pressed into service. The *Montra* made three trips to Europe, carrying general cargo, and after the war the *Montra* was purchased by George W. Cole of New York.

In order to get his return on the steamer, Mr. Cole used her as a coastal steamer, under the command of Captain William P. Bang, who took charge of her in January, 1920. The men who sailed on her felt that she was a jinx. According to Mr. Cole, she was sea worthy and he would use her to transport coal in the Maritime waters. Even though she was an old style steamer and built around 1880, the newly acquired crew aboard her had no knowledge of her past. On one of her many trips to Maritime

100

waters, the *Montra* left Botwood, Newfoundland, and made her way to Louisbourg for a cargo of coal. It was early morning when the steamer reached the southern part of Cape Breton, and a dense fog prevailed. In the midst of the fog, the steamer drifted off course, and just five miles from Louisbourg, at a place known as Gooseberry Cove, she piled up on a reef just a few yards off shore.

The wireless aboard the stricken steamer sent out an S.O.S. which was picked up by the steamer *Bras d'Or*. The cutter *Restless* and the cruiser *Margaret* were sent out from Sydney to assist the *Montra*. When the rescue operations were finished and the survivors landed at Louisbourg, Captain Bang commented on the loss of his steamer:

"We left Botwood, Newfoundland, at noon, August 9th in ballast for Louisbourg, where we were to load a cargo of coal for Newfoundland. Last night was foggy but we made Louisbourg Light about nine o'clock. It was so foggy, however, that we didn't like to risk trying to go in because I am a stranger in these waters. We stood off waiting for daylight and at 5:25 this morning, we piled up at Gooseberry Cove.

"The steamer immediately began to fill with water and I ordered the crew to take to the boats at 7:25. The third mate, two sailors, the boatswain, and I remained on board. At ten o'clock the vessel broke in two, the stern portion being completely submerged. Part of the bow is still firmly fixed on the reef. The officers then joined the men in the boats and made for Louisbourg. When the vessel first went aground, we sent out an S.O.S which was answered by the *Cunander Caronia* at sea, as well as the shore station."

Captain Bang had been at sea for twenty-two years and this was his first serious accident in all that time. He had with him at the time a crew of forty men, which included these officers: First Officer, Captain James Petkin, Boston North, 2nd Officer, Fred. S. Schwarmer, Flushing, N.J., 3rd Officer, Charles Sagling, Philadelphia Chief Engineer, T.S. Mayler, New York, 2nd. Engineer, P.J. Aylward, Halifax, 3rd. Engineer, B. Wise, New York, Wireless operator, Louis Parkin, New York.

—BOHEMIAN—

On February 28, 1920, the 5,544 ton ship *Bohemian,* owned by Leyland and Co. Ltd. of Liverpool, under the command of Captain Hiscoe, sailed out of Boston bound for Liverpool by way of Halifax. Due to a coal shortage in the United States at the time, she was forced to sail for Halifax for a cargo of coal.

As the ship made the approaches to Halifax Harbour, a sudden snow storm came up and visibility became poor. There was no pilot aboard the *Bohemian* at that time, because they were not near enough to a pilot station.

Without warning the ship struck upon Sambro Ledges around 3:10 a.m. on March 5th. The captain immediately sent out messages, stating that they were aground east of Sambro light. The messages were received by the navy and also by C.H. Harvey, the Marine and Fisheries agent. He informed the captain that assistance would be sent to them shortly, and within a half hour the tugs *F.W. Roebling* and *O'Leary Lee* of G.S. Campbell and Company arrived at the scene. The tug *Islander* of the Hendry tugs also set sail for the stricken ship.

The Furness Liner *Maplemore* out of Portland for Halifax had picked up the *Bohemian's* message and the captain of the *Maplemore* asked if he could be of any assistance. Captain Hiscoe requested that he stand by until daybreak.

Most of the passengers and crew were in their berths when the ship struck. There was no sign of panic and those on board dressed quickly and hurried to the upper deck. Four of the ship's life-boats were lowered over the side at 4:00 a.m., even though the ship was in no great danger. But the captain thought it best to play it safe because of the rough weather and for several hours the passengers and crew in the boats managed to keep the boats against the swell and clear of the ship.

When the tug *F.W. Roebling* arrived, those in the life-boats were taken on board and taken directly to Halifax. The captain of the *Maplemore* was later notified of what had taken place and that he could proceed into port. Because of the heavy sea and bad weather, the number one, two and three holds were partially filled with water and the ship began pounding heavily.

The *Bohemian* carried a total of 65 passengers and a crew of 115 officers and men. She also carried a cargo of 7,000 tons in her holds.   When representatives from the London Salvage Association and the Atlantic Wrecking and Salvage Co. were sent to the scene, they found the stern of the ship in 14 fathoms of water, three fathoms at the bow, 9 fathoms at the starboard, and 5 fathoms on her port side amidships.

When the passengers arrived at Campbell's Wharf, they were met by the Red Cross and given dry clothing and then taken to the Halifax Hotel. Some of the passengers were suffering from sea-sickness. The Rev. John Starie, his wife, and two children had sold their home in Marion and were returning to England after twelve years in the United States. They had only their night clothing; their money and valuables were left aboard the ship. Miss K. Hornell of Lynn was also going to England for a ten week visit. Mrs. Sullivan, who had crossed the Atlantic six times, was on her way back to Cork, Ireland. She said that this time she intended to remain in Ireland.

It was later learned that one of the life boats had a little trouble in launching. About 15 persons were in a precarious position and hung suspended until one of the crew hacked away at the rope with a pen knife.

The water was now rising in number four hold and was soon expected to reach the orlop deck. Hopes of saving the ship looked slight. At midnight on Monday her condition became worse and by 2:00 a.m. she began to pound very heavily. The mainmast was swinging until it fell over the starboard side and broke up. By now three lifeboats were put over the starboard side and some of the crew got into them. The remainder of the crew, numbering some seventy, were practically marooned on the ship. A message was sent to the tug *F.W. Roebling* to return to the ship with all speed.

Captain Ormiston had just reached Campbell's wharf with the passengers when he received the urgent message. When all the passengers were ashore, he headed back to the wreck and it was around 3:30 a.m. when he reached the ship.

The sea was breaking heavily over the rocks and it was difficult to put the tug alongside the *Bohemian*. Captain Ormiston got as close as he could to the ship and started taking off the crew by means of a lifeline. Several jumped from the deck of the ship onto the tug and received minor injuries. Some of the men could not hold onto the rope and fell between the ship and the tug. Members of the crew stated that when they left the ship she seemed to be on fire amidships. The forward section began sinking, while the after end protruded at an angle of about 45 degrees. When the tug reached Campbell's wharf with the crew and captain, she was coated with ice and her decks covered in slush. Several of the men from the *Bohemian* had to be sent to the hospital because of injuries sustained while jumping from the ship. One of the officers of the *Bohemian* described the rescue as follows:

"After those who had decided to abandon ship had put out in the boats. There were some forty of fifty men left. The ship was pounding heavily after she broke in two and we were waiting for the tug to come to take us off. A good many of the men froze their hands, and I froze mine!" he said, raising his hands to show the reporter.

The reporter replied, "Did they have any lines from the tug to the ship?"

"Oh, no." answered the officer, "No lines would hold. Some of the men in the tug held life lines in their hands, but the swell often tore them away. The swell kept swinging the tug away from the side of the ship and she had to manoeuvre back into position again. She only swung a few feet, but those men who were lost dropped off the lines at the wrong time. They might have been crushed between the ship and the tug when they came together again.

"There was a little room," he said, "but you simply had to take a chance and drop down the line when your turn came. If you hit on the tug, all right! It was hard coming down the lines hand over hand when your hands were frost bitten. It was 30 to 40 feet from the deck of the ship to the tug."

He also praised the seamanship of the captain and crew of the tug, "It was a great feat they performed in coming alongside and rescuing the men.'

An inquiry into the loss of the *Bohemian* was held in the custom house. The court was presided over by Captain J. Blanchard Henry, acting wreck commissioner. Also acting as nautical assessors were Captain Neil Hall and Captain C.O. Allan. Mr. Rowan, from Ottawa, was the acting secretary taking evidence, while Mr. W.A. Henry, Q.C., acted on behalf of the ship's owners and Captain Hiscoe.

During the morning session Captain Hiscoe, Second Officer Samuel Blackmore, and Captain Fortune, of the *Maplemore*, gave their evidence. At the afternoon session evidence was given by Third Engineer Hugh Smith, Chief Engineer W.G. Lewin, Quartermaster Michael Unthank, Look-out Patrick Walsh, Chief Officer C. Ewing and Third Officer George Kendall. The court was then adjourned until 10:30 the following morning.

The first witness called to the stand was Captain Ernest C.

Hiscoe. He told the court that he had lost his certificate and his money in the wreck and he went on to give a brief history of himself. He stated that he had been a captain for nineteen years and had joined the *Bohemian* seven years ago and had been with her ever since, except for twelve months while he served in the army in the Mediterranean. His only injury during his service was when he tried to handcuff a sailor and the sailor struck him over the head and he was unconscious for three days. When he was sent home, he returned to the *Bohemian* which at that time carried troops and horses during the war. Hiscoe said that while he commanded the *Bohemian,* she was attacked three times by enemy submarines, but he managed to escape them. It appeared that the blow on the head which he claimed to have received had affected his memory and he thought the chief officer had the log book, but he did not. The navigation books and chronometer were missing, and they did have the deviation book.

The chief officer had kept his own log book, in which he made entries each night. It recorded that the ship had passed Brazil Rock buoy at 5:10 on the evening of February the 29th and that the ship's course was set to make that buoy, but was later altered for Sambro lightship. They passed Little Hope Island by 8:28 and the captain left an order on the book to be called when the ship was six miles from the lightship. He was called around 1:30 a.m. when they hit snow squalls, visibility was about three miles and the captain wired ahead to Chebucto Head to get a bearing, but the wireless was unable to give hime one. At 2:00 a.m. the order as given to the engine roome to stand by and cruise at four to five knots. A few miles later he altered course to north 55 degrees, to north 10 degrees east true, and soon after he heard the guns and saw Sambro Island light, which seemed six miles away. He did not see the light long enough to get a two point bearing. The ship then swung on a new course and the light was practically abeam on the old course. That was about 2:45 a.m. and, ten minutes later, the ship struck forward on the rocks. Efforts were made to get her off around 4:30 to 5:00 a.m. with engines full speed astern, but without results.

When later questioned, the captain thought there had been a six mile set to the north the day the ship struck. His course, N.55 E. true, was intended to bring the ship to the lightship, but they never saw it. He said they did not hear any breakers before she hit and the man in the crows-nest could not detect shallow water and the officer who took that last bearing was a certified man. The ship had standard compasses and steering, showing no great error, the steering compass working in sympathy with the standard.

In answer to Captain Hall, Captain Hiscoe said he had not taken soundings and that he did not understand why the sound of the guns was not much louder. He said that he had no complaints to make about his men, and the officer on the bridge with him that morning was more than satisfactory. He had recommended him for captain of the *Lord Kelvin*.

Samuel Blackmore, the second officer, was next and after him came Captain Fortune of the ship *Maplemore*. After his testimony the court adjourned until the afternoon.

The inquiry concluded Saturday morning with Mr. Wilson of Lloyd's taking the stand first. Captain Henry questioned him on the tug *Roebling*. Mr. Henry and Mr. Porter were also questioned on the tug and the part it played in the rescue of the passengers and crew. When J.M. Colton, who was the supervisor of the wireless station at Chebucto Head, was brought in for questioning, he exhibited two copies of the messages between the station and the *Bohemian*. It was not suitable that night to give a correct bearing as such bearings would be only approximate because of atmospheric conditions. John Davies, senior wireless operator on the ship, exhibited the message sent and received from the wireless station. Mr. Blackmore, second officer, was recalled and he showed the court on the chart the course which the ship was steering when he was on duty. Captain Hiscoe was recalled and said that they were working on the first bearing and the reason for asking for a second bearing was to check up. Mr. Henry then addressed the court, summing up the evidence which was submitted. Captain Allen then remarked that the loss of the *Bohemian* was deplorable as was the loss of life whether unnecessary of otherwise.

—ROMSDALSFJORD—

The dreaded Blind Sisters claimed another victim. They gripped the foreign freighter *Romsdalsfjord* and held it firmly in their jaws. It would only be a matter of time before the steel constructed freighter broke under the constant pounding from the relentless sea.

As always, foreign vessels entering our waters are unfamiliar with the coastline and when conditions are unfavorable, they fall prey to the reefs and shoals surrounding Halifax Harbour. In the case of the *Romsdalsfjord,* Mother Nature played but a small part in the fate of this vessel.

The real fault lay with the Department of Transport. If they had placed a lightship off the Sambro Banks, instead of sending it on to Anticosti Island, the *Romsdalsfjord* might have seen many more trips across the Atlantic. It was later learned that this particular lightship was often used in the St. Lawrence to guard the shipping there. Apparently the Department of Transport felt that the buoys around the mouth of Halifax Harbour were sufficient for any vessel to find its way safely into the harbour.

According to the local newspaper, most vessels nearing our coast, trying for Halifax, did so by pure guess work because of the lack of well marked buoys. The truth came out at a formal enquiry which was hold by Harry I. Mathers of the Norwegian Consul, as to what actually had taken place before and during the wreck:

The *Romsdalsfjord* sailed out of Narvick, Norway, on November 17, 1920, under Captain Pay and its destination was Baltimore witha a cargo of 6,300 tons of iron ore. During her trip across the Atlantic the vessel encountered gale force winds and high seas. Because of this, the freighter ran short of fuel and was forced to alter her course for Halifax to refuel.

While making the approaches to the harbour, Captain Pay remained on the bridge with the second officer. He ordered the vessel at half speed, as the wind was east by northeast with heavy seas running. The weather at that time in the morning was a little hazy, Captain Pay had difficulty in distinguishing Sambro Light from Chebucto Light and had to rely on his own judgement. Unknowingly his vessel was approaching the Blind Sisters. There was very little water covering the shoals at that time. Without warning, on December 9, 1920, at 3 o'clock in the morning, the freighter struck headlong onto the rocks. From the moment of impact, Captain Pay knew his vessel was doomed.

Mr. Stander, the Marconi operator, was asleep in his quarters. He was the only British subject on board the freighter. He was awakened by the crash and within minutes he was at his station sending out the S.O.S. signals. At Camperdown the message was promptly picked up and relayed to T.A.S. De Wolf and Sons, agents for the freighter. Their position was recorded as being about half a mile eastward from where the *Bohemian* went down the previous year during the month of February.

The tug *La Canadienne*, along with other tugs from Halifax, were sent to try to help the stricken vessel. The crew meanwhile was busy getting the life boats ready. Blasts from the whistle shattered the air, drowning out the sound of heavy seas as they broke over the reef. The people at Sandy Cove and Ketch Harbour were awakened at the sound of rockets shooting into the night in rapid succession. Residents of that area knew all too well what those signals meant; but they were powerless to help, because of the blackness of early morning and the rough water crashing over the shoreline. They had to wait until daybreak before they could try to assist the freighter. However, by this time the vessel was driven broadside on the rocks because of the wind shifting in an eastwardly direction.

Already her side plates were crumbling due to the constant beating she was taking from the heavy seas. The tugs that were sent out from Halifax could do nothing to help, and only one came within sight of the freighter. For hours the sea pounded away at the vessel, grinding and wrenching the steel hull. Five hours after she struck, the crew had to leave the vessel. The captain and first officer remained on board until the freighter was literally going to pieces beneath their feet. They left the engines running to keep her forced on the rocks in order to break the seas astern of them.

One of the life boats had power but it refused to function at the time when it was most needed and the men had to revert to the oars. They pulled hard against the raging sea and kept themselves away from the rocks as best they could. Within a short time they sighted one of the tugs and headed for her. The men waved their arms and shouted, they flew flages on the staff, but apparently the men on the tug did not see them and headed the tug back to Halifax.

Now the men were left alone to fend for themselves, their drenched bodies shivering each time the spray struck them. They worked hard at the oars to keep their blood circulating. The men pulled hard against the terrific seas while great geysers of spume and spray rose high into the air around them as they worked their way around the shoal. It was sometime later that each life boat landed safely at Sandy Cove. The men were half dead from exhaustion and the cold.

One man suffered a fractured leg in the mishap and he was quickly attended to by the people of Sandy Cove, who helped the survivors to a place of warmth where food and hot drink awaited them.

All that any of them could save was the clothes on their back, except Captain Pay who managed to save his field glasses which were hanging from his neck. With the glasses he watched the last of his ship as it disappeared before his eyes. All that remained by ten that morning was her funnel, the tip of her main mast and a fragment of her stern. Later that morning the men were taken to Ketch Harbour, where trucks from Halifax awaited them. They boarded the covered vehicles and headed for the city.

One of the sad aspects of this disaster was the effect on the reputation of the young captain of the *Romsdalsfjord*. It was understood that this was the first vessel under his command. Apparently he was well known in Halifax and was in the city several times during the First World War. In marine circles he would have received a great deal of sympathy over the loss of his ship. But according to one captain by the name of J.W. Harrison, who had sailed in and out of Halifax for years between London and this city, he stated that if care were used, no ship need have any fear of coming into Halifax Harbour. He was quoted as saying:

"In every case I have watched during recent years, wrecks were caused by failure to use the lead. The lead is part of a ship's apparatus just as much as a compass and should be used. Halifax has an ideal harbour if the lead is used."

As for Captain Harrison, one could consider him very lucky or else that he had sailed under ideal conditions. Nevertheless, many ships met their doom around the mouth of Halifax Harbour and will continue to do so.

The *Romsdalsfjord* was 355.5 feet in length, 50 feet in the beam and 27.8 feet in depth. She was originally the *Vallymete* and later her name was changed to the *Dorington*. She was built at Newcastle-on-Tyne with a net tonnage of 3243 and this was her twelfth year of service.

—SCOTIA—

In August of 1921, the steamer *Scotia* left Halifax around 10 o'clock at night enroute to the Eastern Shore. Later that evening she was sighted off Sheet Harbour and by eight the following morning she tied up at Drum Head to unload cargo. When Captain Paul Cooper concluded his business at Drum Head, he ordered his crew to make ready to cast off. While on the bridge,

Captain Cooper heard the loud cry of a man's voice, "Fire! Fire in the forward hold!"

Just below the purser's office, heavy smoke and flames shot upwards. Apparently the fire had gained a great deal of headway, more than the crew of fourteen and Captain Cooper realized. Unable to subdue the flames, Captain Cooper had his men cut the ropes which held the steamer close to the wharf. Placing the engines in reverse, the Captain edged his steamer away from the wharf and let her drift out to Harbour Island.

He and the crew wasted no time in getting off the smoke enshrouded *Scotia*. With only the clothes on their backs, the men leaped into the water and swam for shore, leaving all their belongings aboard the burning steamer. Safely ashore, the crew and Captain Cooper watched as the *Scotia* burned to the water's edge and sank out of sight.

The steamer's history was a short one: she was built in 1907 for the Halifax and Canso Steamship Company to replace the *Strathcona,* which met a similar fate. The *Scotia* registered in at 266 tons and was of wood construction. She was regarded as the best little steamer operating along the Eastern Shore, running the year round.

Many times over she acted as an ice breaker in small harbours. During the summer months, the *Scotia* operated between Halifax and Canso, taking in such places as: Sheet Harbour, Port Dufferin, Moser River, Isaac's Harbour, Port Hilford, Port Bickerton, Drum Head, Country Harbour, Upper Whitehead, Lower Whitehaven, Queensport, Half Island Cove, Guysboro and Boylston.

Captain Cooper, formerly a resident of Sheet Harbour, was well known along the Eastern coast of Nova Scotia. The loss of his vessel and all its cargo forced the Steamship Company to suspend operations along the Eastern Shore for the time being.

—LADY OF GASPE—

After forty-five years of service, the *Lady of Gaspe* came to rest upon the Thrum Cap Shoal, on August 8, 1921. During her life span, she sailed under the names of *Restigouche* and *Rathlin*. She was an iron built ship and was launched at Port Glasgow,

110

Great Britain, in 1877. The *Lady of Gaspe* registered in at 774 tons and was 229 ft. long, 31 ft. in breadth and 15 ft. in the hold. She was driven by 130 h.p. engines.

Under the ownership of the Nova Scotia Steamship Limited, the *Lady of Gaspe* left Boston at nine o'clock Saturday night on August 7th, bound for Halifax, St. John's and Grand Bank, Newfoundland. Her holds were half filled with food stuffs, consisting of: barrelled beef, flour, meal, canned goods and other items. In dense fog Captain Neil Nicolsen tried to reach the port of Halifax without the aid of a harbòur pilot. Misfortune struck the ship around 6:00 p.m that evening when she grounded on the Thrum Cap Shoal. The ship was inside Lightship Buoy and heading N.W. travelling at half speed when she struck .

Without a wireless, they could not send out an S.O.S. and Captain Nicolsen sent out a boat, under the Chief Officer, to Halifax. They managed to reach Campbell's Wharf around 9:15 that evening. Within fifteen minutes the tugs *G.S. Campbell* and *O'Leary Lee*, left for the scene of the wreck. While heading for the *Lady of Gaspe*, the tugs met the captain and the remaining crew rowing for Halifax. They were picked up just off Meagher's Beach and taken to Campbell's Wharf. They arrived there around 10:30 that night.

According to Captain Nicholsen, five minutes after she hit the rocks, the water put out the fires in the engine room. Heavy swells lifted the ship fore and aft, and let her down hard each time on the ledge. He felt that the bottom would soon give way under such treatment, so he decided it was best that his men leave the ship. Captain Nicolsen managed to save the ship's papers, but he and the rest of the crew of twenty-four left with only what they had on. Those who were napping below took to the life boats with only their shorts on.

When questioned by one of the local reporters about the loss of his ship, Captain Nicolsen said in a raspy voice:

"Last night the thick fog prevailed practically all the way from Boston, and we had to pick our way right up to the time the ship struck. I knew we were well inside of Sambro, but we could not hear the bell on Thrum Cap. Although it was my watch below, I had Chief Officer Wesley Munroe and Third Officer Joseph McDonald remain on the bridge. It was during that watch that the ship struck, and even after the ship fetched on the ledge, we could not hear the bell.

"Before leaving the ship, we discovered that there was 14 ft. of water aft and 10 ft. forward. Once we were in the lifeboats, I knew that the ship would not last, as the sea was taking its toll on her."

—BINGHAMPTON—

Under the command of Captain Mark L. Gilbert, the American steamer, *Binghampton* left Boston around 6:00 a.m. on Sunday July 17th. She was bound for Sydney, Nova Scotia, for bunker coal. Once she took on the coal, she would set her course for Russia. During her trip up the Atlantic sea board, the *Binghampton* encountered heavy fog. Under such conditions, Captain Gilbert took no chances. He stayed in the wheel house to guide his vessel as best he could under the circumstances.

A few hours before dawn on the 18th, Captain Gilbert checked his chart to locate Seal Island Light. He knew that he was somewhere off the south coast of Nova Scotia. Due to the heavy currents, the steamer had drifted off her course and was in the danger zone. Captain Gilbert felt his vessel was in danger and if he did not alter the course he was now on, she would run ashore.

Upon his command, the man at the wheel changed the steamer's direction. Pushing its tremendous weight of 1,549 tons through the water, she moved steadily ahead. Due to the high tide, the men on the steamer had no idea what lay ahead of them. Without warning, the steamer came to a grinding halt around 7:50 a.m. on July 18, 1921, upon the dreaded Gannet Rock.

She slid over the rock some fifty feet before she fetched up solid. Upon contact, the Captain ordered the engines in full reverse, but she would not move from her position. In order to lighten the steamer, the crew began throwing her cargo over the side. Again Captain Gilbert tried to free her by using the engines in full reverse, but the tide had dropped, leaving her bow high out of the water.

Later that day several holes were sighted in the holds with water pouring in. The steam pipes and fittings began to break apart as the steamer shifted its position. Her forward compartments were full of water and six feet of water was in the engine room. In order to help keep her afloat, a great deal of the cargo, valued at $350,000, was thrown into the sea.

About 4:30 that afternoon the thirty crew members including the captain, abandoned her. They reached Chebouge Point in their lifeboats around 5 o'clock that evening. This was an unhappy day for Captain Gilbert, for this was his first loss after thirty-five years of commanding many vessels to every port of the world. That night the sea was heavy and took its toll upon the iron steamer, which was built in 1882. She was another of those vessels that because of the First World War were saved from the scrap heap.

112

—CITY OF BRUNSWICK—

On August 26, 1921, the people of Halifax were astonished to hear that the American steamer *City of Brunswick* had run aground just off Halifax Harbour. They could not understand why this steamer struck the rock ledge, known as the Two Sisters. Weather conditions at that time were ideal for navigation, night or day.

There was a great deal of speculation in the city, as to how the steamer came to be in such a position. Neither the captain nor his crew would divulge to the eager reporters what actually happened. Captain Rossi, of the *City of Brunswick,* told the members of the *Halifax Herald,* that if an investigation into the stranding of his steamer was to be held, it would take place in New York under the United States Shipping Board.

Nevertheless, the truth of the matter leaked out and, through the daily newspaper, it was brought to light the day after the misshap. The headlines read,

'STEAMER STRIKES ROCK OFF HALIFAX!'

With this opening statement, came the following story as recounted by one of the local reporters:

After several days out of Mobile, Alabama, bound for Antwerp, the newly constructed steamer developed engine trouble. Captain Rossi of the steamer, decided to try to reach the port of Halifax, where he could have the engines attended to, as well as obtain more fuel. Sailing conditions could not have been better for the *City of Brunswick,* as she headed for the harbour mouth. Although it was dark and the sea was very calm, the steamer came to a grinding standstill at exactly twelve midnight. Captain Rossi and his officers quickly accessed the situation and, after examining the steamer's hold, it was decided that they should call for assistance, as the engines were unable to pull them free. At 3:30 a.m. an S.O.S. was sent out, as well as signal flares which were sighted by the residents of Sambro. The tugs, *F. W. Roebling* and *Togo,* were dispatched from Campbell's wharf and managed to reach the steamer around 4:00 a.m. that morning. The life-saving crew from Duncan's Cove also went to the aid of the *City of Brunswick.*

Upon arrival, both captains of the tugs were informed that the steamer had developed leaks. Large swells developed which caused the *City of Brunswick* to raise and then come down heavily upon the rocks. Without question Captain Rossi ordered the crew of forty-one to leave the steamer and board the tugs. He would join them later when he thought it was no longer safe to stay aboard.

By daylight the sea had done considerable damage to the bottom of the steamer. The hatches were loosened and the cargo of pine timber in her holds was bulging the sides. With the bottom almost pounded out, the grain which she carried began to spill out under the wave action. From the midships the steamer was submerged and continued to settle. If she shifted either way, she would, without a doubt, slide off and sink to the bottom.

Meanwhile more tugs arrived at the scene, along with the Maritime Wrecking and Salvage Company's steamer *Maggie Marshall*. Operations to try to save the cargo on the upper deck had begun. Later that afternoon Captain Rossie left his steamer and was transported to Halifax. At one time it was estimated that over a hundred crafts of various sizes swarmed around the steamer. Everyone who was there wanted to get into the action and try to salvage whatever they could.

Where the *City of Brunswick* now lies, is not more than half a mile from the Bell buoy on Broad Shoal, and very near the spot where the *Bohemian* went down. It is said that she is practically covering the wreck on the Norwegian steamer *Romsdalsfjord*. Apparently the facts surrounding the circumstances leaked out when one of the crew members was conversing with a resident of Sambro. It was later told to the *Herald* that the captain of the *City of Brunswick* mistook Sambro light for Chebucto Head light. The steamer also did not have a chart of this coast, and the buoys guarding the outside waters of the port of Halifax were duly passed and noted in the log of the steamer.

The *City of Brunswick* was built for the United States Shipping Board by O. Daniels and Company of Tampa, Florida, in 1921. She was a steel screw steamer of 7,225 tons, at a length of 402 ft., breath 54 ft., and depth of hold 34.4 ft. Her agents in Halifax were Pickford and Black, who arranged for the crew members to stay at the new Seaman's Institute. Apparently this was the maiden voyage of the *City of Brunswick* and her last.

—ADVANCE—

Lying about one hundred feet from shore is the Intercolonial Company's steamer *Advance*. She came to an end, just eighteen miles from Halifax, on the eastern end of Shut-In Island. It was logged that, from the time she left Boston en route to Halifax and St. John's, Newfoundland, she had experienced dense fog for most of her voyage. On July 2, 1923, the *Advance* crashed heavily on the rocky shore of this island. The seventy-five passengers and fifty-five crew members were alarmed by the crash. Both passengers and crew rushed to the deck, and for a few moments there was considerable excitement. Captain Nicholson and a few officers surveyed the damages sustained by the steamer, and they indicated to the passengers that they were in no immediate danger.

Conditions on board the steamer soon returned to normal and the crew took charge of making the passengers comfortable. To insure the safety of his passengers and crew, Captain Nicholson ordered the wireless to send out an S.O.S. By the time the Eastern Tow Boat Company's Tug *G.S. Mayes* arrived under Captain William Sitland, the *Advance* began to list. With each swell, the aft section rose and settled again upon the rocks. The Revenue cutter *Grib* arrived with Captain R.F. Coffin in command. G.S. Campbell and Company sent their tug *F.W. Roebling* to the scene and the removal of passengers began.

Within thirty minutes all the passengers were taken aboard the tugs. The greater portion of light luggage was transferred to the *Mayes*. Two tugs returned to Halifax. The *Grib* and *Roebling* remained at the site.

Sometime later, the news that the *Advance* had finally broken in two was brought to Halifax by Captain Coffin of the *Grib*. Shortly after the *Grib* arrived, Captain Ormiston returned with the officers, crew and heavy luggage, as well as the steamer's cat, aboard the *Roebling*. When Captain Ormiston was asked about the condition of the steamer, he replied, "A few minutes after four o'clock, the *Advance* suddenly broke in two forward of her boilers. The width of the break at the top was about two feet. For sometime afterwards the unloading operations were proceeded with and it was not until her stern was almost flush with the water, that the members of the crew abandoned her. When we left her, the bow of the vessel was high out of the water on the rocks."

The only mishap aboard the steamer was sustained by Edward Carey, a crew member of the *Advance*. When the steamer broke in two, Carey was in the galley and he was struck over the back by a falling timber. Unaided, he crawled to the upper deck and over into the tug boat. Several other crew members who were below deck at the time experienced some difficulty in getting out.

One of the passengers aboard the *Advance* was the president and owner of C.E. Creighton of Creighton and Sons, Water Street. He and his wife were returning home from a two week business trip to Boston and gave a personal account of the disaster, "The advance left Boston about seven o'clock on Saturday evening, and her trip up to the time she struck had been a quiet one. The entire journey had been made through dense fog, which did not lift until sometime after the vessel was on the rocks. Yesterday morning shortly after nine o'clock, I was standing on the deck when the lookout suddenly rushed pass me, yelling that there were breakers ahead. Peering through the fog, I could just make out the white foam and, before any action could be taken to reverse the ship's engines, she had struck."

The *Advance* was an iron steamer operating out of New York. She was built in 1883 at Chester, Pa., by John Roach and Son, for the Panama Canal Railway Company. She was employed in the New York Colon Service. The steamer was a combination freight and passenger carrier of 1,650 tons. She was double decked at a length of 295 ft., 38 ft. wide and 23.4 ft. in the hold. Apparently this was Captain Nicholson's first trip to these waters and likely his last.

—MANUATA—

For weeks the schooner *Manuata* lay at anchor near the small community of Riverport. Captain Ritcey was unable to get enough fishermen together to take his schooner to the Grand Banks. Due to lack of funds Captain Ritcey was forced to charter his schooner as a cargo vessel. Under contract with a large firm, he was given a new crew.

His orders were to sail for Newfoundland, where he would pick up a fresh cargo of fish and deliver it to Marseilles. With a full complement of men Captain Ritcey weighed anchor and set his course for Newfoundland. It was September 30, 1927, when the *Manuata* sailed out of Riverport with full sails white against a grey sky.

With the wind at their faces and the spray heavy in their nostrils, the men of the *Manuata* worked the rigging. They were well aware that alertness was the only means of staying alive once a schooner is in motion upon the open sea.

The schooner became enshrouded with fog while approaching the mouth of the LaHave River. Land was soon lost from sight and the *Manuata* was at the sea's mercy.

Unaware of his position, Captain Ritcey tried his best to keep the schooner on course, but the winds and heavy tides altered the course of the schooner. Suddenly, without any warning, the *Manuata* ran hard aground on the west side of Gass Point, near the mouth of the LaHave River. After a series of distress signals, the crew waited patiently for assistance. It would not take long for the wind and sea to take their toll. The signals were picked up on the mainland and the tugs, *Arras, Mascot* and *O.K. Service,* were dispatched to the area.

The crew were taken safely aboard one of the tugs, but Captain Ritcey refused to leave his schooner until there was nothing left to be done to save her.

All three tugs tried for hours to free the *Manuata* from her position. But because of the weather, the tugs were forced to leave. In the midst of the fog, Captain Ricey took one last look at his schooner. He knew the sea would take her and it would only be a matter of time before the schooner broke under the power of the sea.

The *Manuata* was built at Liverpool, Nova Scotia, in the year 1919 and registered in at 114 tons.

—H.M.S. DAUNTLESS—

The 4,700 ton British cruiser *Dauntless* left Bermuda en route to the Martimes, and her first port of call was Halifax. She carried a complement of some 460 men under the command of Captain K.D.W. Macpherson. While steaming slowly towards Halifax, Captain Macpherson had requested bearings from Chebucto Head around 4 o'clock in the morning of July 2, 1928.

Her position was not given and the wireless at the station thought she was some distance off shore. When he did not hear from the cruiser again, he assumed she was proceeding on course without any difficulty. But when the *Dauntless* was some ten miles off Halifax, she ran into heavy fog and at once she lost all sense of direction. Unaware of their position, the captain ordered the cruiser at slow speed ahead. Within a short time she piled up on the jagged Thrum Cap shoals just east of Halifax. Upon contact the *Dauntless* careened and pivoted high out of the water. The tide was half way. When the tide was full, the captain ordered the engine room to put the engines full astern, but the cruiser held fast.

The sea was relatively calm with a steady swell which was sufficient enough to lift the gray steel hull up and set her still further on the shoal with a crunching sound. A message was sent from the *Dauntless* to the dockyard, stating her position and requesting assistance. She hit the shoal shortly after. Immediately the Halifax Towboat company was notified and the tug *Samson* was quickly dispatched to the scene. Later another tug was ordered to the stranded cruiser and both tugs could not move her. The ropes of the tug *Togo* broke at one point and when renewed both tugs again assumed their work to no avail.

Captain Macpherson ordered the wireless to send for more tugs in order to try to get his ship free. The *Landry* and *Grib* of the Eastern Towboat Company, along with the tug *C.B.S. Armstrong,* went in aid of the *Dauntless*. Even with their help the cruiser remained fast on the rocks. While the tugs assembled around the cruiser, the sailors and officers were ordered to abandon ship and with their kits and other personal belongings, the men boarded the mine sweepers *Ypres* and *Festubert* and a few tugs and were taken to Halifax. Only the men and officers thought to be necessary remained on board the *Dauntless* with Captain Macpherson, to act as a working crew in getting all important documents and valuable

118

equipment off the cruiser.

While several tugs clustered around the *Dauntless*, only tow tugs actually doing any work, a large oil tanker loomed out of the fog and disappeared again. Shortly the wrecking tug *Reindeer* arrived with Captain Featherstone and Mr. Scouter who was going to set up a rigging known as a 'ground tackle' or to some more commonly known as a 'redge anchor'. This method gives the tug four times the strength, compared with the regular hauling method.

Captain Macpherson ascertained that the cruiser was ripped open about mid section. As she lay pivoted upon the rocks, he felt that the cruiser might break in two before morning. It was decided that no further attempts would be made to try to pull the *Dauntless* free of the rocks, but the small craft, tugs, and naval cutters stood by during the night. The fear of her breaking up was on the minds of those aboard the cruiser as well as those on the other vessels.

With each roll of the sea, the cruiser lurched and settled down again. The heavy smoke which poured from her funnels had died away, and at one point the small crafts were ordered away from the bow by Commander Moody. He shouted out that the fore-mast had broken away and it might fall with a sudden lurch and tumble over on them. The incoming water extinguished any fires which may have occurred in the engine room. At times the combers reached the taffrail as she lay with a sharp list.

One of the sailors stated that with the last two boatloads of men and petty officers which left the *Dauntless* around 4:30 p.m. that afternoon more than one could be seen casting a last farewell look at their ship. Should the cruiser survive the night they would, as a last resort, try to raise her from her position by means of compressed air. But any hope of doing this with any success was given up as the sea began to roll heavily and her metal began to twist and break apart. Captain Macpherson knew it was useless to remain aboard the cruiser any longer and he ordered the remaining men and officers to leave the *Dauntless*. The captain and men bid the cruiser a farewell before abandoning her, and under a blanket of fog they were escorted to Halifax.

It was later reported that the *Dauntless* was carrying a tombstone, which bore an inscription to the memory of those men who lost their lives on the cruiser *Raleigh* which sank near the shores of Labrador several years ago.

When word of the *Dauntless* reached Vice-Admiral Fuller, Commander of the American and West Indies squadron, he set sail

119

aboard the cruiser *Despatch for Halifax. The Dauntless* was one of the finest vessels under his command.

The *Dauntless* had been launched at Jarrow, England, in 1918. She was a sister ship to the *Danae* and the *Dragon*. She was 445 ft. in length, 46 ft. in the beam, and a draught of 14 ft. 3". The cruiser carried six 6" guns, three 4" anti-aircraft guns, four 3" pounders, two 2" pounders pom pom, two machine guns, eight Lewis guns and twelve torpedo tubes. She had a cruising speed of 29 knots and was powered by engines of 40,000 h.p.

—GOOD HOPE—

Captain Hannaford placed the engines in reverse and slowly eased the trawler *Good Hope* away from the pier. He gently swung the bow southward in the direction of the mouth of Halifax Harbour. The trawler moved forward, increasing speed as Captain Hannaford, with ease of hand, pushed the throttle ahead.

This was just another routine run to the Grand Banks for the men of the *Good Hope*. Many times over they turned a pensive eye towards the waterfront of Halifax Harbour and wondered if they would return with a great catch of fish. Gracefully the trawler cut the water like a large knife, sending the curled waves towards the grey-black sheds which jutted out from the shore.

To the men of the trawler *Good Hope,* this harbour was more than just a sea port, it was their home. Once they passed George's Island, Captain Hannaford kept his vessel well between McNab's Island and the mainland. Looking back over their shoulders, the men took a last look at the great Citadel which, for so many years, had guarded the harbour. Now it was time to look ahead and carry on with their chores. Once beyond the harbour mouth, Captain Hannaford increased the speed to half throttle. The light fog which hung over the harbour faded momentarily as the sun broke through.

Then like a large grey blanket, the fog enshrouded the sun, obscuring it completely. It seemed that within minutes the sea became frosted with great rolling clouds and then silence. The sea was dead calm and the only sound was that which came from the engine room as the men kept the fires going to maintain a steady

120

run.

In the wheel house Captain Hannaford kept a close eye on the compass, while the mate looked over the chart. Both men knew the waters around Halifax Harbour, but in a thick fog the instruments were the only reliable source. What the men of the *Good Hope* did not know, was that their vessel was in fact on a collision course with the Norwegian American Liner *Stavangerfjord*, which was inbound from Norway.

At precisely 11:50 a.m. on Saturday March 16, 1929, the vessels collided. For the men of the trawler, it was like a nightmare. The large liner, like a great sea monster, loomed out of the fog and bore down on them. Captain K.S. Irgens and the pilot were on the bridge of the *Stravangerfjord*. They could see that the trawler made an attempt to pass on the port side of them and they signalled that they would try to alter their course to starboard. But because of the speed at which both vessels were travelling there was no time to try to reverse the engines and the large liner cut through the port side of the *Good Hope*. A gaping hole was left in her side and, when the liner backed off, the sea began to pour in.

The men in the engine room of the trawler rushed to the upper deck and joined those already there. Captain Hannaford, rather than lose his vessel, tried to turn the trawler around and head for shore, but the 12,927 ton liner blocked his way. Rope ladders from the Norwegian liner were thrown over the side for the men of the trawler, and the sounding of the trawler's whistle and the liner's call for help attracted the Eastern Tow Boat Co.'s tug *William S.* which was lying in wait off the breakwater for an incoming steamer.

Within 15 minutes the sea filled the bunkers and the stokeholds, flooded the engine room, and the trawler began to sink. Henrik Laurson and the mate became entangled and were carried below the surface as the trawler sank. As fate would have it, the men somehow freed themselves and swam to the surface, where they were rescued by one of the life boats. By the time the tug arrived, the trawler was gone from sight and the survivors, in their life boats, were on the verge of sinking.

Six of the survivors were picked up by the liner and taken to the Immigration pier. The remaining men of the trawler were landed at the National Fish Company's wharf. The captain of the Norwegian liner was detained for awhile, but no warrant for his arrest was issued. After a statement was taken from both captains the liner sailed out of Halifax at 3:00 that same afternoon, but before leaving she landed several hundred passengers and mail at the Immigration pier.

Captain Irgens before leaving paid tribute to the work of Captain D.D. Clayton of the tug *Williams*, for the manner in which he effected the rescue. Officials of the National Fish Co. and owners of the *Good Hope* stated that she would not be raised because of the damages sustained. The trawler was fully insured by the Standard Indemnity Insurance Co.

The *Good Hope* lies about a half mile from shore between middle ground buoy and Meagher's Beach Light in about sixteen fathoms of water. She was a trawler of 103 tons register, 128.4 ft. long, 22 ft. in the beam, and a depth of 12 ft. She was built at Hull in 1903.

—S.S. GRACE HANKINSON—

Situated in the small town of Margaretsville is a granite stone with the inscription:

"In Memory of Claire Baker, master of the *Ruby L.11* who lost his life in an heroic effort to save his crew from the wreck of his vessel, January 25th, 1930.

Greater love hath no man.

In the same disaster perished Captain Byard Powell, Charles Kennedy and Frederick Hill."

The story behind this commemoration is as follows:

During the First World War the navy built a vessel for coastal service which went under the name of *Canadian Drifter*. After the war was over, a man by the name of Clayton Collins purchased this particular vessel in 1922. For the next two years the naval boat lay at Granville Ferry, while Mr. Collins tried to find a way of making money from this vessel. It was not until a Mr. Byard Powell returned to Digby County after completing his work with the Nova Scotia Steamship Company in Boston that both men concluded that it would be feasible to form a steamship company between Saint John and Weymouth. From this agreement the Weymouth Transportation Company was formed with Mr. Collins as president, George Hankinson as secretary, and Mr. Powell as captain. The naval vessel's name was then changed to the *S.S. Grace Hankinson,* named after Mr. Hankinson's youngest daughter. Two other men, Gus Brooks, a customs officer at Weymouth, and E.C. Bowers of Westport, were investors in the company.

By 1925 the company was in full swing, making regular weekly trips to Saint John and St. Mary's Bay. The *Grace Hankinson* continued to pay dividends to her owners until the spring of 1929, when the Eastern Canada Coastal Company of Saint John purchased her and transferred the management to Saint John. When business slackened she was replaced for a short period by the *Wanda*, which connected with the S.S. *Keith Cann* at Freeport.

Because of dissatisfaction among other patrons of the service, the *Grace Hankinson* was brought out of retirement on the morning of January 23, 1930. She left Saint John at seven o'clock in the morning, with a low barometer reading and with every indication of bad weather approaching. With the *Ruby L.11* in tow, both vessels were bound for Lunenburg to have new diesel engines installed to replace their steam power.

Mr. Baker was cleared as captain and Mr. Powell was the pilot. By mid-day the course which was for Digby Gut was changed and they were now cruising near shore, in order to avoid the full strength of the flood tide. Before they made Petite Passage, a snow squall hit them and at times visibility was almost nil. The winds grew stronger with each hour and, by 5 o'clock, just before high tide, the *Hankinson* struck hard upon the reef. The *Ruby L.11* swung inside the *Hankinson* to the leeward side of her. Within minutes Norman Thurber and the man with him on the *Ruby L.11* tried to launch a lifeboat, but a large wave caught them and flung Thurber against the guard rail, breaking his shoulder.

Both men tried to reach the *Hankinston* but were forced ashore. Thurber tried to warn the men of the *Hankinson* to get into their lifeboat. However, the high wind and crashing waves drowned out his voice. Captain Baker tied a rope to his waist and leaped over the side, in an attempt to get a rope on shore with the help of Mr. Boston the engineer. As he tried to do this, Captain Baker was thrust against the *Hankinson*, he slipped through the loop of the rope and was lost from sight.

The engineer and another of the crew tied themselves to the mast in an effort to keep alive until a rope could be thrown from shore. Meanwhile the heavy seas washed away everything from the upper deck and at high tide the pilothouse was carried away by a large wave. It was not until low tide that a rope was finally secured to the ship and the two men were pulled safely to shore. By morning there was little left of the *Hankinson* and the *Ruby L.11* after the vessels had been battered by the sea.

—HURRY ON—

During the month of September, 1935, a sudden storm swept the Cape Breton coast and, in the midst of this storm of high winds and heavy seas, a small vessel fought its way eastward. The *Hurry On* was a freighter with a cargo of corn, bound for the port of Montreal. While off the coast of Cape Breton near Judique, the *Hurry On,* with a crew of twelve aboard her, ran into difficulty.

Apparently the vessel was thrown off course and during the night she was caught in a shallow water. It was not long afterwards that the sea began to heave this freighter over on her side and the men were left with no choice but to abandon her and take to the life boat. They stood off in the life boat and watched as the freighter turned completely over on her side and sank to the bottom.

The life boat also was turned over in the heavy sea and all twelve men tried to right her. After much difficulty the men managed to get it right again and got into it. In the process some of the men were lost in the darkness in the raging water. Again they were tossed from the life boat and all the provisions and oars were lost. When they again righted the boat, they crawled into it and rode out the storm.

By daylight the captain and five crew members had died. The boat was later washed high up on the beach by the huge waves and strong winds. When the men were picked up, they were questioned as to what happened to the rest of the crew. Second Engineer Albert Boudreau stated,

"We tried to keep the bodies from washing overboard but were without any rope to tie them down. We tried stowing them under the thwarts but the first thing we knew, a man would disappear and we were in no shape to hold them in the boat."

After much questioning, it was obvious that the survivors did all they could to save the captain and the others who had perished.

124

—KENKERRY—

The 6,000 ton British freighter *Kenkerry* left Havana for Halifax in the month of January to take on a cargo of grain. While making the approaches to Halifax harbour during the night of the 17th of January, 1935, Captain Duncan Milne was on the bridge when sudden gale winds and snow blinded his view. He ordered the freighter to dead slow ahead and moved through the darkness of night unaware of his position, as the lights at Chebucto Head could not be seen because of the weather conditions.

Within a short time, the freighter was hard upon the rocks at Black Rock at the mouth of Halifax Harbour. Immediately the shrill blasts of the siren and the sound of rockets were heard by the people of Portuguese Cove who got out of their beds as they knew a wreck had taken place somewhere close at hand.

The villagers searched up and down the coast in the drifting snow for the wreck which was later found by Everette Purcell late Thursday night, piled high against the cliff of Black Rock Point. The wireless aboard the *Kenkerry* had fixed their position with the operator at Chebucto Head, and the message continued for assistance until the water flooded the engine room knocking out all the power.

One of the twenty-eight crew members spotted a light on shore and shouted, "We must be near a village!"

It was not long afterwards that the men of the life saving crew arrived at the scene. They could not use their boats because the sea was a mass of white water and they would have been smashed to pieces against the rocks. The men of the boats that left Halifax for the wreck, because of the weather, could not see more than a hundred yards ahead of them. This prevented them from finding the *Kenkerry* until the following morning. Meanwhile Mr. Spracklin and Charlie Williams came down from the wireless station to assist the men already at the scene. With the use of a flashlight, Williams signalled in Morse Code to shoot another line from the bridge. One had already been shot to the cliff by means of a rocket and it was tied to a tree some fifty feet above the freighter. The attempt to launch another line failed because the line could not be pulled tight. The winches on board the freighter had no more power and the men were too cold to pull by hand, and therefore the line sagged in the water.

One of the crew members, by the name of Davis, made the

first attempt to reach shore. When he was close to the water, the line sagged ever more and, in order to reach safety, he would have had to pull himself through the icy water. The hand over hand method was working until the sea buried him and, since he could not go further, he was pulled back.

Next was a man by the name of Pat O'Day, who had had many years at sea and who proved to the remaining men that it could be done. He eased himself along the breaches buoy and was plunged into the sea. He hung on and pulled himself out and up to the steep incline until he reached the tree at the top of the cliff.

The fishermen from the life saving crew, headed by Captain John Holland, waded into the cold water endangering their own lives but helping those who were threatened by the sea. The rescued were hustled up over the rocks to safety. Captain Milne and the chief engineer remained on board until daylight. They wanted to make sure that the fate of the freighter was certain. During the time they remained on board, the stern snapped off, the freighter turned over on its side and was beaten to pieces.

The hull broke in another spot just beneath the bridge and sagged as if to follow the stern but then held. It was evident to the chief engineer that the vessel was doomed, and he signalled that he was coming ashore, but the captain refused saying he wanted to wait a little longer with the hope that one of the tugs might show up. But because of the heavy seas they were helpless to do anything. The captain stood by the starboard side for awhile looking over the side into the water at the brown scum seeping out of her gaping hull and washing up on the gray-black shore. It was then that he decided to call it quits and started over the side and eased himself onto the breaches buoy. He was the last man on the vessel and he had to cut the rope. As he did this, he lost his grip and slid into the cold dark water. The men quickly pulled the rope in, but he was gone. A small boy who sat on the rocks cried out, "It's awful, why did the captain have to drown? He was a brave man."

When the crew were sheltered in the homes of Mrs. Hildred Purcell, Mr. Ernest Purcell, Mrs. Frank Purcell, Chris Purcell and George Saddler, they talked freely of the wreck and how it actually had happened.

The Chief Engineer Dove was quoted as saying, "We were going at dead slow when I felt her bump and I ordered full speed astern. The fires were low and the steam didn't last long. Then I went into the stokehold. It was awash then and I told them to get out. It didn't take long and we didn't have any trouble in getting out."

126

Second Mate Davis stated, "The water here is colder than it was the day we were wrecked in the Straits of Magellan."

Chief Officer Mabe was quoted as saying, "Yes, I was in Canada before. I was on the *Bright Fan* when she sank, but I was never here before and I don't want to come back."

Jim Keornan, a lad of fifteen and an apprentice aboard the *Kenkerry*, was asked if he had seen what happened to the captain, and he stated with a slight deeping in his voice, "Captain Milne cut that rope, he started to come too fast, he reached up and you could see the splinters of ice stick through his hands. He pulled himself back; stopped himself, the boatswain's chair they were using as a breeches buoy slid from under him but he held on and it seemed for a long time and then he dropped. They cut the line but if fell about two feet away from the captain, he couldn't reach it and we could see him floating there, and then he was gone."

Jim Keornan was then asked about his trip and with a more cheerful expression he replied, "It's better that it's my first voyage and first wreck than if it were my last voyage because it was my last wreck."

When he was asked if he would go to sea again, he smiled and stated, "Sure, I'm going back. All my mother's people and my father's go to sea. My father is chief engineer on an Irish fisheries patrol vessel."

At that moment the wireless operator Robertson interrupted, "Lad, you don't know whether you're going back to sea or not, your father'll decide that."

When they learned that a horse drawn sleigh had arrived from Halifax, Robertson smiled and said, "If we go back by sleigh, it'll be my first trip in one."

In one of the other houses was young William Dumble also from Ireland and an apprentice, fifteen years old. He was from Plymouth and said, "You know where that is — away down on the southwest coast where Drake came from. All my father's people and my mother's people follow the sea. My father is in business now, but he followed the sea for eighteen or twenty years himself. They call him old Joe Dumble, and he'd kill me if ever he heard me calling him that."

Just then one of the seamen came into the room and remarked, "I say, where did I get that drink of whiskey, on the first rock or the second?"

It turned out that he wanted to remember it because it was his first wreck and his first drink of whiskey.

The chief officer said that when he was being rescued, "I couldn't explain to them that I couldn't walk with my sea boots full of water. I'd take two or three steps and fall down and then they'd pick me up. Then I'd fall down again. They thought I was near dead, but I wasn't."

When one of the fishermen of the Cove was questioned as to how they looked for the wreck he said, "We couldn't find the wreck at all for hours. We looked all along the coast as far as Sambro and away beyond Sambro, but we couldn't see a thing."

When the two buses finally reached the isolated Cove after battling heavy snow drifts, the stranded seamen were loaded on board and taken to the city of Halifax, leaving behind the body of Captain Duncan Milne, lost amidst the twisted steel and wreckage of the *Kenkerry*.

Imogene

—IMOGENE—

At the eastern extremity of mainland Nova Scotia lies the little town of Canso. For more than two hundred years, the people of this town derived their livelihood from the sea which almost surrounds them. The barren landscape and granite outcrop of rock is a reminder of the many storms and high winds that frequent this part of the province, and yet the hardy breed of people persist. They, like so many others along the coast, find peace of mind within their surroundings. It is often siad that people born by the sea feel the pull of it, when they are away from it for any length of time.

Despite its sometime gentleness, the sea in a tempest can take its toll upon man and his habitation. Such was the case during the month of September in the year 1940, when the people of Canso experienced a brief gale which caused havoc and sent vessels ashore. Just as suddenly as this gale struck, the weather cleared, leaving the area calm against a background of pale blue sky and a warm sun. The sea turned a deep ultra-marine blue color, crested with white caps. The residents went about their business cleaning up the debris which was left in the wake of the storm. Because of the high winds and heavy seas, the buoys off the coast shifted and changed their position.

On the 22nd of September, just a few days after the storm, a freighter out of Newfoundland under Captain Burden with a crew of twenty-seven neared the coast of Nova Scotia. The 1,625 ton *Imogene* moved lazily on the horizon against a clear sky, under the watchful eye of a few residents of Canso. The freighter carried a full cargo of salt from Turks Island. The salt was destined for Gaspe. As she neared the Strait of Canso, the captain was unaware of his position in relation to the buoys. What he thought to be on course was, in fact, dead reckoning for a reef.

Just six miles off the mainland, the *Imogene* came to a grinding halt, and upon impact the number one hatch was completely torn open. Captain Burden tried to free his vessel from the clutches of the reef but to no avail. When he examined the freighter's condition, he found the holds filling with water and the cargo mixing with the incoming water. Within a short time he had his men lowering the life-boats and making their way to shore. Cape Islanders from the town of Canso came to their rescue and towed them safely to the sheltered harbour.

The captain and his men were cared for by the people of Canso. On the following day, high winds and rough water prevented any salvage work. Later the vessel broke up and went to the bottom. She was owned by Bowring Brothers of St. John's, Newfoundland. To this day a few of the older people of the town can still remember that Saturday afternoon of September 22, 1940, when a vessel came to rest just off their shore.

—GRAIG—

On May 6, 1940, the 2,280 ton British freighter *Graig* ran aground on Flint Rock and became a total loss. Under the cover of darkness and a heavy blanket of fog, the freighter had kept as close as she dared to the coastline without endangering herself. U-boats were common along Nova Scotia and unprotected vessels were their prime targets.

The heavy fog prevented the enemy from spotting the British freighter, but for navigation this kind of weather was dangerous to inbound vessels. Unfortunately for the *Graig,* her sailing days came to an end just off the mainland of Nova Scotia. When the thirty-four crew members of the British freighter *Graig* were brought safely to the Port of Halifax, they were greeted warmly and treated as heroes. The public was anxious to hear of their rescue and how they felt about looking the possibility of death in the face.

Captain D.O. Davies began his story of how they managed to escape death in the disaster that befell their ship by saying, "When the *Graig* ran ashore on Flint Rock Saturday night, we were forced to abandon ship within twenty minutes. We had only one casualty. Seaman Alfred Radford suffered a badly bruised knee. After I examined the freighter, I ordered Chief Officer Frederick Carr to tell the wireless officer, George Burns, to flash the S.O.S. signal.

"This I understand was picked up by Halifax shipping authorities. For a period of five hours, we rowed in the dark in two life-boats, keeping in the light-beam off Egg Island lighthouse."

When Third Officer Dennis J. Neal was questioned about

the shipwreck, he replied, "We didn't know where we were in the dense fog, until the ship grounded. Captain Davies was in the chart room at the time."

Wireless Officer George Burns told how the sea quickly claimed the ship, "When we struck, I was aft and, on Captain Davies' orders, I flashed the S.O.S. signal at 11:11 p.m. I gave two more signals and then the last at 11:20 p.m., telling that we were getting the boats ready to go over the side."

Chief Engineer W.A. Swift stated, "Captain Davies ordered all the men to the boats and he was the last to leave. While we were departing from the craft, she was breaking in two. We used a rope line from the life boats to the ship and some men left without trousers, and others left their shoes and stockings behind. Radford was injured as we were preparing to leave. His leg was smashed against the ship's ladder by a wave. The water at that time was rolling over part of the ship. Once in the boats, we picked up the light beam from Egg Island when the fog lifted for a short time. At first eight men went into the starboard boat under Chief Officer Carr and the remaining twenty-six in Second Officer Morgan's port boat. After we were all safe in the boats we transferred some men to the star board boat."

Sometime later when Mr. Webber, the lighthouse keeper on Egg Island, was interviewed, he said, "I saw the rockets from the ship and learned of the *Graig's* plight. I kept the men of the ship in view by the torches in their life-boats. They approached the island as close as they dared, because the swells were quite heavy. I told them to keep to the north of the island, when they came within shouting distance. For hours they rowed about in the boats, and by dawn, when they were very wet and cold, they attempted a landing which was successful. The following afternoon a craft from the lobster factory at Little Harbour arrived at the island to take the men of the *Craig* five miles across the water to the mainland.

"Just before departure, a plane from Halifax soared overhead and dropped a parcel containing clothing and food. The parcel was picked up by Wireless Operator Burns and the warm clothing was soon put to use. In order to reach the motor craft 200 yards off the island, the men rigged a life line from the shore to the launch.

"Before reaching the craft, several men went under when they missed the boat, but were quickly hauled into the boat by their comrades. As I understand it, they were taken to Little Harbour and later brought to Halifax."

According to Halifax Naval authorities, the *Graig* broke in two and one section was on Flint Rock while the other rested on Egg Island. The *Craig,* and its cargo, both were a total loss.

Hebridean

—HEBRIDEAN—

The two masted pilot boat *Hebridean* for years guided foreign vessels into the port of Halifax. Many times she faced bad weather and rode out fierce gales while at anchor at the entrance to Halifax Harbour. Always she would carry out her duty without a mishap, and on March 29, 1940, she was called out to guide another vessel into port.

While anchored just off the harbour, the men of the pilot boat went about their duties as usual. To them this was just another routine run and, to kill the time, they played cards, listened to the radio or caught a few winks. With a slight sea running, the men of the *Hebridean* were unaware of the ship which loomed out of the darkness and bore down on them. The light on the main mast was on and a watch was posted. Everything seemed in order.

Shortly before midnight, without any warning, the Newfoundland freighter seemed to leap out of the water and come crashing down upon the waiting *Hebridean*. Like a giant knife the freighter cut the pilot boat in half. The men of the pilot boat did not have time to escape. They were lifted into the air and came down with a heavy impact.

Within minutes the *Hebridean* went to the bottom. Those men who were above deck were thrown clear and later were picked up by a naval boat from H.M.C.S. Dockyard. All through the night naval boats searched the area for any other survivors. Of the fifteen men aboard her, only six men were saved. The bodies of pilot James Renner, pilot James Dempsey, Lorni Dempsey, Lionel Pelham, Carleton Dempsey, engineer Matthew Power, boatswain Roy Purcell, Lawrence Thomas and Claude Martin were never found.

—CISS—

On page nine of the *Halifax Herald,* dated February 9, 1941, the newspaper carried the story of the Norwegian freighter *Ciss*:

133

While enroute to Louisbourg from St. John's, the freighter *Ciss* ran into heavy drift ice. During the night she became ice bound and was unable to free herself. In the midst of this ice flow, the currents surrounding Scatarie Island had changed by early morning. The freighter drifted closer and closer to the island and the men aboard her were helpless to do anything.

They watched as they came closer to the treacherous shoal near Point Nova Rock. Captain Danieisen tried his best to clear the shoal by placing the engines in full reverse, with the wheel hard to port. But the currents and heavy ice forced the *Ciss* upon the rocky ledge. The impact ripped her bottom open and she immediately began to fill with water. Examining the freighter's lower section, Captain Danieisen knew it would be only a matter of time before she would sink to the bottom.

He ordered his men to take to the life boats and get away from the freighter as quickly as possible. While in the lifeboats, the crew watched as the stern sank below the waterline. With only the clothes on their backs, the men fought their way through the ice and by 2:00 a.m. that morning, they witnessed the sinking of their vessel. By noon, the men reached a place called Port Morien, and it was here that the survivors, along with their two mascots (a cat and a dog), were cared for.

It was lucky that the 1,159 ton *Ciss* had not been in that area earlier, as a rain storm had lashed the coastline and the men may not have reached shore safely.

—H.M.C.S. OTTER—

During the Second World War, the H.M.C.S. *Otter* was on patrol off the mouth of Halifax harbour. She was near Sambro light when she suddenly caught fire on March 26, 1941. The *Otter* was a luxury craft until war broke out, then she was converted into a patrol boat under the command of Lieutenant D.S. Mossman with a crew of four officers and thirty-seven men.

The vessel was reported to have caught fire around 8:50 a.m. and within a short time the fire spread throughout the *Otter*. Hampered by high seas and strong winds the vessel was helpless, and the men on board could do nothing to save her. It was a

H.M.C.S. Otter

matter of saving those on the *Otter,* and with the help of a passing merchant ship and another vessel most of the men were saved.

According to the report, one of the life boats from the *Otter* was swamped by heavy seas while trying to escape the burning craft.

The men were thrown into the icy water and tried desperately to stay afloat until they were picked up. On one occasion, the merchant ship smashed against the *Otter* destroying two of its lifeboats, leaving the men without a means of escape. Because of this, the men had to use ropes and ladders as a means of trying to get to the merchant ship and, by this method, sixteen men reached the merchant ship safely.

The people on shore, through field glasses, could see all this happening. While they were being tossed about on the high seas, nineteen men out of a crew of forty-one died. Lieutenant Mossman had survived five shipwrecks and he was thankful to live through another. Those unfortunate men who lost their lives were as follows: Lieutenant Alan M. Walker, Chief Skipper Andrew F. Parker, Seaman Lucien J.A. Laurin, Seaman Leonard P. Thibadeau, Seaman John A. Graham, Seaman Wallace O'Hara,

Seaman John Blyth, Chief Meter Mechanic Daniel R. Gillis, Ronald M. Darrach, John G. Drew, electrician, Beverley Johnston, stoker, Edward T. Wall, Lionel E. Sturat, Dudley H. Mason, telegraphist, Irvine C. Armstrong, Elmer A. Mabey, signalman, Norman G. Woods, telegraphist, Karle A. Day, signalling assistant, Gerald J. d'Eon.

—S.S. CLARE LILLEY—

With the war still raging in Europe, the allies of Britian had gathered together a convoy of warships along with supply ships. Bedford Basin was the gathering place for the fleet of ships and together they would sail from there, bringing with them men, weapons, ammunition and vehicles of various kinds.

Among these ships of war was the S.S. *Clare Lilley*, a 3,738 ton British ammunition ship, which was on her way to join with the main task force stationed at Bedford Basin.   Unfortunately this ship never reached the convoy.   With the waters around Halifax harbour infested at times with German U-boats, the *Clare Lilley* steamed near the approaches to Halifax harbour under the cover of darkness.   It was March 22, 1942, that, while attempting to reach the fleet in a blinding squall, the ship ran aground off Portuguese Cove.   There was no way of telling how close she was to shore and under such conditions the ship struck upon the rocks.

The winds began to blow much harder as the early morning hours approached.   The sea threshed heavily against the hull of the ship and the span of water between her and the shore was a mass of white water.   Flares were sent up and a line was shot to the top of the cliffs.   Joseph Thorburn had sighted the *Clare Lilley* from a nearby cliff and quickly contacted the authorities about the ship's predicament.   The people of the area who gathered on the cliffs had taken hold of the rope and made it fast.

Lifeboats were lowered into the water.   Those of the cliffs held flashlights which pierced the thickening fog and revealed bodies thrashing about in the water.   A life raft was lowered into the water, but an attempt to manoeuver it close to shore by means of a lead rope proved useless.   It was ripped free and the raft was thrown hard against the hull of the ship.   The men on shore could

136

do nothing but watch as the men in the water tried desperately to stay afloat. When it became too much for one man to stand by and do nothing, he bravely climbed down the rock face of the cliff and when he was close enough to the water, he plunged into the rough water. Lights from the shore kept him and the men in sight. Burt Spencer guided the first man to safety and he later helped the rest of the men on the raft to reach shore by means of a life line. When the seamen were close enough to the rocks, they were urged to jump into the water and Spencer assisted them to safety. When all but five of the crew members were safely ashore, only then did Spencer need assistance to reach shore himself because he was totally exhausted.

Approximately two hours after she struck, the ship began to break up under the constant pounding from the sea. When questioned as to what happened, the engineer stated, "Everything was fine until there was a heavy crashing noise and then the ship came to a grinding halt. It seemed as if the bottom dropped out of the engine room."

In the confusion and with the rain and darkness, twenty-one men from the ship piled into a life boat and they rowed blindly around most of the night until they were picked up by a naval craft and taken to Halifax. Aboard the life boat was the ship's mascot, a cat by the name of Toots which was owned by F.G. Ford from New Town, North Wales. Thanks were given to W.G. Mitchell of Liverpool who thought of the cat at the last moment and went back for her. When daylight finally did come, the waters were much calmer and small boats came alongside the ship and removed any men left on the ship. The captain and first mate remained but were later removed from the ship which was fast breaking up. The shore line was strewn with debris and smashed wooden piles. A man by the name of Leo Peters from Sydney, Nova Scotia, was the only Canadian member of the crew. When he was questioned concerning the wreck, his only comment was, "I'm going back to Cape Breton and work at my old trade as a steelworker for awhile. One experience like this is enough to suit me for some time to come."

At a later date, a tribute was paid to Burt Spencer for his courage and heroism by Doctor S.H. Keshen. Another man by the name of William Crane who was on the cliffs at the time had stated, "It was a brilliant act of bravery and something I shall always remember."

At the time that the wreck had occurred, the radio was still in operation and they managed to get a call for help through to the naval department. But all the while she sat upon the reef, no one knew of her position except Joseph Thorburn and Burt Spencer, who were the first ones to discover her amidst the fog and light rain. Now, some twenty-eight years later, the Canadian navy's diving team are removing the ammunition from the *Clare Lilley* as she lies broken and scattered over the ocean floor. There would be great danger if the bombs, which once dried out could become active, should be found by sport divers, so in order to insure the safety of the general public, divers of the H.M.C.S. *Gramby* have removed six hundred of these bombs.

Brass Shells from Ship Clare Lilley

—R.B. BENNETT—

A sudden storm caught the schooner *R.B. Bennett* by surprise as she moved slowly along the east coast of Cape Breton. Captain Albert Crouse ordered all the men up on deck and for the rest of that day of May 4, 1942, the men battled the raging storm.

With high winds and a mountainous sea, the schooner pitched and rolled heavily. To make matters worse, a sudden downpour of rain made the deck of the *R.B. Bennett* very slippery. Captain Crouse kept a firm grip on the wheel, while the crew worked the sails. Each man strained his body to keep the schooner from capsizing. Soaked to the skin, the men struggled to secure the boom and furl the sails.

Wave upon wave crashed like thunder over the deck, forcing the crew, in order to keep from being washed overboard, to secure themselves to anything that was attached to the schooner. Unaware of the strong tides, Captain Crouse did not know how close his schooner was to Scatarie Island. In the midst of the storm, the schooner had drifted well within the dangerous shoals of this Island.

Claiming another victim, the Island stretched its tangled webb outward, capturing the disabled schooner. By three o'clock that afternoon, the schooner lifted high out of the water and crashed down upon the shore opposite the mainland side of Main-a-Dieu.

Because of their position and being directly in the line of the storm, the schooner was being pounded to pieces. Captain Crouse ordered all hands to leave the schooner.

The men leaped into the icy water, leaving all their personal belongings aboard the schooner, and made it safely to shore. Very shaken and cold, the men struggled over the rocks to the high ground above.

The residents of the Island came to their rescue and later the men were taken to mainland Cape Breton. The *R.B. Bennett* was out of Lunenburg and bound for North Sydney. She was built at Lunenburg in 1930 by Clifford Romman, at a length of 120 ft., with a beam of 25 ft., and a depth of 12½ ft. Besides her sail, she was powered by a 200 horsepower diesel engine.

—CAMPERDOWN—

On February 24, 1944, the pilot boat *Camperdown* while cruising off the mouth of Halifax Harbour, encountered a rough storm early in the morning. It kept the six pilots and eight crewmen busy to prevent running aground or colliding with another ship. During the blinding snow storm, the men kept a sharp lookout for any vessels that might be trying to reach port.

Captain L.C. Whorrall tried to keep the ship in the lee of Little Thrum Cap reef, to get as much shelter from the storm as possible. All landmarks and the Cap light were lost from view so they had to cruise by time. The ship was running up and down close to shore and, around 5:15 in the morning, the *Camperdown* ran onto the reef.

The events that followed from the time she struck were told by the following:

Captain Whorrall, "We were running up and down close to the beach and finally we got too close and ran on the cap. The ship was run ashore at high tide and with high seas running. We might have easily lost all hands, but only two were soaked."

Captain E.K. Hartling told of how he was wakened from his sleep by the crashing sound, "We tried to launch a boat but it was torn from our grip and lost. The second boat almost got away but we were able to get in and with a line aboard to pass ashore, we started away from the ship. As we pulled away a hundred yards or so, the line fouled and, as we tried to straighten it, the boat capsized. I was sure that we wouldn't make shore but we made our way through the high waves to cap and had to wait until low tide to get across to the shore proper."

Captain de Louchry stated, "It made a dickens of a big noise as it ground on the rocks and we were sure that she would be torn apart in the high waves that broke over her, but thanks to the ship builders she was a tight ship."

The men of the armed forces were thanked by the pilots and crew for their part in towing one of the dories by hand almost two miles from the eastern side of MacNabb's Island, so that the rest of the crew could be taken ashore.

The last to leave the vessel was Captain Whorrall. He examined the *Camperdown* and found the rudder off, part of her

140

keel gone and two gaping holes in the side of the engine room. The *Camperdown* was diesel powered with a weight of 180 tons, 116 ft. in length, and 26 ft. in the beam. She was built at Shelburne in 1940.

—ARKTERINI—

On the night of the 23rd of February, 1944, the inhabitants along the coast of Digby rushed to their windows and some ventured outside their homes into the cold night air. It was very unusual to hear thunder for that time of year and especially when it was snowing. Off in the distance, the people of Long Island and Brier island claimed to have heard three loud explosions which seemed to rumble across the water in their direction. The people of Meteghan said they heard only one loud thunder-like noise, and it seemed to be muffled by falling snow.

There were no flashes of light nor flares of any kind that the people of these areas could see. The only conclusion that they could come to, was that the Royal navy must have encountered the enemy off their shores and, because it was war time, this was the most logical answer. But to the surprise of these people days later, bodies were found along the Bay of Fundy at such places as Tiverton, Whale Cove, and Church Point. At Whale Cove, which is located at Long Island, the body was found by two girls playing on the beach. The corpse had on a life-jacket. In all, there were ten bodies found along the coast. When they were brought ashore, they were kept for identification.

Two men of the United Nations merchant marine, who were captains, along with officers of the local R.C.M.P. detachment inspected the bodies. It was later learned that four of these casualties were crew members of the missing steamer *Arkterini*. Apparently this steamer was a week overdue; she was on a trip from Halifax to Saint John which would ordinarily take a day to complete.

One man, by the name of George Delefes of 38 Morris St., Halifax, was suspected to have been a crew member aboard this steamer. Once the news reached the public's ears, all sorts of

141

theories came to light. Some people surmised that the steamer fell prey to a drifting mine, while others thought the sound they heard was that of the boilers exploding as she went to the bottom. Another theory was that she struck the jagged rock of Northwest Ledges off Long Island. And yet, because of her cargo, it was thought that spontaneous combustion might have been the cause. Whatever the cause, no one will ever know. Not a trace of the steamer was seen by the R.C.N. nor the R.C.A.F. during their search.

At the time the *Arkterini* disappeared, there were two naval gunners, by the names of Mathew Spencer and Alfred Sharpe, aboard her. Both men were buried with full military honours at Digby. Of the twenty-six crew men on her, not another body was found from the coal-laden steamer. The disappearance and the steamer's resting place will probably remain a mystery forever.

—H.M.C.S. MIDDLESEX—

Due to hostilities along the Eastern Atlantic Seaboard, the Canadian Navy transferred H.M.C.S. *Middlesex* to the Halifax force. She was commissioned in June of 1944 and served in the escort group W-3 of the Western escort force until August 28, 1944.

On September 18, 1945, the *Middlesex* became a tender to H.M.C.S. *Cornwallis* for sea training. Her stay in the Bay of Fundy was short lived: she joined the training establishment. During the remainder of the war, the *Middlesex* was restricted to the coastal waters of the Maritimes. She did not get the opportunity to serve in European waters and, after the war, the ship returned to Halifax Naval Base.

For awhile she was used as a ship for dumping ammunition off Halifax Harbour during 1946. Later the *Middlesex* underwent refit and was ordered to southern waters, where she carried out exercises in the waters off Bermuda. The most memorable achievement in the history of the ship was a rescue mission. A call for help went out from the steamship *Alfios*. She went aground on Sable Island in May, 1946. It was not long before the *Middlesex* was at the scene and in a military fashion rescued the men from the

142

wrecked *Alfios.*

Just six months after performing this heroic deed, the *Middlesex,* while making her approach to Halifax Harbour on December 2, 1946, under poor weather conditions, ran aground on Shutin Island. Being so close to the Naval Base, vessels were at her side within a short time. All that could be removed from her was salvaged, and the hulk was left to the fate of the sea.

The H.M.C.S. *Middlesex* was built by the Port Arthur Shipbuilding Company Limited of Port Arthur, Ontario.

H.M.C.S. Middlesex

—MARTIN VAN BUREN—

If you happen to be one of the fortunate people who was in or around Sandy Cove some thirty years ago, you may recall that day, January 15, 1945. To some it was a chance to make a little money; to others it meant booty from the sea. Those who can still recall that day clearly in their minds, may chuckle at the antics which took place so close to their homes, and at how the attitudes of people will change when opportunity presents itself.

A fisherman, tending his boat that day, saw the awesome sight of a large ship looming out of the fog momentarily. It was not more than five hundred feet from shore lying broadside on the rocks. His first reaction was to get into his dory and row out to where the ship was and get a closer look. Much to his surprise, when he got alongside the ship, he found it abandoned and he was the only person in sole possession of this large ship.

The sight of two Baldwin locomotives on her decks must have bewildered the fisherman. When he climbed on board the ship, he found motor vehicles, a variety of war machinery, dry-goods, boxes of canned rations, cartons of American cigarettes, and other items which were destined for the men of the military overseas. When news of this great find reached the ears of the public, it turned out to be a great field day for those who lived near the wreck. What they could not carry overland, they loaded in their boats to get the things safely back to their homes. Within a short time people from the city emerged upon the wreck in droves to take whatever they could carry off.

Many came to the scene of the wreck by dories, row-boats, motor boats, launches, sail craft, tugs, and those with cars came by road. They were like ants scurrying about the ship in search of whatever they could find. Before too long the R.C.M.P. were called in to put a stop to the looting. While they stood guard, no one was allowed to board the ship. It then became the task of the soldiers, sailors, and stevedores to unload what was left aboard the ship. The local salvage companies moved their heavy equipment into the area after being notified, and with the help of large cranes the heavy machinery was removed.

With her back broken, the *Martin Van Buren* held firmly upon the rocks and it was the hope of all concerned that the weather would remain stable. Should a sudden southeast gale

144

Martin Van Buren

spring up, it would mean disaster for the ship and everything that remained on her. As it was, the shoreline was covered with flour, evaporated potatoes, matches, tobacco, field ration kits, chocolate, biscuits, and other items which were light in weight and easily carried away by the changing of the tides.

With willing men and many hours of hard work, a great deal of the equipment and the two locomotives were finally removed. This, along with the rest of the cargo which was salvaged, were later placed aboard another vessel enroute to Europe. To this day the ship lies in a heap of twisted, rusted steel, the remnant of another unfortunate ship which fell prey to the rocks along our coast. To the younger generation who would question as to how the ship got there in the first place, the only answer one can give is to relate the circumstances. In January of that year the Second World War was in ful swing and the waters off the coast of Nova Scotia at times were threatened by German U-boats. Shipping was always a danger, especially for those vessels which were unarmed and at times unattended by allied war ships. It happened that on one of these occasions, a small convoy of ships was making its way towards Camperdown under the cover of a light snow storm on the 14th of January, 1945. Their objective was to reach the port of Halifax safely without coming in contact with the enemy. Under such weather conditions, visibility was poor and, though they were so close to port, the opportunity presented itself for the U boats lurking off the coast to sink them. Conditions were ideal for them to move in closer to shore in search of their prey.

Somewhere off the Blind Sisters a U boat discovered the convoy, and within minutes there was a sudden explosion. Immediately the British tanker *Freedom* began to list as she took in water after being hit by a torpedo. The second victim was the ship *Athelviking,* and she only lasted about twenty minutes before going to the bottom, taking four men with her.

Apparently an hour later the *Freedom* sank with the loss of one man, and during this time the other ships escaped under the cover of fog. One of these ships to escape with minor damages was the 10,000 ton American liberty ship *Martin Van Buren.* She drifted aimlessly about in the fog somewhere off Sambro along the treacherous rock bound coast. For several days the coast of Nova Scotia was lockbound by a heavy blanket of fog and during the period the American ship drifted ashore near Sandy Cove.

At the time she struck the rocks, the people of that area heard a loud crunching noise about 5:00 a.m. They paid little attention to it, as they were accustomed to strange noises from the sea. Little did they know that a ship with 6,000 tons of war cargo, valued at two and a half million dollars, had come to rest at their door step. How she escaped the outer reefs of that area no one will ever know, for she was abandoned at sea. She now rested upon a reef known as Duck Reef which is located less than a mile down the coast from Sandy Cove, just inside Lobster Claw reef. If you stood next to her on shore, on a clear day, you could see Sambro Island and the lighthouse.

—ODYSSEUS—

About the same time as the *Martin Van Buren* went aground, the steamer *Odysseus* escaped the threat of being sunk by an enemy submarine. She was later found fetched up on a reef just off Ketch Harbour with a cargo of coal and dry grain. With her crew gone, the old steamer was left to the fate of the sea or the possiblity of being blasted out of the water by the enemy should the opportunity arise.

But the people of Ketch Harbour did their best to secure as much of the coal and grain as they could carry off. Most of the light equipment were removed by the fishermen, and such things as heavy brass from the engine room were left because it was too difficult to get at, and how long she would remain on the reef was hard to tell. The wheel-house was stripped of its instruments, except for a bundle of marine charts from other parts of the world.

It was obvious that someone tried to remove the brass name plate which indicated the company that had built the steamer, because only a few bolts remained in place. Because of the water in the engine room it was impossible for them to get the plate off the wall. Most of the rooms, which were lined with mahogany, showed signs of decay because of age and lack of upkeep. Sometime later the *Odysseus* slipped unknowingly from where she sat and vanished from sight, leaving no trace of her ever being there. She now lies somewhere on the bottom of the ocean just off the small settlement of Ketch Harbour.

—RAINBOW—

The eighty-nine ton Boston dragger *Rainbow* left Yarmouth in November, 1947, after spending a week in dry-dock having its engine repaired. She carried a crew of seven and was owned by Dennis Boland of Boston. The dragger was on her way home when she encountered engine trouble after passing Lurcher lightship.

The captain turned the dragger around and had started

back to Yarmouth when the engine gave out. She began drifting with the heavy seas and soon began to take on water. A signal was sent out but the other fishing boats in the area could not tell whether she was operating or just drifting with the tide.

After many attempts to start the engine and to try to keep the water from raising any further in the hold, the captain ordered the anchor over the side to try to prevent the dragger from going ashore on Sunday Point. Within a short time the anchor began to drag and they were unable to help themselves. The men watched and waited until the fatal moment came when she struck the rocky ledges at Sunday Point, just beyond the mouth of Yarmouth harbour, around 6:30 p.m.

The waves crashed heavily over the decks and within a short time all hell broke loose as she began to break up under the constant pounding of the sea. The distress signal was picked up by J.M. Lamb at Saint John and he requested that all available fishing crafts in the area assist the stricken dragger. A Yarmouth fishing boat under Wentworth Porter headed for the area. When he reached the dragger, he found no life on board, and he thought they must have tried to reach the shore by means of their life jackets.

He further searched the area in the darkness and found the bodies of three of the fishermen. He could not get any closer to the dragger because the sea was too strong, and he feared that his boat would be smashed against the rocks.

Of the crew of seven, only two survived the wreck and they managed to swim ashore by means of life jackets. After a long struggle through icy waters, they reached the ragged shore and later they were taken to the General hospital at Yarmouth. While in the hospital, George Walsh gave his personal account of what had taken place:

"We left Yarmouth last Saturday morning after having been here a week for engine repairs and sailed out to the fishing grounds outside the Lurcher lightship. We made a couple of sets there before the strong southeast wind sprang up. We then headed for Boston but that same evening developed engine trouble again. We drifted all Saturday night and most of Sunday, meanwhile working on the engines. We got five of the six cylinders working and Monday noon we were at the lightship again, fourteen miles from Yarmouth.

"We hoped to make port here before dark and we telephoned the owners in Boston and reported where we were going and to tell the Coast Guard we could make it under our own power. All this time for two days, the ship had been leaking badly and the pump was out of order so we kept bailing by hand. The skipper was at the wheel and we were nearing the Yarmouth light when the engineer came on deck and reported the ship was leaking badly and was taking a heavy pounding by the heavy gale and breakers. The engine stopped again, and the skipper decided to turn her around for the open sea rather than take a chance smashing up on the rocky shores at the mouth of the harbour. The engineer got the motors started again for a few minutes, but then they gave out for good. We dropped anchor but that wouldn't hold. We started drifting, and after about twenty minutes we struck the reef on the tip end of Sunday Point.

"By then it was dark. The pounding seas were breaking all over the craft which was already on her side and taking a heavy beating. The engineer was washed overboard and disappeared, we got one dory in the water but couldn't hold it and it smashed itself to pieces. The remainder of the crew, with the exception of Goodwin, the sixty year old cook who felt he was too old to attempt to swim ashore, all jumped in the water to try and make the beach about four hundred yards away.

"That was the last I saw of O'Hearn and Melanson, but the skipper, Cavanaugh, and myself started out together. Cavanaugh couldn't swim so skipper Linehan and myself were helping him along. We all wore lifebelts, we struck rocks and Cavanaugh disappeared but skipper and I kept going, calling to each other every few minutes. I saw a small beacon ahead and realized that must be land and struck out for it. I never saw the skipper after that. Reaching the shore, I landed on a rocky section with the breakers making it extremely hard to get a good hold. That was the hardest experience I've ever had.

"I finally made dry land and lay there exhausted for some minutes, by then I was down to my underclothes and nearly perishing with cold. I struggled up and started up over a hill until I came to a house. The people there were at the beach looking for us, having heard the horn which we had been sounding when we struck. There were two little girls there and they let me lie down on a couch. Their mother arrived soon after that, gave me hot tea and sent for her husband who drove me to the hospital."

The cook, Henry White aged sixty, stated that he had supper ready when the boat struck the reef. He said, as he sat up in his bed, "I knew I could never make it by trying to swim at my age so I decided to take a chance by climbing in the rigging. After the others left I blew the horn and worked the blinker until I was forced to climb higher by the breaking waves. It was very hard trying to hold on. The cold was terrific, and finally I lost consciousness. The next thing I can remember was being picked up and on my way to the hospital."

Apparently this was the second bad experience for Walsh that year. He was knocked overboard in the Boston harbour in the month of April while serving on the trawler *Brookline,* now the *Rainbow* was a total loss on the rocks at Sunday Point.

The names of those who perished on the *Rainbow* are as follows: Captain Ronald Lenihan, Chelsea, Mass.; Engineer Elmer Sawyer, Newton, Mass.; Malachi O'Hearn, East Broadway, South Boston; Raymond Melanson, East Boston; and Daniel Cavanaugh of Boston.

—DORTHY AND ETHEL THIRD—

The seventy-five foot American owned dragger *Dorthy and Ethel third* left Gloucester on Monday, November 3, 1947, for the fishing grounds. Aboard the dragger was Captain Roderick F. Dunphy and four other crew members. While they were south east of Seal Island, the captain received a radio warning that a storm was approaching and, for the safety of his vessel and those on board, he headed for Yarmouth with 15,000 pounds of red fish on board.

As the dragger made its approach for Yarmouth Harbour under blinding rain and strong south easterly gales, the captain could not locate Cat Rock buoy nor the Hen and Chicken buoy, as the lights from both buoys were out. They continued on without the aid of the buoys until the dragger struck Gunners Point, a ledge on the north side of John's Cove, on the Cape side of the harbour. There the dragger held fast and the sea pounded heavily over her. The captain and crew, with the aid of fishermen in the area, made their way ashore in a dory. The fishermen used flashlights to guide the men from the dragger safely to the sandy beach, which was only a hundred yards from the wreck. That night the men were sheltered in the homes of Alex Sweeney, Allan Sweeney, and Stanley Doane.

An inquiry was later held concerning the reason for the buoys not being in working condition on the night of the storm.

—KISMET 11—

In the midst of a raging storm, a distress signal was picked up and quickly relayed to Air Command Base, C.F.B. Shearwater. Upon receiving the call for help, the Base Commander ordered a helicopter made ready. Weather conditions in the Halifax area were fair, and the men of squadron HU-21 were eager to effect their mission. Within minutes four men entered the Sourski H04S (commonly known as the 'Horse').

When they were in their respective places, the Commander in charge primed the cylinders. Following the correct procedure, he warmed the engine up until the instrument panel showed the proper R.P.M'S. The propeller overhead whined to a high pitch and soon it was just a blur to the naked eye. Gradually the helicopter rose from its pad, and in no time at all they were well over the harbour, following the compass eastward.

Keeping in constant touch with home base, the men of the helicopter prepared themselves for a rough ride. Visibility was poor on that November day of 1955, and after two hours of flying, the men were moving up the coast of Cape Breton. They experienced a strong head wind and heavy snow. Lieutenant Commander F. Roger Fink, Lieutenant Commander T.H. Beeman, Petty Officer Vipond and Leading Seaman Smith kept a watchful eye below.

The only conversation aboard the helicopter was that of the commander in charge and the radio operator at Shearwater. The co-pilot checked their course on the map and noted that they were nearing the site. Looming up out of the water below was a wall of sheer rock of nine hundred feet or so. Cape St. Lawrence on a fine day was a magnificent sight, but under storm conditions, it is a dangerous place to be near.

Held fast against the cliff, bow first, lay the ill fated *Kismet 11*. With all its fury, the sea smashed heavily over the helpless ship. The commander knew it would be an impossible task to try to rescue the men from the stricken ship; the gale force winds only added to the problem. With each attempt, the men of the helicopter held fast, the wind gusting through and around the cliffs, causing the helicopter to dip and rise with each up lift of the under thrust of the wind.

The swirling snow only added to the dilemma. The men of

the ship clung to whatever they could and watched with hope in their eyes. Due to sheer courage and determination, the men of the helicopter made one more attempt to try to reach the ship, and, this time, they got close enough to lower a rope ladder over the deck of the ship. The commander, with the help of his co-pilot, managed to keep the helicopter steady enough so that the first of the rescued climbed onto the ladder. He was very cold, wet, and almost exhausted.

One by one they climbed into the helicopter until the last of them was aboard. Twenty-one in all huddled close together and watched as the door of the helicopter closed. Steadily the helicopter rose upwards, straining under the newly acquired weight. The grey-black cliffs, crested with drifting snow, seemed to reach out for them. Below them the sea roared and lashed against the *Kismet*, slowly crushing the steel hull.

In the blinding snow, the ship was soon lost from sight and the elements outside were drowned by the continuous roar of the helicopter's engine. Turning westward, the commander headed in the direction of Halifax, where the men of the *Kismet 11* were landed safely. Sometime later, because of their heroic deed in saving the lives, all four men were cited for bravery and were presented with the George Medal.

—MAID OF LA HAVE—

The ship *Maid of La Have* unloaded a cargo of potatoes at Long Island, New York. She then started back for Halifax to pick up another cargo of potatoes for Norfolk, Virginia. When just five miles off Cape Sable Lighthouse, around 3:00 a.m. on the morning of February 5, 1957, the ship caught fire. The men were quickly aroused by Captain Jules Jourdan. With 500 barrels of diesel fuel on board, the ship was a floating bomb.

Captain Jourdan ordered the holds sealed off to prevent the fire from spreading any faster. For the safety of his men the captain altered the ship's course and headed her for land. By 4:30 that same morning the bow of the *Maid of La Have* was high out of the water. The men were soon scrambling over the side and onto the beach. Within a short time the ship was a mass of flames and the glow from the burning ship was sighted by the light keeper.

Immediately Benjamin Smith radioed the R.C.A.F. Search and Rescue section of Halifax. As the ship lay burning, people from all around Cape Sable came by foot or by boat to get a glimpse of the ship. Just a mile from the lighthouse lies the remains of the *Maid of La Have*. She was formerly an American corvette and was purchased by Captain A.D. Publicover of Lunenburg and converted into a cargo ship.

—MARGARET H.M.—

Before the discovery of mercury in swordfish, the large fishing vessels around Nova Scotia searched the waters off our coast for this large fish. It was a delight to see that large black fin protruding just above the water, sometimes stationary or moving ever so slowly through the water.

When swordfishing was at its peak and the fishing boats lined the docks with their catch, it was a sight to behold. Among these fine vessels was a particular one known as the "The Queen of Swordfishers". She was well known around the Maritime waters for her vast quotas of fish. Always she filled her holds and sailed back home to deliver her booty. The captain and crew were paid well for their fish and money flowed freely.

Now with the swordfishing industry gone, so died the legend of "The Queen of Swordfishers". Her life ended upon the jagged rocks near Rocky Bay, Cape Breton. It happened during the month of November, 1958, when she was out of Petit De Grat and bound for Sydney, Cape Breton. She was caught in a strong easterly gale, and before too long she was at the mercy of the sea.

The ship *Red Diamond 4* came to her aid, but under such harsh conditions the ship was unable to free her from the rocks. It was not long before this fine vessel became a total wreck under the constant pounding from the sea.

During her life upon the open sea, the *Margaret H.M.* was credited with saving the lives of six crewmen of the burning trawler *Sheila Patricia* out of Mulgrave. The *Margaret H.M.* was built in 1948 by John Barkhouse at East Chester. She was later purchased by Smith and Rhuland's of Lunenburg and cut in two and was then lengthened to 85 feet with a weight of 75 tons. Under the ownership of Bill Miller of Chester, she was hired out to Booth Fisheries just before her life ended.

—GLOUCESTER—

Returning from the fishing grounds just forty miles off Egg Rock, with a cargo of 40,000 pounds of cod, the American trawler *Gloucester* ran into a blanket of fog while off the mouth of Halifax Harbour. Upon entering the thick fog, Captain Michel Clarke turned on the radar and, very much to his surprise, the radar did not function. Without this instrument to guide them, the trawler was at a loss.

To add to their problem, the men were faced with winds from 30 to 40 m.p.h., followed by high seas. Captain Clarke had no alternative but to turn to his charts and compass and try to figure out their position as best he could. In the midst of the heavy fog, and in the hopes of picking up a sounding buoy, the trawler moved steadily through the water.

The men of the trawler knew how dangerous it was to be in such a predicament, and they kept a sharp ear to try to catch the sound of a buoy. Operating a vessel along the coast of Nova Scotia in the middle of winter is no picnic, and to be land locked is very dangerous, especially without the use of radar.

Unknowingly, on February 19th, 1960, the men of the *Gloucester* fell prey to the sea. They came to a grinding stop at a place known as Sandwich Point and fetched up solid on the reef. Under her own power she was unable to free herself from this rocky reef. In this position, the white combers began breaking over the deck of the trawler, sending fear through the hearts of those aboard her.

Captain Clarke managed to maintain his cool and got his men safely ashore without loss of life. Their location was picked up by a radio operator and quickly passed onto the proper authorities. The *Foundation Valor* and the *Maritime Limited* were dispatched to assist the stricken trawler. After many attempts to free her without too much damage, it proved unsuccessful. The *Gloucester* slipped from the reef's grip, rolled off and sank to the bottom with all its cargo.

—CAPE AGULHAS—

Returning home from the fishing grounds during the month of January, 1956, the trawler *Cape Agulhas* experienced much difficulty. While at sea, she lost the use of her sounding gear and radar. Operating in the north Atlantic under such conditions can be very dangerous, especially during the winter months. Due to the circumstances, Captain Jack Lilly did his best to keep spirits high among his crew of nineteen. The men kept a close watch and listened very carefully for the sound of waves breaking. In the early hours of the morning, it was still dark and visibility was almost nil.

Each turn of the prop, brought them that much closer to the mouth of Halifax Harbour. A heavy sea was running at that time and this altered the trawler's course slightly. Using the compass as best he could under the circumstances, Captain Lilly brought his vessel very close to Portuguese Cove. Close to the rocky coast, a dense fog enshrouded the trawler adding further complications.

Just off the bow, the men could hear the faint sound of

waves. By the time Captain Lilly placed the engines in full reverse and changed course, it was too late. She struck a covered reef, careened and righted herself again. Her hull was ripped open, allowing the sea to rush in adding more weight to the trawler. As suddenly as it happened, the men knew without saying that possible death stared them in the face. Mate Ernest Thornhill tied a life line to himself and donned a life-jacket.

He leaped over the side in the midst of white water and large combers. Ernest fought to keep himself from being smashed against the jagged rocks. The darkness and fog only added to his problem, but he kept his head and swam for shore. Unfortunately a large wave caught him and lifted him high against the large rock. He was stunned momentarily from the impact. His felt numb as he lay motionless, he knew something was wrong when he tried to swim. One of his legs would not function properly, and because of the shock, the pain did not hit him immediately.

Again he turned towards shore and struggled for all his worth. He knew that without the life line, his friends would perish. Without that life-jacket, his chances of survival would have been slim. Even with his fractured leg, Ernest made it to shore. He wasted no time in securing the line, so those on board the trawler could escape.

Gripping the rope tightly, each man in a hand over hand motion, pulled himself safely ashore. The people of Portuguese Cove came down to the scene of the wreck and assisted the survivors as best they could. Ernest was taken to Camp Hill Hospital, where he underwent treatment for his injuries.

When interviewed, Captain Lilly stated that there was nothing that he or his men could have done to prevent the sinking of the trawler. He said that they were moving at about three knots when they struck. It all happened so fast that they could only think of saving themselves from the sea and within ten minutes the trawler sank in about fifty feet of water.

The hundred and fifty foot trawler was owned by National Sea Products Ltd.

To this day I have no idea if Ernest Thornhill was ever honoured for his brave deed. Acts of heroism too often pass into obscurity with time and it is too bad that our memories are short lived. Our hurried life style prevents us from taking a brief moment to reflect upon great deeds of the past.

—JANET IRENE—

The *Janet Irene* was a sixty foot double end displacement type of longliner.   She was built at Meteghan River in 1954 and owned by Warren Levy.   On February 21, 1963, the *Janet Irene* set sail from Shelburne enroute to Liverpool to pick up the rest of her crew.

Whatever took place aboard the longliner remains a mystery to this day.   When she did not show up at Liverpool, the air and search rescue unit along with the R.C.M.P. were called into action.   Together they combed the shore line and found pieces of the wreckage of the longliner strewn over an area of four miles.

The only section of the vessel intact was that of the forward end, from the bow stem to the cabin door.   There were also fishing gear, life jackets, and buoy markers found within the same area. There was no sign of an explosion or fire and weather conditions were not all that bad.

Some fishermen at Shelburne concluded that the vessel may have ventured too close to shore and struck the rocks at Black Point, which jutted out from land about a mile east of Shelburne. The body of Mr. Fralick was found floating close to shore.   He was clad in light clothing and wore a life jacket.   Upon examination of the body, authorities found injuries sustained to the head believed to be caused by smashing against the rocks.

The search for Warren Levy and Thomas Winters continued with the help from volunteers from Little Harbour, but to no avail.   Mr. Levy, who was the skipper of the longliner, was the last surviving member of a family of nine brothers and it is believed that his vessel was lost in the Ram Island-Hemeon's Point area.

—FURY—

The 3,000 ton Liberian freighter *Fury* was built in Hamburg, Germany, in the year 1944, during the Second World War. She served in the German Mercantile Marine under the name of *Weserwehr*. When the war ended, she was sent to Canada and given the name of *Empire Gangway*. The firm of Clarke Steamship Ltd., of Montreal, took the freighter over and renamed her *Novaport*. She was used to carry cargo to and from Newfoundland and often visited Halifax.

Some years later, this same vessel had its name changed for the last time. Under Captain Pateras, she was called the *Fury* and he took command of her at Quebec City. With a crew of seventeen, he set sail for Halifax and Newfoundland. While passing Canso on Tuesday afternoon, December 2, 1964, the vessel and crew experienced heavy seas which became much worse as they sailed westward in the direction of Halifax.

Fury

As the freighter tossed and dipped into the oncoming waves, her superstructure took a tremendous beating and, because of this, the captain was forced to sent out an S.O.S. to Halifax. Shortly afterwards confirmation was received that help was on its way. Under high winds and strong currents, the vessel made it as far as Barachois Point, at the mouth of St. Mary's River. It was here that she lost the use of her steering gear.

Captain Pateras tried his best to keep her into the wind, but she was driven sideways. He then gave the order to let go the anchors in order to keep her from drifting towards shore, but the sea with its mountainous waves prevented the anchors from taking hold. With each strain upon the heavy chains, the ship lifted high out of the water and disappeared in the valley of each trough. Panic stricken, the wireless operator sent out messages to any ships in the area. Shortly before the ship struck Steering Reef, both the short wave radio and the medium wave radio were put out of order.

All through the night flares were shot into the air at intervals. In the morning they released a few more flares which were spotted by a tug that replied to their signals. By now all the ship's hold had filled with water, and because of the steady pounding which she had taken, a gaping hole developed in her. The Foundation Maritime tug *Valiant* stood by the stricken vessel all the following day, until they received orders to assist the Greek freighter *Ogious Nicolas 111* which was grounded near Summerside, P.E.I., and in serious condition.

With most of her life boats gone, the crew of the *Fury* could do nothing but wait until the seas subsided. The coast guard ship *Narwhal* out of Halifax attempted to reach the *Fury,* and later an aircraft from search and rescue was sent to the scene. By nightfall the tide had fallen and the sea died down a little. The captain and crew knew this would be their only chance to try to make shore safely before the sea rose again.

They all climbed over the side and waded into the icy water. Once ashore they were met by an R.C.M.P. officer and a local fisherman. They, along with the captain and crew, marched overland through the woods and stayed at the motel in Sherbrooke for the night. In an interview the following day, Captain Pateras stated that he had relived an experience similar to one his father had had fifteen years earlier. It was in 1951 that his father, who was the captain of a Liberty ship, ran aground in the Phillippines. Recalling the similarities, the young captain said:

"I'm the fourth generation of captains. I'm a captain, my father is a captain, my father's father was a captain, and my father's father's father was a captain. I had one element to battle which my father didn't and that was extreme cold. It was awful. All of us were on the ship's bridge all night, and the weather got colder and colder. Water splashing on us made it even worse.

"None of us was scared, but I was frightened for the crew's safety. They are all a great bunch and they came through this wonderfully. We were all cold and thirsty, but who could eat? There was lots of food aboard, but the men just couldn't eat. We were all in the chart room during the night, in an area no bigger than nine feet by four feet. Some of the men looked like they would doze, but just as their eyes closed, a smash from a wave would bring them back to the realism of it all.

"We ere tossed about like a feather by waves as big as thirty feet."

Some of the crew members could speak no English and, when questioned through an interpreter, one sailor said, "Awful."

Another sailor, with a piece of bread in one hand and a spoon in the other, grinned as he dipped into the soup bowl and uttered in his native tongue, "Cold! Very cold!"

Old Bottles found in North West Arm

—TEGEAN—

A light fog rolled in over the approaches to Halifax Harbour on November 28, 1966, with gentle breezes. The waves rolled steadily towards shore, setting the scene of dark water against a grey misty background. In the distance could be heard the steady sound of rumbling engines moving through the water in the direction of Halifax.

Unfamiliar to our waters, the foreign Panamanian freighter *Tegean,* manned by a Greek crew, loomed up out of the fog like a great sea monster out of the deep. She moved forward, bold and unafraid of what awaited her, under the cover of darkness. About 2:00 a.m. the *Tegean* struck hard upon a reef known as the Sisters.

Upon impact the freighter began to fill with water and within minutes she started to list. The men in the engine room hurried to the upper decks, and amidst the confusion the radio operator sent out an S.O.S. Shortly thereafter a salvage tug and the coast guard were sent to aid the freighter.

Of the forty-one men aboard the *Tegean,* only thirty-nine of them were taken aboard the *Auk.* The captain and the first mate remained aboard until night fall. They refused to leave their vessel until after much persuasion from the other captains.

With the increasing rise in swells from the open sea, they feared that the 7,300 ton freighter might slip free and roll back into deeper water. In order to rescue the two remaining men, a helicopter was used. The *Tegean* was built at Houston, Texas, in 1943. She was formerly the *James W. Fannin* and later renamed the *St. Malo.* Its owner was listed as CIA, Santo Kalliopi, S.A.

—ICELAND 11—

A sudden snow storm struck the east coast of Cape Breton and, during the peak of this blinding storm, the winds forced the sea to rise to a record height. The inhabitants along the eastern coast of the Island were faced with a terrifying experience. The coastline echoed with the sound of thunder, as mountainous waves crashed heavily upon the shoreline. All through the night the storm raged and, by early morning, the coastline had changed considerably.

The area surrounding Fourchu lay in a blanket of white and the air was sharp and crisp. It was cold, very cold, and as a young boy by the name of Brian Hill took his early morning walk along the beach near the settlement of Fourchu, he kept a close eye for objects which may have washed ashore during the storm. The air cut his lungs like a knife, and he found it hard to breathe, which made it difficult for him to walk through the snow drifts.

Occasionally he would pick up an object and examine it and then throw it at an incoming wave. The sea was deep green, with tones of grey-brown, and overhead the clouds of dark grey were moving out to sea. On that morning of February 26, 1967, Brian raised his head and squinted his eyes, as he protected them from the glaring sun by cupping his hands over his forehead. What he saw before him seemed like a mirage. The bright reflection from the snow caused him to blink and rub his eyes, and then he looked again. There high and dry on the beach was a large trawler. He walked closer to it and read the name plate. The name *Iceland 11* was engraved high up on the bow.

Brian quickly returned home and told his parents. The people of Fourchu were alerted to the fact that a vessel was ashore. They figured that she must have struck the reef at Fourchu and drifted ashore during the night of the storm.

Corporal Dan Morsden of the Royal Canadian Mounted Police arrived at the scene and took charge. He tied a life line to

162

himself and crawled along a twenty foot ladder and squirmed through the bulkhead. He could find no sign of life aboard the trawler and returned to the beach, where a crowd awaited him.

Later a man was found naked about four miles east of the wreck, his body was frozen and battered. Another was found by the coast-guard icebreaker *Sir William Alexander*. The icebreaker took the bodies to the scene of the wreck and waited for the air search and rescue helicopter to arrive, so they could remove the bodies. Two dories and a rubber raft were found washed up on the rocks and all hope of finding any of the crew alive was given up.

When an inquest was held into the matter, it was discovered that the trawler was out of Souris, P.E.I., and she was trying to make the port of Fourchu. The records showed that those men who lost their lives during that storm of 1967 were as follows: Captain Thomas Hodder, Mate Leslie MacDonald, Chief Engineer Albert MacDonald, Crewmen James Carter, Clarence Malone, Lee Jenkins, David O'Handley, John Hendsbee, all of Souris, Clovis Golland of Rustico, and Reginold Foote from Burin, Newfoundland. The trawler was owned by Jonas Bjornsson.

Costarican Trader

—COSTARICAN TRADER—

High winds and heavy seas on April 28, 1967, forced the Liberian ship the *Costarican Trader* off her course and consequently the 4,100 ton ship struck stern first upon the rocks at Halibut Bay. Because of the strong currents and large waves, the ship was heaved withing ten yards of the rugged cliffs of that area.

Almost within the approaches to Halifax harbour, the ship lies hard against the granite wall with her back broken and a gaping hole close to her mid-section. The twenty-six crew members of the *Costarican Trader* were fortunate enough to reach the cliffs above by means of a gaping plank. While the ship lay helplessly upon the rocks, people in the nearby area began looting the ship on Saturday night and carried off anything they could carry. But on Sunday several R.C.M.P. officers were ordered to the scene of the wreck to guard her from further looting.

Upon close examination by salvage companies, they found that most of the lower holds were full of water and it was further decided that she would never be saved in one piece. It was thought that it would be only a matter of time before the sea would tear her structure apart and she would slip into deeper water. The tugs *Foundation Valiant* and *Foundation Vigilant* made an unsuccessful attempt to pull her free from the rocks at high tide, but their lines snapped. Later because of her position and the condition she was in, it was decided that the only way to get her off the rocks was to cut her into many sections which could be used as scrap iron. Before this took place, thousands of curious onlookers lined the highway to try to get a glimpse of the wrecked ship so close to our shore line. We can be thankful that this ship was using diesel fuel and carried no bunker oil, or our waters and nearby beaches would have suffered for years to come.

—CAPE BONNIE—

In the winter of 1967 during the month of February the coast of Nova Scotia was swept with high winds upwards of one-hundred miles per hour. The coastal waters raged with high walls of white water and, to the mariner, it meant sure death for those who would venture into this kind of weather upon the open seas.

To the wives and families of the crew of the *Cape Bonnie,* this dreadful storm brought tragedy, and with it a scar which will remain in the hearts of those who lost their loved ones on board the ship. As it happened, the 400 ton trawler was on its way back to Halifax from the Grand Banks off Newfoundland with a cargo of fish. With no way of avoiding it, the *Bonnie* ran into this storm of high winds and blinding snow. They were within sight of land when the trawler ran upon the rocks of Woody Island. Within a distance of some sixteen miles from the mouth of Halifax harbour, the trawler was helpless against the heavy seas which washed over her. When she did not show up as scheduled, the air and sea rescue teams went in search of the trawler.

A helicopter from H.M.C.S. Shearwater was sent out to search for the eighteen men aboard the *Cape Bonnie.* For a period of three hours the men of the helicopter battled high winds dropping down at times to within forty feet of the mountainous seas. When they finally located the trawler, the *Bonnie* was a mass

Cape Bonnie

165

of wreckage. They could see no life aboard her and later a search by the coast guard confirmed that all the members of the crew of the *Bonnie* had perished while trying to escape from the wrecked trawler. One body from the trawler was later found and brought to Terrence Bay.

With the trawler still upon the rocks, hopes of reaching her looked good, until another storm struck with even greater force and this time the *Bonnie* was lost from view. It was also reported that a stern trawler by the name of *Iceland 11*, 91 ft. in length, out of Souris P.E.I., was lost near Forchu on the east coast of Cape Breton. The wreckage was discovered by an eleven year old boy, who was playing near the jagged rocks of that area. The storm had claimed the lives of the ten crew members.

Old Bottles found in North West Arm

—ARROW—

While trying to make the approaches to the Strait of Canso on February 4, 1970, the Greek oil tanker *Arrow* out of Monrovia under Captain Anata Sobolos struck upon Gabarus Rock around 9:00 a.m. in view of those who were watching her. She was carrying in her holds at that time approximately 6,000 tons of fuel oil, which later proved to be fatal to the marine and animal life of the nearby coast.

How this tanker struck the rock is not clear in the minds of many people of that area. It would have been a different story if she had been in these waters twenty-four hours earlier, and it would have been understandable if she had been facing gale force winds of up to sixty m.p.h. But following a course in daylight hours and in fairly good sailing weather poses questions to the minds of sea faring men of the Strait area. Even though the tides in that area are a little tricky at times, there is no excuse for negligence with all the modern equipment and navagational charts supposedly aboard these vessels.

There is some reason to believe that the Rock must have been covered over at the time she struck. This would account for the gaping hold in her mid section when later examined by salvage divers. Because of her position and the heavy seas which were building up, it became necessary for some of the men to abandon the tanker around 3:40 a.m. on Thursday. More of them left at 6:10 that same day. Captain Sobolos and three others remained aboard the *Arrow* until it was too dangerous to remain on her any longer.

As she sat upon the rock, some of the fuel that she was carrying began to leak out and spread like a black plague upon the water. Later the slick was reported to have reached as far east as Cape Hogan, taking with it the life of many sea birds and animals. Salvage divers, Curley Vemp of Halifax, Edward Barrington and Joe Vigneau of Sydney, went aboard the *Arrow* to examine her condition and to conclude their findings the following morning. Those who had a really good look at the *Arrow* discovered that the original name of this vessel was the *Olympic Games,* and it was said to be now under the control of her new owner, Aristotle Onassis. Onassis, however, has never been legally proven to be the owner. The 11,379 ton Liberian tanker ironically was trapped upon the rock whose name was taken from Greek mythology, a three headed

167

dog which guarded Hades. The locals also have a name for this rock, which is Shara MacLeod. It lies about five miles from Arichat in Chedabucto Bay.

Old bottles found in North West Arm

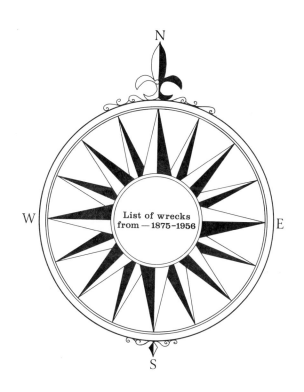

List of wrecks
from — 1875-1956

LIST OF SHIPWRECKS 1875 — 1956

(1875)— VOLANT, a brigantine of 242 tons register, sailed from a place unknown and was wrecked one mile inside Low Point Light, Cape Breton, on January 10. Her port of registry was St. John's, Newfoundland. Cause: bad weather. Value of vessel was $4,800.

WM. NASH, a brigantine of 124 tons register, sailed from Apple River, N.S., to Havana and was wrecked at Lobster Cove east of Dipper Harbour, N.S., on January 8. Her port of registry was Windsor. Cause: a snow storm. Value of vessel was $3,500.

W. JENKINS, a schooner of 117 tons register, sailed from Demerara to Boston and was wrecked at Blanche Point, Shelburne Co., N.S., on February 23. Her port of registry was Lunenburg. Cause: an error of judgment. Value of schooner was $9,000.

WM. H. THURSTON, a schooner of 54 tons register sailed from a fishing trip and was wrecked at Gull Rock near Liverpool, N.S., on February 29. Her port of registry was Gloucester, U.S.A. Cause: fog. Value of schooner was $2,700.

(1876)—AEROLITE, a schooner of 110 tons register, sailed from St. Martins, W.I., to Yarmouth and was wrecked at Seal Island on June 28. Her port of registry was Yarmouth. Cause: an error of judgment. Value of schooner was $4,500.

ANNIE AMELIA, a schooner of 95 tons register, sailed from Canso to Boston and was wrecked at Lawrencetown Beach near Halifax on December 30. Her port of registry was Souris P.E.I. Cause: bad weather. Value of schooner was $5,000.

AGO, a schooner of 34 tons register, sailed from Argyle, N.S., to Halifax and was wrecked at Brampton Rock off Port Hebert, N.S., on October 30. Her port of registry was Shelburne. Cause: bad weather. Value of schooner was $4,000.

ADELA, a barkentine of 200 tons register, sailed from Bangor to Port au Prince, W.I., and was wrecked at Woods
170

Harbour, Barrington, on date unknown. Her port of registry was Liverpool, N.S. Cause: low tide. Value of vessel was $3,000.

AMSTERDAM, a barkentine of 723 tons register, sailed from Sydney, C.B., to Quebec and was wrecked at Little Duck Island, Lunenburg, on December 13. Her port of registry was Sunderland. Cause: bad weather. Value of vessel was $16,000.

ANGIE RUSSELL, a schooner of 25 tons register, sailed from St. John, N.B., to Cannington, N.S., and was wrecked at West Bay, Parrsboro, N.S., on December 19. Her port of registry was Windsor. Cause: bad weather. Value of schooner was $500.

BLOOMING BELLE, a schooner of 15 tons register, sailed from a fishing voyage to place unknown and was wrecked at Porter's Passage, N.S., on October 18. Her port of registry was Halifax. Cause: fog. Value of schooner was $400.

BLUE WAVE, a schooner of 62 tons register, sailed from Sydney, C.B., to Marble Head and was wrecked at Black Rock Reef, Main a Dieu, C.B., on October 28. Her port of registry was Marble Head, Mass. Cause: high winds. Value of schooner $3,000.

BEVERELY, a schooner of 72 tons register, sailed from Port Gilbert, N.S., to Gloucester and was wrecked at Cranberry Head, Bay of Fundy, on October 16. Her port of registy was Digby. Cause: bad weather. Value of schooner was $2,100.

CHINA, a brigantine of 201 tons register, sailed from La Have to St. Martins, W.I., and was wrecked at Covey's Island Harbour off La Have on April 11. Her port of registry was Lunenburg. Cause: parting of chains. Value of vessel was $3,200.

DUKE OF NEWCASTLE, a schooner of 86 tons register, sailed from Joggins, N.S., to Saint John, N.B., and was wrecked one mile west of Digby light on April 27. Her port of registry was Saint John, N.B. Cause: leakage. Value of schooner was $1,500.

D.B. DOANE, a schooner, tons unknown, sailed from Port Caledonia, C.B., was wrecked at Negro Island, N.S., in November. Her port of registry was the U.S.A. Cause: bad weather. Value of schooner was $4,700 and three lives were lost.

EMELIE BARABINO, a barkentine of 737 tons register, sailed from Londonderry to Sydney, C.B., and was wrecked at Cranberry Head, C.B., on June 16. Her port of registry was Liverpool. Cause: fog. Value of vessel was $20,000.

ELIZABETH, a brigantine of 400 tons register, sailed from Quaco, N.B., to Cork and was wrecked at Porter's Passage, N.S., on November 4. Her port of registry was New York. Cause: fog. Value of vessel was $10,000.

(1876)—FRED E. SCAMMELL, a schooner of 234 tons register, sailed from St. John's, Newfoundland, to Saint John, N.B., was wrecked at Beaver Harbour, N.S., on January 3. Her post of registry was Saint John, N.B. Cause: bad weather. Value of schooner was $12,600.

FOX, a schooner of 68 tons register, sailed from Fogo, Newfoundland, to Sydney, C.B., was wrecked at Boutilier Ferry, Glace Bay, on July 6. Her port of registry was St. John's, Newfoundland. Cause: bad weather. Value of schooner was $1,000.

FLORIDE, a schooner of 84 tons register, sailed from St. Pierre Miquelon to C.B., was wrecked 40 miles south east of Scatarie Island on October 20. Her port of registry was Quebec. Cause: bad weather. Value of schooner was $3,600.

G.T. WINDSOR, a brigantine of 98 tons register, sailed from Barbadoes to Yarmouth and was wrecked at North Passage, Briar Island, on February 10. Her port of registry was Yarmouth. Cause: miss stays. Value of vessel was $1,000.

GLENCOE, a barkentine of 546 tons register, sailed from Sydney, C.B., to Richibucto, N.B., was wrecked south east side of St. Paul's Island on June 5. Her port of registry was Pictou. Cause: bad weather and strong currents. Value of vessel was $30,000.

GLENORA, a brigantine of 263 tons register, sailed from Liverpool, G.B., to Halifax and was wrecked at Gabarus, Cape Breton, on May? Her port of registry was Liverpool. Cause: fog. Value of vessel was $15,000.

JENNIE QUEROLE, a barkantine of 459 tons register, sailed from Dunkirk to Quebec, was wrecked at Little Glace Bay on May 22. Her port of registry was Rome. Cause: fog. Value of vessel was $10,000.

JUVENTA, a ship of 1,324 tons register, sailed from Liverpool to Saint John, N.B., was wrecked at Cape Sable on June 21. Her port of registry was Liverpool, G.B. Cause: fog. Value of vessel was $12,000.

KINGSTON, a brigantine of 81 tons register, sailed from Cunfuegos, Cuba, to Halifax, was wrecked at Cranly Point near Chebucto Head on December 12. Her point of registry was Halifax. Cause: snow storm. Value of vessel was $6,000.

LIVE OAK, a barkantine of 423 ton register, sailed from Saint John, N.B., to Liverpool, was wrecked near Seal Island lighthouse on March 16. Her port of registry was Saint John, N.B. Cause: bad weather. Value of vessel was $10,000.

MARY, a brigantine of 130 tons register, sailed from Halifax to Jamaica, was wrecked on west side of Ketch Harbour on April 28. Her port of registry was Halifax. Cause: snow storm. Value of vessel was $10,000.

MORNING STAR, a schooner of 33 tons register, sailed from Sydney, C.B., to Lockeport, was wrecked at Little Hope, N.S., on October 27. Her port of registry was Yarmouth. Cause: bad weather. Value of schooner was $900.

MAGGIE II, a schooner of 90 tons register, sailed from Boone Bay, Newfoundland, to Georgetown, P.E.I., was wrecked at Port Hood, C.B., on December 17. Her port of registry was Port Hawkesbury. Cause: bad weather. Value of schooner was $6,100.

MARIA CATHERINE, a schoooner of 87 tons register, sailed from Cow Bay, C.B., to Yarmouth, was wrecked at Brooklyn Roadstead, Liverpool, N.S., on date unknown. Her port of registry was Miramichi. Cause: collision. Value of schooner was $400.

NATHANIAL STEVENS, a schooner of 162 tons register sailed from Yarmouth, N.S., to Liverpool, was wrecked at Yarmouth Sound on February 6. Her port of registry was Boston. Cause: parting of chains. Value of schooner was $4,000.

NORTHERN CHIEF, a schooner of 52 tons register, sailed from Cheticamp to Arichat, was wrecked near Cape Marbon, C.B., on October 16. Her port of registry was Arichat. Cause: bad weather. Value of schooner was $2,300.

PRARIE BIRD, a schooner of 149 tons register, sailed from Cow Bay, C.B., to Saint John, N.B., was wrecked 12 miles south of White Head Light, N.S., on May 30. Her port of registry wa Saint John, N.B. Cause: bad weather. Value of schooner was $6,750.

RAINBOW, a schooner of 36 tons register, sailed from Yarmouth to Weymouth, was wrecked at Cape St. Mary's Ledges on July 20. Her port of registry was Yarmouth. Cause: fog. Value of schooner was $2,200.

R.B. MULHALL, a barkentine of 242 tons register, sailed from Cardenas, Cuba, to New York, was wrecked one mile east of West Head, Shelburne Co., N.S., on October 1. Her port of registry was Gloucester, Mass. Cause: bad weather. Value of vessel was $22,000.

S.M. RYERSON, a schooner of 41 tons register, sailed from a fishing voyage to Argyle, was wrecked at Argyle Harbour on June 13. Her port of registry was Yarmouth. Cause: burning. Value of schooner was $1,300.

TRIAF, a schooner of 53 tons register, sailed from Newfoundland to Halifax, was wrecked at Indian Brook, C.B., on January 7. Her port of registry was Pictou. Cause: bad weather. Value of schooner was $2,400.

THOMAS COCKRAN, a barkentine of 627 tons register, sailed from London to Boston, was wrecked at Scatarie Island on June 4. Her port of registry was Saint John, N.B. Cause: fog. Value of vessel was $2,000.

WILD HORSE, a brigantine of 165 tons register, sailed from Whycocomagh to Leith, G.B., was wrecked 40 miles south west of Yarmouth on December 16. Her port of registry was Maitland, N.S. Cause: bad weather. Value of vessel was $4,000.

WESTWOOD, a brigantine of 149 tons register, sailed from Turk's Island to Halifax, was wrecked at Herring Cove on December 12. Her port of registry was Halifax. Cause: bad weather. Value of vessel was $14,500 and four men lost their lives.

(1877)—ADA, a schooner of 113 tons register, sailed from Georgetown, P.E.I. to Boston, was wrecked at St. George's Bay, N.S., on January 8. Her port of registry was Charlottetown. Cause: ice. Value of schooner was $9,500.

ANNIE FLEMING, a barque of 855 tons register, sailed from Quebec to Ardrossan, G.B., was wrecked off Schooner Pond, C.B., on August 30. Her port of registry was Greenock, G.B. Cause: hitting unknown rock. Value of vessel was $40,500.

AMELIA, a steamer of 1090 tons register, sailed from Montreal to Great Britain, was wrecked off Sydney Harbour, N.S., on September 22. Her port of registry was South Shields, G.B. Cause: bad weather. Value of vessel was $500.

ASSYRIAN, a brig of 295 tons register, sailed from Montreal to Queenstown, was wrecked off Cape North, N.S., on September 22. Her port of registry was Sunderland, G.B. Cause: shifting of cargo and bad pumps. Value of vessel was $2,500.

ANTELOPE, a schooner of 28 tons register, sailed from Margaree, C.B., to Halifax, was wrecked at north entrance to Canso Harbour on December 1. Her port of registry was Port Hawkesbury. Cause: error of judgment. Three lives were lost and the value of schooner was $400.

CAMBRIA, a schooner of 109 tons register, sailed from Georgetown, P.E.I., to Boston, was wrecked at Pond Cove, Brier Island, on January 14. Her port of registry was Saint John. Cause: bad weather. Value of schooner was $4,400.

174

DREADNOT, a schooner of 105 tons register, sailed from Shelburne to Philadelphia, was wrecked at the mouth of Shelburne Harbour on May 21. Her port of registry was Windsor, N.S. Cause: misstayed. Value of schooner was $6,000.

DOMITILLE, a schooner of 17 tons registry, sailed from Port Hastings, N.S., on a fishing voyage, was wrecked at Smith's Island, Port Hood, on September 22. Her port of registry was Port Hawkesbury. Cause: bad weather. Value of schooner was $400.

ELIZA JANE, a schooner of 48 tons register, sailed from Shelburne to La Have, was wrecked at Big Rock, Shelburne Harbour, on January 23. Her port of registry was Gloucester, Mass. Cause: error in judgment. Value of schooner was $2,000.

EVERGREEN, a schooner of 106 tons register, sailed from Portsmouth, U.S.A., to Dunsport, was wrecked at Green Island, Bay of Fundy, on July 18. Her port of registry was Saint John, N.B. Cause: fog. Value of schooner was $4,000.

ENOCH BANNER, a schooner of 32 tons register, sailed from Canso to Halifax, was wrecked at Outer Ledge, Canso Harbour, on September 28. Her port of registry was Baddeck. Cause: error of judgment. Value of schooner was $2,600.

GEO. PEABODY, a schooner of 63 tons register, sailed from Port Hawkesbury to Arichat, was wrecked off Arichat, Western Channel, on date unknown. Her port of registry was U.S.A. Cause: squall. Five lives were lost and the value of schooner was $2,500.

G.S. DeFOREST, a schooner of 74 tons register, sailed from St. John, N.B., to Crookhaven, was wrecked at Cape Rouge, C.B., on September 18. Her port of registry was Saint John, N.B. Cause: fog. Value of schooner was $4,500.

HOWARD M., a schooner of 54 tons register, sailed from Georgetown, P.E.I., on trading voyage, was wrecked at Long Point, St. Georges Bay, on January 13. her port of registry was Port Hawkesbury. Cause: ice. Value of schooner was $4,400.

H.D. HOLSTEAD, a schooner of 135 tons register, sailed from Saint John, N.B., to New York, was wrecked at Dipper Harbour, Bay of Fundy, on January 20. Her port of registry was Saint John, N.B. Cause: bad weather. Value of schooner was $1,450.

HELENE, a ship of 760 tons register, sailed from Bristol, G.B., to Sydney, C.B., was wrecked at Cape St. Esprit, C.B., on September 18. Her port of registry was Grimstad, Norway. Cause: fog. Value of vessel was $25,000.

JUAN F. PEARSON, a barque of 507 tons register, sailed

from Saint John, N.B., to Amsterdam, was wrecked at Big Mud Island, N.S., on June 10. Her port of registry was London. Cause: fog. Value of vessel was $22,000.

JULIAN, a schooner of 64 tons register, sailed from Bank Offen to Provincetown, was wrecked at Little Judique Beach, C.B., on September 22. Her port of registry was Provincetown. Cause: bad weather. Value of schooner was $1,800.

JANE STEWART, a barkentine of 195 tons register, sailed from St. John's, Newfoundland, to Sydney, C.B., was wrecked at Cranberry Head, C.B., on December 3. Her port of registry was St. John's, Newfoundland. Cause: bad weather. Two lives were lost and the value of vessel was $6,000.

KATE AGNES, a barque of 545 tons register, sailed from Saint John, N.B., to New port, G.B., was wrecked at Flat Mud Island, N.S., on June 10. Her port of registry was Saint John, N.B. Cause: fog. Value of vessel was $15,000.

MORNING LIGHT, a schooner of 82 tons register, sailed from Boston to Liverpool, was wrecked on west side of Seal Island on June 10. Her port of registry was Liverpool, N.S. Cause: bad weather. Value of schooner was $5,500.

MARY LUCIA, a schooner of 79 tons register, sailed from Little Glace Bay to Halifax, was wrecked at Main a Dieu Bar on August 16. Her port of registry was Halifax. Cause: fog. Value of schooner was $1,500.

MARIA, a schooner of 17 tons register, sailed from Port Medway, was wrecked at Spruce Point, Port Medway, on August 27. Her port of registry was Liverpool. Cause: main boom carried away. Value of schooner was $500.

MARY, a schooner of 75 tons register, sailed from Charlottetown to Lingan, C.B., was wrecked at Lighthouse Point, Louisburg, on August 27. Her port of registry was Charlottetown. Cause: misstayed. Value of schooner was $2,250.

THOMAS GREEN, a schooner which struck Cow Ledge near Long Island and became a total wreck.

MAY QUEEN, a schooner of 42 tons register, sailed from Sydney, C.B., on a trading voyage, was wrecked at entrance to Big Bras d'Or. Her port of registry was Halifax. Cause: fire in forecastle. Value of schooner was $900.

MARY, a schooner of 59 tons register, sailed from Gabarus, C.B., to Halifax, was wrecked at south side of Scatarie Island on November 15. Her port of registry was Sydney, C.B. Cause: bad weather. Value of schooner was $1,100.

MARTIN, a schooner of 30 tons register, sailed from Saint

John, N.B., to Grand Manan, N.B., was wrecked in Bay of Fundy on January 18. Her port of registry was Saint John, N.B. Cause: foremast going through her bottom. Value of schooner was $1,100.

NINETH OF JUNE, a schooner of 93 tons register, sailed from Halifax to L'Ardoise, N.S., was wrecked at L'Ardoise Shoal, C.B., on May 7. Her port of registry was Halifax. Cause: bad weather. Value of schooner was $7,000.

PRISCILLA MAY, a brigantine of 200 tons register, sailed from Georgetwon, P.E.I., to New York, was wrecked at Strait of Canso on January 26. Her port of registry was Pugwash. Cause: ice. Value of vessel was $8,000.

PETRONILLA, a barque of 576 tons register, sailed from Philadelphia to Queenstown, G.B., was wrecked at Belfry Beach, C.B., on October 21. Her port of registry was Genoa, Italy. Cause: a leak. Value of vessel was $17,000.

W.S. McLEOD, a schooner of 25 tons under Captain Archibald Newell out of Argyle for Yarmouth, went ashore at Calf Island during the month of September and became a total wreck. She was owned by A.F. Stoneman and Co.

REBECCA ANN, a schooner of 122 tons register, sailed from Sydney, C.B., to Halifax, was wrecked at Crooks Island, N.S. on November 19. Her port of registry was Sydney, C.B. Cause: misstayed. Value of schooner was $2,400.

SWALLOW, a brigantine of 184 tons register, sailed from Maderia to Liscomb, N.S., was wrekced at White Point Rock, C.B., on August 10. Her port of registry was Lanelly, G.B. Cause: fog. Value of vessel was $10,000.

TIDAL WAVE, a barque of 487 tons register, sailed from Halifax to North Sydney, was wrecked at Gabarus Cape, C.B., on December 14. Her port of registry was Saint John, N.B. Cause: error of judgment. Value of vessel was $16,000.

VICTORIA, a schooner of 135 tons register, sailed from Falmouth, G.B., to place unknonwn, was wrecked at South Point, Neils Harbour, C.B., on September 22. Her port of registry was Falmouth. Value of schooner was $2,700.

WM. CROSSCUP, a barkantine of 461 tons register, sailed from Liverpool, G.B., to Sydney, C.B., was wrecked at White Point near Louisburg, C.B., on April 26. Her port of registry was Annapolis. Cause: fog. Value of vessel was $18,000.

(1878)—ADRIA, a schooner of 118 tons register, sailed from St. John, N.B., to Queenstown, Ireland and was wrecked at west side of Gannet Rock Ledge on September 6. Her port of registry was

Parrsboro. Cause: fog. Value of schooner was $2,764.

ALICE MAY, a schooner of 22 tons register, sailed from Yarmouth to Cape Breton and was wrecked at Wining Point Beach, C.B., on July 10. Her port of registry was Yarmouth. Cause: fog. Value of schooner was $1,600.

AMELIA, a schooner of 114 tons register, sailed from Boston to Arichat and was wrecked at Green Island off Cape Sable Island. Her port of registry was Arichat. Cause: fog. Value of schooner was $1,200.

ALCYONE, a schooner of 66 tons register, sailed from Campbellton, Big Bras d'Or to Halifax and was wrecked at Little Harbour on September 28. Her port of registry was Halifax. Cause: bad weather. Value of schooner was $2,400.

ANNIE B., a schooner of 96 tons register, sailed from Charlottetown to New York and was wrecked at Ship Harbour Bay on November 20. Her port of registry was Saint John, N.B. Cause: fog. Value of schooner was $5,960.

CARCAND, a schooner of 69 tons register, sailed from Cape Canso to St. Pierre Miquelon, was wrecked at Madame Island, C.B., on November 13. Her port of registry was New Carlisle. Cause: fog. Value of schooner $5,800.

BARBARA, a brig of 229 tons register, sailed from Limerick, Ireland, to Miramichi, N.B., was wrecked at St. Paul's Island on April 5. Her port of registry was Dublin, Ireland. Cause: fog. Value of vessel was $10,000.

BETA, a brig of 155 tons register, sailed from Boston to Lunenburg, was wrecked at Rose Head, N.S., on June 24. Her port of registry was Lunenburg. Cause: fog. Value of vessel was $5,000.

CHEBUCTO, a barque of 802 tons register, sailed from Rotterdam to Halifax, was wrecked at Black Rock, at the mouth of Halifax Harbour, on May 8. Her port of registry was Windsor, N.S. Cause: fog. Value of vessel was $30,000.

CONFEDERATE, a brigantine of 221 tons register, sailed from Philadelphia, U.S.A., to Saint John, N.B., was wrecked at Brier Island, N.N.E. about 20 miles on June 23. Her port of registry was Digby. Cause: fog. Three lives were lost and the value of vessel was $5,435.

CENTREVILLE, a schooner of 25 tons register, sailed from Cardigan, P.E.I., to Halifax, was wrecked at south east end of St. Andrews Channel, Canso, N.S., on November 5. Her port of registry was Charlottetown. Cause: error of judgment. Value of schooner was $550.

CALEDONIA, a schooner of 112 tons register, sailed from Yarmouth to Hantsport, was wrecked at Libby Island on December 7. Her port of registry was Windsor, N.S. Cause: error in judgment. Six lives were lost and the value of schooner was $3,000.

CONQUEST, a schooner of 102 tons register, sailed from Halifax to Port Caledonia, N.S., was wrecked at Whitehead, N.S., on December 22. Her port of registry was Saint John, N.B. Cause: bad weather. Value of schooner was $2,000.

D.M. SMITH, a schooner of 18 tons register, sailed from Saint John, N.B., to Weymouth, was wrecked at Outer Point of Petite Passage, Bay of Fundy, on March 13. Her port of registry was Weymouth. Cause: heavy winds and darkness. Value of schooner was $1,000 and three lives were lost.

E.L. HAMMOND, a schooner of 57 tons register, sailed from Charlottetown to Margaree, C.B., was wrecked at Chimney Corner on August 20. Her port of registry was Halifax. Cause: bad weather. Value of schooner was $1,700.

EMMA J. SHANKS, a schooner of 135 tons register, sailed from Halifax to Port Caledonia, C.B., was wrecked at Aspe Bay, Cape North, C.B., on August 22. Her port of registry was Saint John, N.B. Cause: parting of chains. Value of schooner was $6,500.

EMBLEM, a schooner of 59 tons register, sailed from Louisburg to Yarmouth, was wrecked 10 miles south of Shelburne Light on November 18. Her port of registry was Yarmouth. Cause: bad weather. Value of schooner was $5,000.

GLENDORA, a schooner of 42 tons register, sailed from West Arichat to Halifax, was wrecked at entrance to Canso Harbour on December 10. Her port of registry was Arichat. Cause: error in judgment. Value of schooner was $600.

HARMONIDES, a ship of 1,564 tons register, sailed from Havre, France to Saint John, N.B., was wrecked at Gulliver's Hole near Digby on July 27. Her port of registry was Saint John, N.B. Cause: bad weather. Value of vessel was $20,000.

HEBE, a barque of 748 tons register, sailed from Antwerp to Saint John, N.B., was wrecked south west Wolf, Bay of Fundy, on August 27. Her port of registry was Porsgrund, Norway. Cause: fog and error of judgment. Value of vessel was $13,000.

JULIA WOOD, a schooner of 93 tons register, sailed from Gloucester to fishing banks, was wrecked at Emulow Breakers near Lockeport, N.S., on April 26. Her port of registry was Gloucester, U.S.A. Cause: fog. Value of schooner was $17,000.

JOHN D. TUPPER, a brigantine of 289 tons register,

sailed from Sackville, N.B., to Great Britain, was wrecked at Port George, Bay of Fundy, on August 3. Her port of registry was Halifax. Cause: fog. Value of vessel was $10,000.

LEADER, a brigantine of 146 tons register, sailed from Halifax to Yarmouth, was wrecked 10 miles W.N.W. of Seal Island on April 9. Her port of registry was Arichat, C.B. Cause: error of judgment. Value of vessel was $1,800.

LIGHT OF HOME, a schooner of 56 tons register, sailed from Argyle to Prospect, was wrecked at Emulous Breakers near Lockeport on April 14. Her port of registry was Portsmouth, U.S.A. Cause: error of compass. Value of schooner was $2,000.

LINDA ABBOTT, a barque of 248 tons register, sailed from Demerara, B.G., to Bridgewater, was wrecked at Liverpool Harbour, N.S., on December 11. Her port of registry was Liverpool. Cause: parting of chains. Value of vessel was $5,000.

MIRIAM, a schooner fo 122 tons register, sailed from La Have,N.S., to St. John's, Newfoundland, was wrecked at Spectacle Island, La Have Harbour, on January 5. Her port of registry was St. John's, Newfoundland. Cause: parting of chains. Value of schooner was $4,000.

MIGUMOWESOO, a schooner of 31 tons register, sailed from Eastport, U.S.A., to Yarmouth, was wrecked at Petite Passage on March 30. Her port of registry was Digby. Cause: a snow storm. Value of schooner was $1,900.

MARY, a brigantine of 215 tons register, sailed from Antigua, W.I., to Saint John, was wrecked at Ledge off Marie Joseph on June 24. Her port of registry was Digby. Cause: fog and currents. Value of vessel was $15,400.

MAGGIE B., a schooner of 84 tons register, sailed from Newcastle, N.B., to Pictou, was wrecked at Pictou on August 17. Her port of registry was Miramichi, N.B. Cause: fire. Value of schooner was $6,400.

MARY JANE, a schooner of 84 tons register, sailed from Pictou to Chatham, N.B., was wrecked at Cape Tormentine on September 22. Her port of registry was Arichat. Cause: bad weather. Value of schooner was $1,770.

M, a schooner of 29 tons register, sailed from Tusket Wedge to Halifax, was wrecked at Port Herbert on November 20. Her port of registry was Yarmouth. Cause: fog. Value of schooner was $2,000.

PHOPERO, a schooner of 75 tons register, sailed from La Have to Rose Blanche, Newfoundland, and was wrecked at

Samson Rocks south side of Scatarie Island on June 24. Her port of registry was St. John's, Newfoundland. Cause: bad weather. Value of schooner was $2,250.

POTOMAC, a schooner of 147 tons register, sailed from Yarmouth to Saint John, N.B., and was wrecked at Dartmouth Ledges on December 21. Her port of registry was Saint John, N.B. Cause: darkness. Value of schooner was $3,000.

ROCKLAND, a brigantine of 237 tons register, sailed from New York to Sydney, N.S., and was wrecked at St. Esprit, N.S., on May 6. Her port of registry was Sydney, C.B. Cause: fog. Value of schooner was $12,000.

SNIPE, a schooner of 55 tons register, sailed from Sydney, N.S., to Charlottetown, P.E.I., and was wrecked off Petit de Grat, Richmond Co., on June 17. Her port of registry was P.E.I. Cause: fog and tides. Value of schooner was $800.

SECRET, a schooner of 47 tons register, sailed from Halifax to Aspey Bay, N.S., and was wrecked at Wreck Cove near Little Lorraine on June 27. Her port of registry was Halifax. Cause: bad weather. Value of schooner not known.

SARAH, a schooner of 46 tons register, sailed from Burges, Newfoundland, to Halifax and was wrecked 14'E.N.E. from Flint Island, N.S., on August 19. Her port of registry was Halifax. Cause: bad weather. Value of schooner was $1,000.

SUSAN, a brigantine of 146 tons register, sailed from North Sydney, N.S., to St. John's, Newfoundland, and was wrecked at Lingan Head, N.S., on December 13. Her port of registry was St. John's, Newfoundland. Cause: snow storm. Value of vessel was not known.

SWAN, a schooner of 46 tons register, sailed from Canso to Halifax and was wrecked at St. Andrew's Island, Canso, on December 24. Her port of registry was Lunenburg. Cause: wheel gear parting. Value of schooner was $690.

SPEED, a schooner of 104 tons register, sailed from St. John's, Newfoundland, to P.E.I. and was wrecked at Caribou Cove, Gut of Canso, on December 22. Her port of registry was St. John's, Newfoundland. Cause: misstayed. Value of schooner was $5,000.

VENEZIA, a steamer of 507 tons register, sailed from Montreal to North Sydney, N.S., and was wrecked at Swivel Point, N.S., on October 1. Her port of registry was Montreal. Cause: error of judgment. Value of vessel was $63,000.

WALTON, a barque of 557 tons register, sailed from Carnarvon, G.B., to Saint John, N.B., and was wrecked at western

Muro Ledge, Bay of Fundy, on September 14. Her port of registry was Liverpool, G.B. Cause: fog. Value of vessel was $10,000.

WATSON BAKER, a schooner of 51 tons register, sailed from New London, P.E.I., to Boston and was wrecked at western entrance to Barrington, N.S., on December 12. Her port of registry was U.S.A. Cause: bad weather. Value of schooner was $1,500.

ACORN, a schooner of 81 tons register, sailed from Cheverie, N.S.,to Bangor, Maine, and was wrecked in the Bay of Fundy on April 26. Her port of registry was Windsor. Cause: currents. Value of schooner was $1,275.

MAY, a schooner of 28 tons under Captain Eli Richards out of Tusket for Halifax with a cargo of dye and pickled fish. She struck upon the rocks at Port L'Hibert on November 25 and became a total loss. She was owned by John Rodgers.

HARRIET, a schooner of 60 tons out of Poulamont was wrecked at St. Esprit during the month of August. She was owned by Henry and Simon Boudrot.

(1879)—ARMADA, a schooner of 131 tons register, sailed from Bear River to Boston and was wrecked at Briar Island, Bay of Fundy, on May 17. Her port of registry was Digby. Cause: collision. Value of schooner was $1,500.

ATALIA, a schooner of 34 tons register, sailed from Liscomb to Charlottetown and was wrecked at Cape Jack, N.S., on October 19. Her port of registry was Halifax. Cause: bad weather. Value of schooner was $1,000.

A.E.DATER, a schooner fo 45 tons register, sailed from Sydney, C.B., to Halifax and was wrecked as Main-a-Dieu, C.B., on December 3. Her port of registry was Yarmouth. Cause: error of judgment. Value of schooner was $1,440.

WIER, a schooner of 56 tons register, sailed from Newfoundland to Halifax and was wrecked at St. Andrews Island, Canso, on July 19. Her port of registry was Quebec. Cause: error of judgment. Value of schooner was $1,600.

BLUE WAVE, a schooner of 61 tons register, sailed from Main-a-Dieu to Halifax and was wrecked at Whitehaven, N.S., on October 29. Her port of registry was Sydney, C.B. Cause: parting of chains. Value of schooner was $2,500.

CAMILLA, a schooner of 126 tons register sailed from St. John's, Newfoundland, to Sydney, C.B., and was wrecked at Bird Rock on April 26. Her port of registry was Quebec. Cause: ice. Value of schooner was $5,060.

DEFIANCE, a schooner of 25 tons register, sailed from

Cardigan, P.E.I., to Halifax and was wrecked at Bear Island, Little Dover, on October 28. Her port of registry was Halifax. Cause: bad weather. Value of schooner was $1,000.

ELIZA B. BEARD, a schooner of 101 tons register, sailed from Saint John, N.B., to Halifax and was wrecked one mile south west of Chebucto Head on May 14. Her port of registry was Saint John, N.B. Cause: error of judgment. Value of schooner was $2,500.

ENTERPRISE, a schooner of 42 tons register, sailed from Clam Harbour to Halifax and was wrecked off Shut-in Isalnd, N.S., on April 18. Her port of registry was Saint John, N.B. Cause: fog. Value of schooner was $500.

GOODWIN, a schooner of 82 tons register, sailed from Yarmouth to Sydney, C.B., and was wrecked at Jedore Ledges, N.S., on August 25. Her port of registry was Shelburne. Cause: error of judgment. Value of schooner was $3,500.

EMELIA B., a schooner of 29 tons register, sailed from Halifax to Shelburne and was wrecked at McNutt's Island, Shelburne Harbour, on October 29. Her port of registry was Port Hawkesbury. Cause: parting of chains. Value of schooner was $1,010.

ECLIPTIC, a brigantine of 149 tons register, sailed from St.John's, Newfoundland, to Sydney, C.B., and was wrecked at Cranberry Head on November 10. Her port of registry was St. John's, Newfoundland. Cause: bad judgment. Value of vessel was $2,000.

ELIZABETH ANN, a brigantine of 173 tons register, sailed from Bayfield, N.S., to St. John's, Newfoundland, and was wrecked at Bayfield, N.S., on November 29. Her port of registry was Halifax. Cause: bad weather. Value of vessel was $5,000.

ELIZA, a brigantine of 199 tons register, sailed from Charlottetown to Malpeque and was wrecked at Carter's Cove, N.S., on November 19. Her port of registry was Charlottetown. Cause: a snow storm. Value of vessel was not known.

G.W. JOHNSON, a steamer of 72 tons register, sailed from Parrsboro to Wolfville, and was wrecked at Partridge Island, Minas Basin, on April 3. Her port of registry was Yarmouth. Cause: fire. Value of vessel was $10,000.

IDA, a brigantine of 149 tons register, sailed from St. John's, Newfoundland, to Sydney, C.B., and was wrecked at Black Rock, C.B., on November 15. Her port of registry was St. John's, Newfoundland. Cause: a snow storm. Value of vessel was $1,200.

JANIE R., a schooner of 44 tons register, sailed from

Shelburne to Boston and was wrecked at Shelburne Harbour on February 15. Her port of registry was Liverpool, N.S. Cause: snow squall. Value of schooner was $3,900.

JOSEPH MILBURY, a ship of 1,078 tons register, sailed from Honfleur, France, to Delaware Breakwater and was wrecked at For Bay Point, N.S., on August 24. Her port of registry was Yarmouth. Cause: fog. Value of vessel was $43,000.

JESSIE, a schooner of 55 tons register, sailed from Georgetown, P.E.I., to Halifax and was wrecked at Scraggy Ledge, N.S., on Arpil 24. Her port of registry was Charlottetown. Cause: error of judgment. Value of schooner was $1,500.

J.P. BLAKE, a schooner of 115 tons register, sailed from Hillsboro, N.B., to West Indies and was wrecked at Sister's Rock, N.S., on August 1. Her port of registry was Parrsboro. Cause: never known. Value of schooner was $1,000.

JUVENILE, a schooner of 49 tons register, sailed from Banqureaux to Lockeport and was wrecked at Jedore Ledges on October 9. Her port of registry was Yarmouth. Cause: unknown. Value of schooner was $3,200.

JANE McKAY, a schooner of 59 tons register, sailed from Boston to P.E.I. and was wrecked at Spry Head, N.S., on October 20. Her port of registry was Charlottetown. Cause: misstayed. Value of schooner was $2,500.

LASSIE, a schooner of 40 tons register, sailed from Pictou to Charlottetown and was wrecked one mile west of Pictou Harbour on July 4. Her port of registry was Charlottetown. Cause: bad weather. Value of schooner was $540.

LIZZIE GILLESPIE, a barque of 429 tons register, sailed from Sydney, C.B., to Saint John, N.B., and was wrecked at Walkers Reef, Cape Island, N.S., on December 10. Her port of registry was Saint John, N.B. Cause: error of judgment. Value of vessel was $17,000.

MAGGIE, a brigantine of 266 tons register, sailed from Lunenburg to Liverpool, N.S., and was wrecked at Neal's Ledge on January 22. Her port of registry was Liverpool, N.S. Cause: bad weather. Value of vessel was $15,450.

MELITA, a schooner of 70 tons register, sailed from Hantsport to Saint John, N.B., and was wrecked at Spencer Island, N.S. Her port of registry was Parrsboro. Cause: bad weather. Value of schooner was $500.

MARIE EMMA, a schooner of 65 tons register, sailed from Pictou to Digby and was wrecked at High Island near Beaver Harbour on October 10. Her port of registry was Charlottetown.

184

Cause: bad weather. Value of schooner was $833.

MARY, a schooner of 43 tons register, sailed from New Campbellton to Halifax and was wrecked at Glasgow Harbour on October 29. Her port of registry was Port Hawkesbury. Cause: bad weather. Value of schooner was $900.

MAGGIE, a schooner of 118 tons register, sailed from Pictou to Halifax and was wrecked west Arichat on October 29. Her port of registry was Arichat. Cause: bad weather. Value of schooner was $2,000.

NORA MATHILDE, a brigantine of 150 tons register sailed from Halifax to Lisbon and was wrecked at McDonald Rock, Sheet Harbour, on date unknown. Her port of registry was Portuguese. Cause: unknown. Value of vessel was $2,000.

NANCY, a schooner of 63 tons register, sailed from Richibucto to Pictou and was wrecked at Caribou Island on October 19. Her port of registry was Shelburne. Cause: bad weather. Five lives were lost, and the value of the schooner was $950.

OCEAN GEM, a schooner of 51 tons register, sailed from Cape Canso to Halifax and was wrecked at Whitehead on November 18. Her port of registry was Port Hawkesbury. Cause: snow storm. Value of schooner was $4,000.

P. BLAKE, a schooner of 83 tons register, sailed from Saint John to Cardenas and was wrecked at Digby Harbour on February 21. Her port of registry was Parrsboro. Cause: bad weather. Value of schooner was $2,900.

SULTAN, a steamer of 11 tons, sailed from Charlottetown to Wallace and was wrecked five miles north of Malagash Point on November 11. Her port of registry was Saint John, N.B. Cause: bad weather. Value of vessel was $8,000.

SNIPE, a schooner of 53 tons register, sailed from North Sydney to Halifax and was wrecked at Petite de Grat on October 29. Her port of registry was Arichat. Cause: bad weather. Value of schooner was $1,380.

SPARKLING WAVE, a schooner of 38 tons register, sailed from Louisburg to Halifax and was wrecked at Gunning Rocks near Louisburg on October 27. Her port of registry was Port Medway. Cause: fog. Value of schooner was $2,300.

THDI FIGLIA, a barque of 671 tons register, sailed from Boston to New Ross, Ireland, and was wrecked off McNutt's Island, N.S., on February 17. Her port of registry was Italy. Cause: fire. Value of vessel was $45,000.

TURKISH EMPIRE, a ship of 1,502 tons register, sailed

from Saint John, N.B., to Dublin and was wrecked at Big Duck Island, Bay of Fundy, on March 7. Her port of registry was London. Cause: vessel on beam ends. Seven lives were lost and the value of vessel was $40,221.

TWO SISTERS, a schooner of 58 tons register, sailed from Sydney, C.B., to Halifax and was wrecked at St. Archeveque, N.S. Her port of registry was Arichat. Cause: heavy swell. Value of schooner was $1,200.

VOLUNTEER, a schooner of 120 tons register, sailed from Sydney, C.B., to Halifax and was wrecked at Whitehaven, N.S., on October 29. Her port of registry was Halifax. Cause: bad weather. Value of schooner was $100.

WILLIAM G. PUTMAN, a barque of 771 tons register, sailed from Quebec to Marseilles and was wrecked off Cape Egmont, C.B., on August 4. Her port of registry was Liverpool, G.B. Cause: leakage. Value of vessel was $15,000.

CRESCENT, a schooner of 75 tons register, sailed from St. Pierre Miquelon to Canso and was wrecked eight miles north of Cape Canso on November 29. Her port of registry was Lunenburg. Cause: bad weather. Value of schooner was $4,000.

EXCELSIOR, a schooner of 87 tons register, sailed from Cow Bay to Halifax and was wrecked at Battery Island Ledge, Louisburg Harbour, on November 19. Her port of registry was Sydney, C.B. Cause: snow storm. Value of schooner was $1,500.

ELEANOR JANE, a schooner of 74 tons register, sailed from Spencer Island to Canning and was wrecked at Balls Bluff, Diligent River, N.S., on December 4. Her port of registry was Saint John, N.B. Cause: misstayed. Value of schooner was $500.

EMMA B., a schooner of 11 tons register, sailed from Crapaud, P.E.I., to Pugwash and was wrecked at Jackson's Head, N.S. Her port of registry was Charlottetown. Cause: bad weather. Value of schooner was $200.

J.P. MILLEDGE, a schooner of 97 tons register, sailed from Halifax to Sydney, C.B., and was wrecked at Louisburg Harbour on October 29. Her port of registry was Halifax. Cause: bad weather. Value of schooner was $1,500.

LORD MAYO, a schooner of 97 tons register, sailed from Demerara to Halifax and was wrecked at Emulous Rock, near Lockeport. Her port of registry was Liverpool. Cause: bad weather. Value of schooner was $2,800.

LENA, a brigantine of 136 tons register, sailed from Jamaica to Halifax and was wrecked at Mud Island on December 29. Her port of registry was Liverpool, N.S. Cause: fog and gale.

Value of vessel was $12,000.

MARY, a schooner fo 58 tons register, sailed from Cocaigne, N.S., to Arichat and was wrecked at Black Rock, West Arichat, on October 20. Her port of registry was Arichat. Cause: bad weather. Value of schooner was $1,200.

N. NOYES, a schooner of 60 tons register, sailed from Halifax to New York and was wrecked at Abbot's Point, Cape Negro, N.S. Her port of registry was St. Andrews, N.B. Cause: bad weather. Value of schooner was $2,000.

NATIVE LASS, a schooner of 101 tons register. While at West Arichat, she was wrecked at Creighton's Beach on February 20. Her port of registry was Arichat. Cause: ice. Value of schooner was $600.

O.K., a brigantine of 199 tons register, sailed from Halifax to Lingan, C.B., and was wrecked at Indian Point, C.B., on December 20. Her port of registry was Halifax. Cause: a snow storm. Value of vessel was $7,000.

PLOVER, a schooner of 22 tons register, sailed from Port Richmond to Port Hastings and was wrecked at Port Hastings on November 20. Her port of registry was Arichat. Cause: parting of chains. Value of schooner was $320.

SPECULATOR, a schooner of 71 tons register, sailed from Cow Bay to Summerside and was wrecked at Mouth of Canso Harbour on December 16. Her port of registry was Saint John, N.B. Cause: a leak. Value of schooner was $750.

SOPHIA, a schooner of 20 tons register, sailed from River Bourgeois, C.B., to Halifax and was wrecked at Cape Canso on October 7. Her port of registry was Arichat. Cause: parting of chains. Value of schooner was $500.

(1880)—BELLONA, a barque of 295 tons register, sailed from Boston to Saint John and was wrecked at Split Rock Cove on May 10. Her port of registry was Norway. Cause: fog. Value of vessel was $7,000.

EBLANA, a barque of 651 tons register, sailed from Newport to Saint John and was wrecked at Negro Head on March 8. Her port of registry was Saint John. Cause: error in judgment. Seven lives were lost and the value of vessel was $18,000.

SEA LARK, a schooner of 69 tons register, sailed from Saint John to Boston and was wrecked at Head Harbour on December 10. Her port of registry was Saint John. Cause: a snow storm. Value of schooner was $1,400.

ALONZO, a schooner of 45 tons register, sailed from Yarmouth to Shelburne and was wrecked at Wraton's Harbour,

N.S., on May 26. Her port of registry was Yarmouth. Cause: lightning. Value of schooner was $450.

ACTIVE, a barque of 344 tons register, sailed from Ganderfoird to Parrsboro and was wrecked at Mouth of Parrsboro Harbour. Her port of registry was Ganderfoird, Norway. Cause: a squall. Value of vessel was $8,000.

ABDIEL, a schooner of 55 tons register, sailed from Jordan River to St. Pierre Miquelon and was wrecked 12 miles off Liverpool Light on November 19. Her port of registry was Shelburne. Cause: fire. Value of schooner was $2,750.

BORNEO, a ship of 737 tons register, sailed from New Orleans to Trieste and was wrecked at Beaver Island Ledge, N.S., on April 24. Her port of registry was New York. Cause: loss of spars. Value of vessel was $130,000.

CLARA JANE, a schooner of 46 tons register, sailed from Sydney, C.B., to Port Medway and was wrecked at Mira Bay, C.B., on July 15. Her port of registry was Port Medway. Cause: bad weather. Value of schooner was $1,320.

CLYDESDALE, a barque of 994 tons register, sailed from Liverpool to Parrsboro and was wrecked at West Bay, Parrsboro, on October 23. Her port of registry was Liverpool, G.B. Cause: bad weather. Value of vessel was $6,000.

DELTA, a schooner of 109 tons register, sailed from Harvey, N.B., to Boston and was lost 20 miles north west from Briar Island on March 25. Her port of registry was Saint John, N.B. Cause: a leak. Value of schooner was $3,300.

ELLEN C., a brigantine of 295 tons register, sailed from Sydney, C.B., to Annapolis and was wrecked at Cape Negro on September 28. Her port of registry was Digby. Cause: fog. Value of vessel was $9,650.

FRANK NEWTON, a schooner of 41 tons register, sailed from Aspey Bay to Bay St. Lawrence, C.B., and was wrecked at entrance to Ingonish Harbour. Her port of registry was Lunenburg. Cause: bad weather. Value of schooner was $1,000.

FREEDOM, a schooner of 152 tons register, sailed from Louisburg to Halifax and was wrecked at St. Peter's Bay, C.B., on December 5. Her port of registry was Halifax. Cause: fog. Value of schooner was $3,000.

JOHN C. NEWELL, a schooner of 80 tons register, sailed from Boston to P.E.I. and was wrecked at entrance to Lockeport on October 30. Her port of registry was Yarmouth. Cause: misstays. Value of schooner was $6,400.

LUCRETIA, a schooner of 36 tons register, sailed from

Louisburg to Halifax and was wrecked 4 miles s.s.west of Green Island, Cape Breton, on November 26. Her port of registry was Halifax. Cause: a leak. Value of schooner was $2,800.

MARY McKENZIE, a schooner of 24 tons register, sailed from Halifax to Arichat and was wrecked at Jerseyman's Island on October 7. Her port of registry was Halifax. Cause: darkness. Value of schooner was $400.

PRONTO, a brigantine of 139 tons register, sailed from Boston to Yarmouth and was wrecked at Grand Eddy Point, N.S., on February 3. Her port of registry was Yarmouth. Cause: bad weather. Value of vessel was $5,000.

PROVIDENCE, a schooner of 77 tons register, sailed from Georgetown, P.E.I., to Halifax and was wrecked at Nancy Shoal, N.S. Her port of registry was Chatham, N.B. Cause: error of judgment. Value of schooner was $3,000.

PARA, a steamer of 704 tons register, sailed from Boston to West Hartlepool and was wrecked at Cape Sable, N.S., on February 26. Her port of registry was West Hartlepool, G.B. Cause: error of judgment. Value of vessel was $145,000.

REPEAL, a schooner of 60 tons register, sailed from Cow Bay, C.B., to Saint John, N.B., and was wrecked off Lingan, C.B., on April 6. Her port of registry was Sydney, C.B. Cause: unknown. Value of schooner was $1,200.

REVIEWER, a barque of 991 tons register, sailed from Antwerp to Philadelphia and was wrecked at Harbour Island, N.S., on August 6. Her port of registry was Yarmouth. Cause: fog. Value of vessel was $25,000.

ROSE STANDISH, a schooner of 49 tons register, sailed from Halifax on a fishing trip and was wrecked at La Have Ledge, N.S., on August 17. Her port of registry was Barrington. Cause: misstayed. Value of schooner was $1,600.

RETRIEVER, a brig of 183 tons register sailed from Madeira to Charlottetown and was wrecked at Shoal Point, N.S., on October 12. Her port of registry was Aberystwith, G.B. Cause: strong currents. Value of vessel was $5,000.

ROYAL ARCH, a schooner of 67 tons register, sailed from Halifax to Lockeport and was wrecked at Jumping Jack Lodge, N.S., on November 25. Her port of registry was Shelburne. Cause: fog. Value of schooner was $3,800.

SAMUEL, a schooner of 54 tons register, sailed from Louisburg to Halifax and was wrecked on West Black Ledge, entrance to Canso Harbour, on March 9. Her port of registry was Guysboro. Cause: bad weather. Value of schooner was $1,875.

SARAH E. SNOW, a schooner of 51 tons register, sailed from Halifax on a fishing voyage and was wrecked at Strawberry Point, Ketch Harbour, on June 10. Her port of registry was Halifax. Cause: misstayed. Value of schooner was $1,600.

SYLVAN, a schooner of 61 tons register, sailed from Cow Bay to Halifax and was wrecked at Main-a-Dieu Beach, C.B., on October 31. Her port of registry was Sydney, C.B. Cause: bad weather. Value of schooner was $1,500.

STRANGER, a schooner of 31 tons register, sailed from Coddles Harbour to Halifax and was wrecked at Black Prince Rock off Liscomb on October 17. Her port of registry was Guysboro. Cause: error of judgment. Value of schooner was $3,000.

TROPIC BIRD, a schooner of 46 tons register, sailed from Lunenburg to Liverpool and was wrecked at Eastern Head, entrance to Liverpool Harbour, on July 14. Value of schooner was $3,000.

WILLIE, a brig of 282 tons register, sailed from Barbadoes to Weymouth, N.S., and was wrecked at Gull Rock, south west of Briar Island, on March 22. Her port of registry was Yarmouth. Cause: tides. Value of vessel was $5,000.

W.H. SMITH, a schooner fo 19 tons register, while at Port Medway was wrecked in Medway Harbour on October 22. Her port of registry was Port Medway. Cause: unknown. Value of schooner was $600.

ZYPHYR, a schooner of 48 tons register, sailed from Main-a-Dieu to Halifax and was wrecked at Sheet Harbour Passage on November 11. Her port of registry was Sydney, C.B. Cause: bad weather. Value of schooner was $1,500.

(1881)—ANNIE BOGART, a brigantine of 148 tons register, sailed from Dorchester, N.B., to Newburyport and was wrecked at Grindstone Island, Bay of Fundy, on December 22. Her port of registry was Digby. Cause: buoys were lifted. Three lives were lost and the value of the vessel was $7,896.

BONITA, a schooner of 38 tons register, sailed from Glace Bay to Halifax and was wrecked at Ecum Secum on October 17. Her port of registry was Halifax. Cause: bad weather. One life was lost and the value of the schooner was $608.

CANONBURY, a steamer of 1,079 tons register, sailed from Liverpool, G.B., to Sydney, C.B., and was wrecked three miles east of Flint Island on May 5. Her port of registry was London, G.B. Cause: ice. Value of vessel unknown.

CLARA B. WARREN, a schooner of 52 tons register,

sailed from Gloucester to Western Bank and was wrecked at Duncan's Reef, entrance to Halifax Harbour, on August 7. Her port of registry was U.S.A. Cause: fog. Value of schooner was $2,750.

CORTES, a steamer of 1,246 tons register, sailed from Halifax to St. John's, Newfoundland, and was wrecked at Thrump Cap Shoal, entrance to Halifax Harbour, on August 7. Her port of registry was U.S.A. Cause: error in judgment. Value of vessel was $85,000.

CYCLONE, a schooner of 90 tons register, sailed from Saint John to Boston and was wrecked at Cow Ledge, Mouth of Westport, Brier Island, on December 3. Her port of registry was Saint John, N.B. Cause: a snow strom. Value of schooner was $1,000.

EMMA, a brigantine of 167 tons register, sailed from Philadelphia to Halifax under Captain Charles Dowling and was wrecked 22 miles south west from Sambro Light on November 15. Her port of registry was Lunenburg. Cause: collision with the steamship *Howards* of Sunderland, England, under Captain Shotton. Both vessels sank within minutes after colliding.

FRANKLIN, a schooner of 32 tons register, sailed from Pictou to Halifax and was wrecked at Cape Jack Shoal on September 7. Her port of registry was Halifax. Cause: mistook shore light for Cape Jack Light. Value of schooner was $1,000.

GREEN LEAF, a schooner of 69 tons register, sailed from Lunenburg to Boston and was wrecked at Iron Bound Island on March 5. Her port of registry was Lunenburg. Cause: misstayed. Value of schooner was $7,500.

GRAND MASTER, a schooner of 108 tons register, sailed from Georgetown, P.E.I., to New York and was wrecked at Cape Jack Shoal, Antigonish County, on November 21. Her port of registry was Yarmouth. Cause: hit Cape Jack Shoal. Value of schooner was $5,600.

HAPPY HOME, a barque of 884 tons register, sailed from Hamburg to Saint John, N.B., and was wrecked at Trinity Ledge 7 miles off Yarmouth on January 3. Her port of registry was Windsor, N.S. Cause: a snow storm. Three lives were lost and the value of vessel was $25,000.

HOPE, a schooner of 90 tons register, sailed from St. Kitts, B.W. Indies, to Halifax and was wrecked at Oven's Reef, entrance to Lunenburg Harbour, on June 11. Her port of registry was Lunenburg. Value of schooner was $10,000.

HADJI, a steamer of 959 ton register, sailed from Cow Bay,

C.B., to Portland and was wrecked at Blond Rock, 10 miles south of Seal Island, on August 25. Her port of registry was Sunderland, G.B. Cause: error in judgment. Value of vessel was $9,000.

HERBERT J. OLIVE, a brigantine of 315 tons register, sailed from Darien to Saint John, N.B., and was wrecked at Whipper's Point, Brier Island, on August 27. Her port of registry was Saint John, N.B. Cause: error in ship's position. Value of vessel wa $10,000.

HOWARDS, a schooner of 696 tons register, sailed from Sydney, C.B., to Portland and was wrecked 22 miles south west of Sambro Light on November 15. Her port of registry was Sunderland, G.B. Cause: lights. Value of schooner was $82,500.

JENNIE M. HAMMOND, a schooner of 98 tons register, sailed from Nevis, W.I., to Halifax and was wrecked at Thrum Cap Shoal on February 16. Her port of registry was Shelburne. Cause: dragging of anchors. Value of schooner was $4,200.

J.A. HATFIELD, a schooner of 132 tons register, sailed from White Head, N.S., to New York and was wrecked off Thatcher's Island on December 10. Her port of registry was Parrsboro. Cause: collision. Value of schooner was $10,000.

MORTON, a schooner of 96 tons register, sailed from Yarmouth to New York and was wrecked at Naddy's Point, Westport, on December 12. Her port of registry was Yarmouth. Cause: winds. Value of schooner was $3,900.

LARNAX, a steamer of 898 tons register, sailed from Baltimore to Sydney, C.B., and was wrecked at Charles Island, near Tangier, N.S., on May 18. Her port of registry was Sunderland, G.B. Cause: fog. Value of vessel was $105,000.

LIONEL, a brigantine of 273 tons register, sailed from Plymouth, G.B., to Charlottetown, P.E.I., and was wrecked at Herron Rock, Chedabucto Bay, N.S., on August 11. Her port of registry was Charlottetown. Cause: bad weather. Value of vessel was $12,200.

LIGHT OF HOME, a schooner of 51 tons register, sailed from Labrador to Halifax and was wrecked at Seven Island Ledge on August 20. Her port of registry was Halifax. Cause: unmarked ledge on chart. Value of schooner was $2,000.

LINDA AND LIZZIE, a schooner of 56 tons register, sailed from Canso to Pictou and was wrecked at Sand Point, Gut of Canso, on November 24. Her port of registry was Pictou. Cause: bad weather and buoy out of place. Value of schooner was $2,144.

METTE MARGRETHE, a barque of 429 tons register, sailed from Miramichi to place unknown and was wrecked at St. Paul's Island on July 5. Her port of registry was Sauwig, Norway. Cause: fog. Five lives were lost and the value of vessel was $4,000.

MELLO, a schooner of 110 tons register, sailed from Caledonia, C.B., to Saint John, N.B., and was wrecked off Spry Harbour, Halifax County on December 11. Her port of registry was Saint John, N.B. Cause: ice. Value of swas $5,500.

S.B. NICKERSON, a schooner of 35 tons register, sailed from Canso to Halifax and was wrecked 7 miles S.S.E. from Beaver Island Light on September 18. Her port of registry was Yarmouth. Cause: fire. Value of schooner was $800.

SARAH, a schooner of 46 tons register, sailed from Glace Bay to Halifax and was wrecked 15 miles east of Scatarie Island on October 23. Her port of registry was Halifax. Cause: a leak. Value of schooner was $850.

TWO SISTERS, a schoner of 130 tons register, sailed from Saint John, N.B., to Ireland and was wrecked at South shore, Bay of Fundy, on September 21. Her port of registry was Digby. Cause: dragging of anchors. Value of schooner was $3,000.

THRASHER, a schooner of 80 tons register, sailed from Gloucester on a fishing trip and was wrecked at Cape Sable on September 27. Her port of registry was U.S.A. Cause: fire. Value of schooner was $2,500.

HAPPY HOME, a barque of 884 tons register, sailed from Hamburg to Saint John and was wrecked at Trinity Ledge on January 3. Her port of registry was Windsor, N.S. Cause: a snow storm. Three lives were lost and the value of the vessel was $25,000.

CYCLONE, a schooner of 90 tons register, sailed from Saint John to Boston and was wrecked at Brier Island on December 3. Her port of registry was Saint John. Cause: a snow storm.

(1882)—AGENORA, a schooner of 77 tons register, sailed from Halifax to Main-a-Dieu and was wrecked at Grand River, C.B., on January 2. Her port of registry was Sydney, C.B. Cause: bad weather. Value of schooner was $1,800.

AMAZON, a schooner of 42 tons register, sailed from Banks to Yarmouth and was wrecked at Pudding Island, Queen's County, N.S., on August 10. Her port of registry was Yarmouth. Cause: fog. Value of schooner was $1,500.

ABBOT LAWRENCE, a brigantine of 160 tons register, sailed from Lynn, Mass., to a place unknown and was wrecked at

Nags Head Point, at entrance to Louisburg Harbour, on November 1. Her port of registry was St. John's, Newfoundland. Cause: fog. Value of vessel was $24,000.

ERIN, a brigantine of 199 tons register, sailed from Halifax to Saint John, N.B., and was wrecked at Little Hope Island on March 17. Her port of registry was Halifax. Cause: bad weather. Value of vessel was $8,000.

EDITH WEIR, a schooner of 96 tons register, sailed from Cienfuegos to Halifax and was wrecked at Blanche Island, Barrington, N.S., on April 12. Her port of registry was Halifax. Cause: bad weather. Value of schooner was $10,750.

J.W. FALT, a schooner of 56 tons register, sailed from Halifax to Mud Island and to Pubnico and was wrecked at Bald Head, entrance to Pubnico Harbour, on April 1. Her port of registry was Halifax. Cause: bad weather. Value of schooner was $3,000.

J.M.S., a schooner of 170 tons register, sailed from Cow Bay, C.B., to Boston and was wrecked at Petit de Grat Harbour, Isle Madame, C.B., on May 10. Her port of registry was Arichat. Cause: dragging of anchors. Value of schooner was $5,350.

MALAGA, a brigantine of 268 tons register, sailed from Boston to Glace Bay and was wrecked at Rocky Isle, Madame, C.B., on May 31. Her port of registry was Saint John, N.B. Cause: bad weather. Value of vessel was $7,000.

MARTHA AND HARRIET, a schooner of 140 tons register, sailed from Sydney, C.B., to Gardiner, Me., and was wrecked 4 miles south of Cape Sable Lighthouse on October 28. Her port of registry was Aberystwith. Cause: too close to land. Value of schooner was $14,560.

MAGGIE, a schooner of 49 tons register, sailed from Charlottetown to N.S. and was wrecked at entrance to Sheet Harbour on December 11. Her port of registry was Lunenburg. Cause: misstayed. Value of schooner was $3,000.

ORION, a schooner of 99 tons register, sailed from Philadelphia to Shelburne and was wrecked at Shelburne Harbour on January 2. Her port of registry was Shelburne. Cause: parting of chains. Value of schooner was $4,500.

OLIVER CUTTS, a brig of 253 tons register, from New York to Hantsport and was wrecked at Hantsport on date unknown. Value of vessel was $1,200.

PIONEER, a schooner of 91 tons register, sailed from Gloucester to Halifax and was wrecked at Seal Island on July 11. Her port of registry was Lunenburg. Cause: fog. Value of

schooner was $5,000.

ROSEBUD, a schooner of 46 tons register, sailed from Saint John to Alma, Albert Co., N.B., and was wrecked at Port Lowe, N.S., on February 6. Her port of registry was Saint John, N.B. Cause: bad weather. Value of schooner was $6,400.

SCUD, a steamer of 482 tons register, sailed from Boston to Lunenburg and was wrecked at Owen's Reef, entrance to Lunenburg Harbour, on August 8. Her port of registry was St. John, N.B. Cause: fog. Value of vessel was $16,300.

WILD ROSE, a schooner of 25 tons register, sailed from Wrayton's Island to Yarmouth and was wrecked at Cat Rock Ledges on November 6. Her port of registry was Liverpool, N.S. Cause: misstayed. Value of schooner was $400.

(1883)—A.B. CROSBY, a schooner of 198 tons register, sailed from Arichat to Boston and was wrecked at Half-moon Rock, Barrington, N.S., on August 12. Her port of registry was Halifax. Cause: error in judgment. Value of schooner was $8,560.

AMELIA, a schooner of 35 tons register, sailed from D'Escouse to L'Ardoise, C.B., and was wrecked at L'Ardoise on August 30. Her port of registry was Arichat. Cause: a gale. Value of schooner was $650.

AMERICA, a schooner of 86 tons register sailed from Boston to Cornwallis and was wrecked south shore Kings Co., N.S., on January 20. Her port of registry was Windsor, N.S. Cause: a leak. Value of schooner was $800.

ANNIE INGRAM, a brigantine of 190 tons register, sailed from Sydney to Halifax and was wrecked at entrance to Petit de Grat, C.B., on January 18. Her port of registry was Halifax. Cause: winds. Value of vessel was $3,500.

ATLAS, a brigantine of 402 tons register, sailed from North Sydney to Cow Bay and was wrecked at Cow Bay Harbour on August 29. Her port of registry was Pensacola, U.S.A. Cause: a gale. Value of vessel was $4,020.

A. FRED. ARCHER, a brigantine of 169 tons register, sailed from Antigua to Yarmouth and was wrecked at Sunday Point on November 12. Her port of registry was Yarmouth. Cause: parting of chains. Value of vessel was $15,500.

ANNIE SIMPSON, a schooner of 169 tons register, sailed from Halifax to Wallace, N.S., and was wrecked at Gull Rock, off Sambro, on November 16. Her port of registry was Saint John, N.B. Cause: bad weather. Value of schooner was $6,000.

BLUE WAVE, a schooner of 37 tons register, sailed from North Sydney to Halifax and was wrecked at Cow Bay Harbour on

August 29. Her port of registry was Sydney, C.B. Cause: a gale. Value of schooner was $1,100.

BLOMIDON, a barkantine of 563 tons register, sailed from New York to Eatonville, N.S., and was wrecked at Eatonville on January 21. Her port of registry was Windsor, N.S. Cause: winds and tide. Value of vessel was $8,000.

BONETTA, a schooner of 114 tons register, sailed from Saint John, N.B., to Cornwallis and was wrecked at Canada Creek, N.S., on February 19. Her port of registry was Windsor. Cause: ice. Value of schooner was $1,800.

BRANTFORD CITY, a steamer of 1,566 tons register, sailed from Halifax to Boston and was wrecked at Arnold's Point, Shelburne Co., on August 10. Her port of registry was West Hartlepool. Cause: fog. Value of vessel was $30,000.

BROTHERS, a barkantine of 537 tons register, sailed from Holyhead to Yarmouth and was wrecked at Cape Sable on March 22. Her port of registry was Yarmouth. Cause: a snow storm. Value of vessel was $10,000.

CHERUB, a schooner of 40 tons register, sailed from Halifax to Port Medway and was wrecked at Port Mouton Head on March 23. Her port of registry was Halifax. Cause: a snow storm. Value of schooner was $1,800.

ECHO, a schooner of 23 tons register, sailed from Herring Cove to fishing Banks and was wrecked at Morris Point, Ketch Harbour, on March 6. Her port of registry was Halifax. Cause: wind and a snow squall. Value of schooner was $1,600.

ETHEL GRANVILLE, a schooner of 109 tons register, sailed from Port William to New York and was wrecked at Minas Channel, north Cape Sharp, N.S., on March 21. Her port of registry was Saint John, N.B. Cause: ice. Value of schooner was $4,500.

GERTRUDE E. SMITH, a schooner of 279 tons register, sailed from Rockland to Windsor, N.S., and was wrecked at Gannet Rock on July 21. Her port of registry was Rockland, Me. Cause: fog. Value of schooner was $3,500.

HITTERO, a barkantine of 456 tons register, sailed from Chatham to Bordeaux and was wrecked at Cape St. Lawrence, C.B., on November 13. Her port of registry was Norway. Cause: a gale. Twelve lives were lost and the value of vessel was $23,600.

I.C. TUPPER, a schooner of 117 tons register, sailed from Sydney to Halifax and was wrecked at Cow Bay Harbour on August 29. Her port of registry was Sydney, C.B. Cause: a gale. Value of schooner was $3,250.

196

ISABELLA, a brigantine of 198 tons register, sailed from Liverpool, G.B., to Charlottetown, P.E.I. and was wrecked at Isle Basque, C.B., on July 15. Her port of registry was Charlottetown. Cause: bad weather. Value of vessel was $8,000.

JOHN MURPHY, a ship of 147 tons register, sailed from Havre to Saint John, N.B., and was wrecked at Tusket Island, Shelburne, on June 20. Her port of registry was Yarmouth. Cause: fog. Value of vessel was $40,000.

LILIAN, a schooner of 48 tons register, sailed from Halifax to Port Hawkesbury and was wrecked at Shut-in-Island, Three Fathom Harbour, on January 5. Her port of registry was Halifax. Cause: compass out of order. Value of schooner was $1,500.

LORNE, a schooner of 87 tons register, sailed from Bear River to Boston and was wrecked at Lighthouse Point, Digby, on November ? Her port of registry was Digby. Cause: misstays. Value of schooner $1,200.

LAVINIA ELIZABETH, a schooner of 49 tons register, sailed from Montague, P.E.I., to Halifax and was wrecked at Thomas Head, Guysboro Co., N.S., on November 12. Her port of registry was Halifax. Cause: a leak. Value of schooner was $1,600.

MARY WHITE, a schooner of 110 tons register, sailed from Charlottetown to Arichat and was wrecked at Arichat Harbour on August 29. Her port of registry was Arichat. Cause: a gale. Value of schooner was $600.

MARY THEALL; a schooner of 99 tons register, sailed from Saint John to Port Williams, N.S., and was wrecked at Port Williams on February 7. Her port of registry was St. John, N.B. Cause: ice. Value of schooner was $2,600.

MARY E. BANKS, a schooner of 50 tons register, sailed from Petit de Grat to L'Ardoise, C.B., and was wrecked at North East Reef, L'Ardoise, on August 30. Her port of registry was Halifax. Cause: a gale. Value of schooner was $3,500.

PLOVMANDEN, a barkantine of 446 tons, sailed from Pugwash to U.K. and was wrecked at Green Island, C.B., on November 16. Her port of registry was Norway. Cause: heavy gale. Ten lives were lost and the value of vessel was $11,000.

PHOENIX, a brigantine of 197 tons register, sailed from Halifax to Port Medway and was wrecked at mouth of Port Medway Harbour on March 23. Her port of registry was Digby. Cause: a snow storm. Value of vessel was $5,500.

PRINCESS LOUISE, a steamer of 364 tons register, sailed from Maccan to Halifax and was wrecked near Point Prim, Digby

Co., on December 3. Her port of registry was Ottawa. Cause: heavy gales. Eight lives were lost and the value of vessel was $30,000.

SHELBURNE, a schooner of 59 tons under Captain William Larkin, while lying at anchor five miles east of Louisburg, C.B., with a cargo of salt fish, parted both chains and went ashore during a gale on the 2nd of October and became a total loss.

RESTLESS, a schooner of 25 tons register, sailed from La Have to fishing banks and was wrecked off south coast of N.S. on August 29. Her port of registry was Lunenburg. Cause: a hurricane. Eight lives were lost and the value of schooner was $1,500.

RHIWINDDA, a steamer of 1,329 tons register, sailed from New York to Miramichi and was wrecked at Torbay, N.S., on June 25. Her port of registry was Cardiff. Cause: deviation of compass and currents. Value of vessel was $28,000.

RINGLEADER, a schooner of 119 tons register, sailed from Lynn, Mass., to Louisburg and was wrecked at Cape Breton on June 29. Her port of registry was Sydney, C.B. Cause: fog. Value of schooner was $3,500.

SILVER MOON, a schooner of 57 tons register, sailed from Western Banks to Whitehaven, N.S., and was wrecked at Yellow Stone Beach, Guysboro, N.S., on June 5. Her port of registry was Yarmouth. Cause: fog and a gale. Value of schooner was $3,800.

SWAN, a schooner of 92 tons register, sailed from Sydney to Halifax and was wrecked at Point Micheauds, C.B., on August 5. Her port of registry was Halifax. Cause: bad weather. Value of schooner was $3,300.

TEAL, a schooner of 147 tons register, sailed from Saint John to New York and was wrecked at Bay of Fundy on February 20. Her port of registry was Saint John, N.B. Cause: capsized. Six lives were lost and the value of schooner was $4,000.

TWILIGHT, a schooner of 15 tons register, sailed from a fishing trip and was wrecked at Cranberry Head, Yarmouth Co., on July 1. Her port of registry was Yarmouth. Cause: dragging of anchors. Value of schooner was $600.

VALETTA, a steamer of 507 tons register, sailed from Halifax to Boston and was wrecked at Port Mouton Island, N.S., on April 25. Her port of registry was Montreal. Cause: deviation of compass and currents. Value of vessel was $45,000.

VOLUNTEER, a schooner of 22 tons register, sailed from Isaacs Harbour to Cow Bay and was wrecked at Cow Bay on

August 29. Her port of registry was Halifax. Cause: a gale. Value of schooner was $1,000.

ZEBENIA, a brigantine of 251 tons register, sailed from Hantsport, N.S., to Hillsboro, N.B., and was wrecked at Ratchford's River, N.S., on November 13. Her port of registry was Parrsboro. Cause: parting of chains. Three lives were lost and the value of vessel was $7,000.

ALPHETA, a brigantine of 299 tons register, sailed from Liverpool, G.B., to Charlottetown and was wrecked at Long Point, Canso, on December 18. Her port of registry was Charlottetown. Cause: dragging of anchors. Value of vessel was $13,500.

ARGO, a schooner of 91 tons register, sailed from Bear River to Boston and was wrecked at Joggins Bridge on September 7. Her port of registry was Digby. Cause: a submerged pier. Value of schooner was $1,050.

BERTHA, a brigantine of 140 tons register, sailed from Boston to Lockeport and was wrecked at Chebogue Point, N.S., on November 16. Her port of registry was Shelburne. Cause: a gale. Value of vessel was $5,000.

BETSEY, a schooner of 78 tons register, sailed from St. John's to Sydney and was wrecked at Gabarus on October 29. Her port of registry was Newfoundland. Cause: a gale. Value of schooner was $800.

HARMONY, a schooner a 102 tons register, sailed from North Sydney to Halifax and was wrecked at Red Island, C.B. Her port of registry was Halifax. Cause: hit rocks. Value of schooner was $1,800.

J.N.A., a schooner of 63 tons register, sailed from Port Hastings to Magdalen Islands and was wrecked at Cape George on December 4. Her port of registry was Magdalen Islands. Cause: a gale. Value of schooner was $4,000.

J.E. GRAHAM, a schooner of 22 tons register, sailed from Parrsboro to Port Lawrence and was wrecked at Apple River on December 3. Her port of registry was Windsor. Cause: a snow strom. Value of schooner was $500.

LOUISA MONTGOMERY, a schooner of 27 tons register, sailed from Charlottetown to Marble Mountain and was wrecked at McRae's Island, Bras d'Or, on August 29. Her port of registry was Charlottetown. Cause: anchor did not hold. Value of schooner was $400.

JOHN MURPHY, a ship of 1,471 tons register, sailed from Havre to St. John and was wrecked at Tusket Island on January

20. Her port of registry was Yarmouth, N.S. Cause: fog. Value of ship was $40,000.

TEAL, a schooner of 147 tons register, sailed from St. John to New York and was wrecked at Bay of Fundy on February 20. Her port of registry was St. John. Cause: capsized. Six lives were lost and the value of the schooner was $4,000.

(1884)—J.F. WHITTAKER, a schooner of 210 tons register, sailed from New York to St. John and was wrecked at Goose Island on August 31. Her port of registry was St. John. Cause: fog. Value of schooner was $9,000.

PLEVNA, a barque of 656 tons register, sailed from St. John to Carnarvon and was wrecked at Bliss Island on October 22. Her port of registry was Liverpool. Cause: error. Value of vessel was $18,000.

MARY, a schooner of 101 tons, out of West Arichat, was wrecked at Great Bras d'Or, during the month of November. She was owned by Valenten and Alex Bouten.

ALPIN, a schooner of 26 tons register, sailed from Beaver Harbour to Halifax and was wrecked near Lunenburg on July 9. Her port of registry was Charlottetown. Cause: a leak. Value of schooner was $1,020.

A.C. MAJOR, a schooner of 88 tons register, sailed from Cow Bay to Halifax and was wrecked at Cranberry Island on August 8. Her port of registry was Halifax. Cause: a leak. Value of schooner was $1,900.

ABBIE ALICE, a schooner of 72 tons register, sailed from Louisburg to Halifax and was wrecked off Foshay on April 10. Her port of registry was Halifax. Cause: ice. Value of schooner was $2,000.

ALOE, a schooner of 84 tons register, sailed from Parrsboro to Saint John and was wrecked at Bay of Fundy on October 26. Her port of registry was Parrsboro. Cause: a gale. Value of schooner was $400.

ARROW, a schooner of 50 tons register, sailed from Green Island to Liscomb and was wrecked at Crook's Ledge on May 27. Her port of registry was Halifax. Cause: a gale. Value of schooner was $2,700.

ADAH E., a schooner of 119 tons register, sailed from St. Martins to Medway and was wrecked at Pennant Bay on December 22. Her port of registry was Port Medway. Cause: a gale. Value of schooner was $3,740.

BREAK OF DAY, a schooner of 36 tons register, sailed from Port Hood to Margaree and was wrecked at Margaree on September 16. Her port of registry was Pictou. Cause: a gale. Value of schooner was $1,750.

CORA, a brig of 233 tons register, sailed from Yarmouth to Bridgewater and was wrecked at Little Hope Island on July 5. Her port of registry was Yarmouth. Cause: fog. Value of vessel was $9,000.

CLARA ROGERS, a schooner of 121 register, sailed from Canso to Halifax, and was wrecked at Sheet Harbour on August 31. Her port of registry was Arichat. Cause: currents. Value of schooner was $4,900.

CHS. VALENTINE, a schooner of 120 tons register, sailed from Halifax to Gabarus and was wrecked at Bull Rock on October 11. Her port of registry was Sydney. Cause: a gale. Six lives were lost and the value of schooner was $3,000.

DUNTULM, a schooner of 78 tons register, sailed from Glace Bay to Baddeck and was wrecked at Baddeck on April 18. Her port of registry was Sydney. Cause: unknown. Value of schooner was $3,000.

ETHEL EMERSON, a schooner of 176 tons register, sailed from Portsmouth to New Bandon and was wrecked along the coast of Nova Scotia on July 7. Her port of registry was Dorchester. Cause: fog. Value of schooner was $8,500.

ELLA BLANCHE, a schooner of 123 tons register, sailed from St. John's to Sydney and was wrecked at Rocky Bay on December 15. Her port of registry was Digby. Cause: a gale. Value of schooner was $4,000.

FORENCE, a schooner of 114 tons register, sailed from Halifax to Boston and was wrecked at Jordan Bay on January 9. Her port of registry was Shelburne. Cause: a gale. Value of schooner was $6,000.

FYLGIA, a steamer of 963 tons register, sailed from Pictou to Montreal and was wrecked at Perces, C.B. on July 9. Her port of registry was London. Cause: fog. Value of vessel unknown.

FINCHLEY, a steamer of 1,265 tons register, sailed from South Carolina to London and was wrecked at Issaac's Harbour on September 29. Her port of registry was London. Cause: fog. Value of vessel was $120,000.

INVERALT, a steamship of 841 tons register, sailed from Montreal to Pictou and was wrecked at Pictou Island on July 4. Her port of registry was Liverpool. Cause: fog. Value of vessel unknown.

JANIE, barkantine of 254 tons register, sailed from Bahia to Halifax and was wrecked at Tusket on January 13. Her port of registry was Greenock. Cause: a squall. Value of vessel was $6,500.

J.F. WHITTAKER, a schooner of 210 tons register, sailed from New York to St. John's and was wrecked at Goose Island on August 31. Her port of registry was Saint John. Cause: fog. Value of schooner was $24,000.

JOHN WESLEY, a schooner of 45 tons register, sailed from Liverpool to Halifax and was wrecked at Devil's Island, Halifax, on September 4. Her port of registry was Lunenburg. Cause: fog. Value of schooner was $1,000.

LAURA GERTRUDE, a schooner of 47 tons register, sailed from Yarmouth to Quero Bank and was wrecked at Saint Esprit, C.B., on June 20. Her port of registry was Yarmouth. Cause: a gale. Value of schooner was $3,200.

L.H. DeVEBER, a barkantine of 600 tons register, sailed from Saint John to Avonmouth and was wrecked at Lurcher Shoal, Yarmouth Co., on May 25. Her port of registry was Saint John. Cause: error. Value of vessel was $10,900.

LORD LYONS, a schooner of 51 tons register, sailed from River Inhabitants to Halifax and was wrecked at Seal Harbour on November 17. Her port of registry was Halifax. Cause: a gale. Value of schooner was $2,000.

Oi KAZE, a sloop of 9 tons register sailed from Halifax to Sydney and was wrecked at Country Harbour on August 23. Her port of registry was Port Medway. Cause: fog. Value of sloop was $800.

PARA, a brigantine of 281 tons register, sailed from Pernambuco to Halifax and was wrecked at Berry Head, Guysborough. Her port of registry was Saint John, N.B. Cause: ice. Value of vessel was $18,000.

QUEEN OF THE EAST, a schooner of 24 tons register, sailed from Halifax to Main-a-Dieu and was wrecked on east coast of Nova Scotia on May 19. Her port of registry was Halifax. Cause: a leak. Value of schooner was $2,100.

ROTHESAY, a brigantine of 148 tons register, sailed from Saint John to Sydney and was wrecked at Scatarie Island on August 6. Her port of registry was Saint John. Cause: fog. Value of vessel was $17,000.

SIR JOHN A, a schooner of 25 tons register, sailed from St. Peter's to Guysborough and was wrecked at Lennox Passage on September 11. Her port of registry was Guysborough. Cause: fire. Value of schooner was $2,300.

VICTOR, a schooner of 123 tons register, sailed from St. John's to Bridgewater and was wrecked at Grand River on July 10. Her port of registry was Charlottetown. Cause: fog. Value of

schooner was $2,000.

XEBEC, a schooner of 195 tons register, sailed from Buctouche to Boston and was wrecked off Pictou Island on October 2. Her port of registry was Digby. Cause: fire. Value of schooner was $6,600.

YARMOUTH, a barkantine of 698 tons register, sailed from Gloucester to Yarmouth and was wrecked at Yarmouth Island on January 4. Her port of registry was Yarmouth. Cause: a snow squall. Value of vessel was $17,000.

(1885)—A.S. TOWNSHEND, a schooner of 74 tons register, was wrecked by ice, while at anchor in Main-a-Dieu Harbour. Her port of registry was Parrsboro, and the value of the schooner was $2,500.

A.E. McDONALD, a schooner of 148 tons register, sailed from Boston to Sydney and was wrecked at Scattarie Island. Her port of registry was Sydney. Cause: fog. Value of schooner was $2,000.

ANNIE BELL, a schooner of 42 tons register, sailed from Halifax to Cow Bay and was wrecked at Minas Gut on September 23. Her port of registry was Halifax. Cause: bad weather. Value of schooner was $500.

ALERT, a schooner of 36 tons register, sailed from Guysborough to Halifax and was wrecked at Fisherman's Harbour on November 26. Her port of registry was Guysboro. Cause: bad weather. Value of schooner was $2,550.

CLANDEBOYE, a barkantine of 872 tons register, sailed from London to Sydney, C.B., and was wrecked at Schooner Rock on May 16. Her port of registry was Chatham, N.B. Cause: fog. Value of vessel was $17,000.

EDGAR STUART, a steamship of 183 tons register, sailed from Liverpool to Yarmouth and was wrecked at Gull Rock on July 15. Her port of registry was Halifax. Cause: currents. Value of vessel was $20,000.

HELENA MORRIS, a schooner of 106 tons register, sailed from Philadelphia to Halifax and was wrecked near Sambro on February 4. Her port of registry was Windsor. Cause: ice. Value of schooner was $8,700.

HOWARD D. TROOP, a ship of 1,543 tons register. While at anchor at Mary Island, N.S., she was wrecked due to bad weather on January 6. Her port of registry was Saint John. Value of vessel was $50,000.

IMPERO, a schooner of 136 tons register, sailed from Sydney to Halifax and was wrecked at Marie Joseph on November 13. Her port of registry was Sydney. Cause: error of judgment.

Value of schooner was $3,150.

MARY, a schooner of 92 tons register, sailed from St. Martin's to Lockeport and was wrecked at Lockeport on February 5. Her port of registry was Shelburne. Cause: fire. Value of schooner was $4,800.

MAGGIE, a schooner of 71 tons register, sailed from Pictou to Halifax and was wrecked at Three Fathom Harbour on May 19. Her port of registry was Charlottetown. Cause: fog. Value of schooner was $2,650.

MADGE WILDFIRE, a barkantine of 842 tons register, sailed from West Hartlepool to Sydney and was wrecked at Scatarie Island. Her port of registry was Liverpool. Cause: bad weather. Value of vessel was $12,000.

PALESTINE, a barkantine of 1,350 tons register, sailed from Liverpool to Shelburne and was wrecked at Black Rock, Shelburne, on May 18. Her port of registry was Saint John. Cause: fog. Value of vessel was $55,000.

RICHMOND, a steamship of 44 tons register. While at wharf at Grandique Ferry the vessel was wrecked due to unknown causes. Her port of registry was Arichat. Value of vessel was $4,000.

RISE AND SHINE, a brigantine of 162 tons register, sailed from Portland to Lingan and was wrecked at Beaver Harbour on October 30. Her port of registry was Parrsboro. Cause: bad weather. Value of vessel was $5,500.

ROUGH AND READY, a schooner of 46 tons register, sailed from Georgetown to Halifax and was wrecked at Three Fathom Harbour on November 14. Her port of registry was Charlottetown. Cause: fog. Value of schooner was $1,200.

STANDARD, a schooner of 77 tons register, sailed from St. Martin's to Newfoundland and was wrecked at Scatarie, C.B., on January 29. Her port of registry was St. John's, Newfoundland. Cause: ice. Value of shcooner was $3,800.

SMILING WATER, a schooner of 54 tons register, sailed from Jeddore to L'Ardoise and was wrecked along the coast of Nova Scotia on June 11. Her port of registry was Mahone Bay. Cause: bad weather. Value of schooner was $5,300.

ST. PETER, a schooner of 15 tons register, sailed from Mabou to Pictou and was wrecked at Little Harbcur on October 9. Her port of registry was Port Hawkesbury. Cause: a gale. Value of schooner was $500.

SPIRIT OF THE DAY, a schooner of 33 tons register, sailed from Pictou to Chatham and was wrecked at Cape

Tormentine on October 21. Her port of registry was Pictou. Cause: fog. Value of schooner was $1,615.

TORDENSKJOLD, a barkantine of 673 tons register, sailed from Norway to Sydney and was wrecked at Halifax Harbour on May 15. Her port of registry was Norway. Cause: fog. Value of vessel was $8,500.

WILD ROSE, a schooner of 25 tons register, sailed from place unknown and was wrecked at Cape Sable on November 12. Her port of registry was Liverpool. Cause: a gale. Value of schooner was $300.

W.H. HATFIELD, a schooner of 115 tons register, sailed from Halifax to Arichat and was wrecked at Frying Pan Shoal on November 9. Her port of registry was Halifax. Cause: fog. Value of schooner was $1,000.

ALBERT, a schooner of 45 tons register, sailed from Lockeport to Halifax and was wrecked at Jeddore on December 22. Her port of registry was Shelburne. Cause: bad weather. Value of schooner was $3,300.

ANN HILTY, a schooner of 16 tons register, sailed from Port La Tour to Yarmouth and was wrecked at Wood Harbour on November 12. Her port of registry was Liverpool. Cause: bad weather. Value of schooner was $300.

CANNING PACKET, a schooner of 105 tons register, sailed from Cornwallis to Boston and was wrecked at Point Prim, N.S., on December 25. Her port of register was Windsor. Cause: ice. Value of schooner was $3,000.

ERATO, a schooner of 24 tons register, sailed from Lunenburg to Halifax and was wrecked off Liverpool, N.S. Her port of registry was Shelburne. Cause: a leak. Value of schooner was $500.

EMELLE, a schooner of 101 tons register, sailed from Perce to Quebec and was wrecked at Caribou Island on November 4. Her port of registry was Quebec. Cause: bad weather. Value of schooner was $7,000.

F. TOWNSEND, a schooner of 161 tons register, sailed from Saint John to Windsor and was wrecked at Port Greville on August 7. Her port of registry was Parrsboro. Cause: fire. Value of schooner was $8,000.

HARRY WETMORE, a schooner of 56 tons register, sailed from Sydney to Channel and was wrecked South Bar, Sydney, on October 8. Her port of registry was Great Britain. Cause: collision with steamship. Value of schooner was $14,000.

JANE PORTER, a schooner of 37 tons register, sailed from

205

Annapolis to Yarmouth and was wrecked at Westport on December 30. Her port of registry was Yarmouth. Cause: currents. Value of schooner was $750.

JULIA ANN W., a schooner of 21 tons register, sailed from Jeddore to Halifax and was wrecked near Jeddore on December 14. Her port of registry was Halifax. Cause: fog. Value of schooner was $1,550.

KINGFISHER, a schooner of 20 tons register, sailed from Mabou to Pictou and was wrecked at Port Hood Harbour. Her port of registry was Halifax. Cause: a gale. Value of schooner was $300.

LILLIAN BOURQUE, a schooner of 79 tons register, sailed from Pictou to New London and was wrecked at St. Peter's Harbour on September 20. Her port of registry was P.E.I. Cause: bad weather. Value of schooner was $2,500.

LADY CAROLINE, a schooner of 36 tons register, sailed from LaHave to Lunenburg and was wrecked at LaHave River on October 8. Her port of registry was Lunenburg. Cause: misstayed. Value of schooner was $1,100.

MARY ANN, a schooner of 143 tons register sailed from Meteghan to Belliveau Cove and was wrecked at this Cove. Her port of registry was Digby. Cause: bad weather. Value of schooner was $2,000.

MARY A. NELSON, a barkantine of 408 tons register, sailed from Pernambuco to Arichat and was wrecked off Arichat. Her port of registry was Charlottetown. Cause: bad weather. Value of vessel was $5,000.

SUMMERVILLE, a schooner of 129 tons register, sailed from Louisburg to Halifax and was wrecked on the south coast of Nova Scotia on August 30. Her port of registry was Liverpool. Cause: unknown. Six lives were lost and the value of schooner was $2,300.

TIGER, a steamship of 28 tons register, sailed from Halifax and was wrecked at Black Point on February 27. Her port of registry was Pictou. Cause: faulty compass. Value of vessel was $4,000.

UNICORN, a schooner of 29 tons register, sailed from Sydney to North Sydney and was wrecked at North Sydney on December 13. Her port of registry was Sydney. Cause: bad weather. Value of schooner was $600.

BRIGHT STAR, a schooner of 18 tons out of River Bourgeois was wrecked at West Arichat. She was owned by Urban and David Sampson.

BESSIE M. WELLS, a schooner of 82 tons under Captain

Robert Porper out of Gloucester, Mass., sailed for the fishing Banks and struck on the western point of Seal Island on March 16 and went to pieces.

(1886)—ARLINGTON, barkentine of 850 tons register, sailed from St. Ann's, C.B., to Montreal and was wrecked on a reef near Bird Islands on June 7. Her port of registry was Yarmouth. Cause: high winds. Value of vessel was $1,400.

ANNIE DUNCAN, a schooner of 57 tons register, sailed from Glace Bay to Charlottetown and was wrecked at Scatarie Island on September 9. Her port of registry was Charlottetown. Cause: a leak. Value of schooner was $2,100.

ANNIE JANE, a schooner of 103 tons register, sailed from Sydney to Halifax and was wrecked at New Harbour on October 3. Her port of registry was Baddeck. Cause: a gale. Value of schooner was $1,000.

BEULAH, a schooner of 107 tons register, sailed from Boston to Tignish and was wrecked at White Head, N.S., on May 5. Her port of registry was Shelburne. Cause: a gale. Value of schooner was $4,000.

BENONA, a steamer of 872 tons register, sailed from North Sydney to Montreal and was wrecked at Aspey Bay, N.S., on July 11. Her port of registry was Liverpool. Cause: fog and currents. Value of vessel was $43,900.

BIRDIE, a brigantine of 126 tons register, sailed from Boston to Sydney, N.S., and was wrecked at Tor Bay, N.S., on August, 31. Her port of registry was Charlottetown. Cause: fog. Value of vessel was $5,000.

CLIFTON, a barkentine of 1,717 tons register, sailed from London to Halifax and Chatham and was wrecked at Port Hawkesbury on May 6. Her port of registry was London, England. Cause: ice. Value of vessel was $2,700.

CYGNET, a schooner of 95 tons register, sailed from Bridgewater to St. John's, Newfoundland, and was wrecked at St. Peter's Bay on May 20. Her port of registry was Lunenburg. Cause: fog. Value of schooner was $1,600.

ELIZA HOOPER, a schooner of 50 tons register, sailed from Halifax to Sydney and was wrecked at Port Nova, C.B., on July 21. Her port of registry was Sydney, N.S. Cause: fog and bad weather. Value of schooner was $700.

EMMA, a schooner of 98 tons register, sailed from Salmon River, N.B., to Eastport, Me., and was wrecked at Bay of Fundy on December 16. Her port of registry was Saint John. Cause: a snow storm. Value of schooner was $1,000.

GARIBALDI, a schooner of 49 tons register, sailed from Gloucester, Mass., to fishing grounds and was wrecked at Minow Island, N.S., on October 3. Her port of registry was Gloucester, Mass. Cause: explosion. Value of schooner unknown.

JOHN NORTHRUP, a schooner of 125 tons register, sailed from Paspebiac, P.Q., to Boston and was wrecked at Little Harbour, N.S., on August 14. Her port of registry was Halifax. Cause: fog. Value of schooner was $700.

MINNIE, a schooner of 24 tons register, sailed from Grand Harbour, Grand Manan, to Campobello, N.B., and was wrecked in Bay of Fundy on February 21. Her port of registry was Saint John. Cause: unknown. Seven lives were lost and the value of schooner was $950.

MILLIE B., a schooner of 88 tons register, sailed from Liverpool, N.S., to Lockeport and was wrecked at Port Mouton Island on August 23. Her port of registry was Shelburne. Cause: error of judgment. Two lives were lost and the value of schooner was $5,500.

MAGNOLIA, a barkentine of 405 tons register, sailed from Portsmouth, U.S.A., to Little Glace Bay, C.B., and was wrecked at Scatarie Island on November 5. Her port of registry was Halifax. Cause: bad weather. Value of vessel was $10,000.

NESBIT, a schooner of 440 tons register, sailed from Windsor, N.S., to New York and was wrecked at Bay of Fundy, Gannet Rock, on August 14. Her port of registry was Windsor. Cause: fog. Value of schooner was $2,200.

OLIVETTE, a barkentine of 289 tons register, sailed from Summerside, P.E.I., to Bridgewater and on to England and was wrecked at St. Paul's Island on May 26. Her port of registry was Charlottetown. Cause: fog and currents. Value of vessel was $9,000.

PHILISTINE, a schooner of 44 tons register, sailed from Halifax to Pugwash and was wrecked at Goose Point, N.S., on May 7. Her port of registry was Pugwash. Cause: fog. Value of schooner was $440.

REGINA, a schooner of 128 tons register, sailed from Richibucto to Portland, Me. and was wrecked at Ironbound Island on south coast of Nova Scotia on August 8. Her port of registry was Quebec. Cause: misstays. Value of schooner was $2,200.

RIPPLE, a schooner of 17 tons register, sailed from Canso to Port Mulgrave and was wrecked at Arichat Harbour on November 26. Her port of registry was Lunenburg. Cause:

winds. Value of schooner was $500.

RACER, a barkentine of 251 tons register, sailed from Bahia to Sydney, C.B., and was wrecked at Cape Breton Island on December 4. Her port of registry was Greenock. Cause: high winds. Value of vessel was $5,000.

SISTERS, a schooner of 15 tons register, sailed from Yarmouth to fishing grounds and was wrecked off Barrington, N.S., on August 11. Her port of registry was Yarmouth. Cause: collision with barque *Midas* of U.S.A. Value of schooner was $12,000.

SANDNAES, a brig of 230 tons register, sailed from Boston to St. Mary's, N.S., and was wrecked at Halifax County on July 28. Her port of registry was Norway. Cause: fog. Value of vessel was $9,000.

WILLIAM LAW, a ship of 1,599 tons register, sailed from Havre to Sydney and was wrecked at Michael's Point, C.B., on May 20. Her port of registry was Yarmouth. Cause: currents. Two lives were lost and the value of vessel was $40,000.

W.R. PAGE, a schooner of 81 tons register, sailed from fishing trade to Halifax and was wrecked at Hay Island, Scatarie, on November 8. Her port of registry was Sydney, C.B. Cause: a gale. Value of schooner was $6,500.

ELIZABETH, a schooner of 32 tons register, sailed from Halifax to Sheet Harbour and was wrecked at South East Passage, Halifax Harbour, on December 26. Her port of registry was Halifax. Cause: bad weather. Value of schooner was $1,000.

FLORA BELL, a schooner of 39 tons register, sailed from Mabou and was wrecked at this place on December 23. Her port of registry was Port Hawkesbury. Cause: the wheel, some how, got tangled. Value of schooner was $2,400.

HERBERT, a schooner of 29 tons register, sailed from Halifax to Magdalen and was wrecked at Madame Island on December 12. Her port of registry was Halifax. Cause: bad weather. Value of schooner unknown.

HEATHER, a schooner of 139 tons register, sailed from St. John's Newfoundland, to Antigonish and was wrecked at Cow Bay on October 15. Her port of registry was Halifax. Cause: bad weather. Value of vessel unknown.

LAURA M. BRUCE, a schooner of 84 tons register, sailed from Arichat to New York and was wrecked at Petit de Grat on December 12. Her port of registry was Halifax. Cause: bad weather. Value of schooner was $3,200.

MARIA, a schooner of 45 tons register, sailed from

Margaree to Halifax and was wrecked at Broad Cove. Her port of registry was Halifax. Cause: bad weather. Value of schooner was $4,000.

MAYFLOWER, a brigantine of 193 tons register, sailed from St. John's to Glace Bay and was wrecked off Scatarie Island on December 20. Her port of registry was St. John's, Newfoundland. Cause: bad weather. Value of vessel unknown.

MARY, a schooner of 21 tons register, was wrecked on October 20 while at anchor at Petit de Grat. Her port of registry was Arichat. Cause: bad weather. Value of schooner was $200.

NIMBLE, a schooner of 59 tons register, sailed from Halifax to Little Glace Bay and was wrecked at Louisburg on December 6. Her port of registry was Halifax. Cause: bad weather. Value of schooner was $1,000.

UNION STAR, a schooner of 33 tons register, sailed from Halifax to Margaree and was wrecked at Turtle Reef on March 29. Her port of registry was Halifax. Cause: misstayed. Value of schooner was $330.

(1887)—AFTON, a schooner of 84 tons register, sailed from Saint John, N.B. to Portland, Me., and was wrecked at Cranberry Island on January 14. Her port of registry was Saint John, N.B. Cause: a gale. Value of schooner was $1,500.

ARTHUR, a schooner of 28 tons register, sailed from Port Hood to Margaree and was wrecked in this harbour on January 3. Her port of registry was Lunenburg. Cause: ice. Value of schooner was $500.

ANNA McGEE, a schooner of 57 tons register, sailed from Pubnico to Western Banks and was wrecked at Musquodoboit on June 3. Her port of registry was Yarmouth. Cause: a gale. Value of schooner unknown.

ACACIA, a steamer of 1,150 tons register, sailed from Maryport to North Sydney and was wrecked at Schooner Pond Wedges on June 9. Her port of registry was Sunderland. Cause: fog. Value of schooner unknown.

ALICE L.M. CROWDIS, a schooner of 53 tons register, sailed from Sydney to Halifax and was wrecked at S.W. Braker, Wedge Island, on July 6. Her port of registry was Halifax. Cause: fog. Value of schooner was $1,400.

ARIADNE, a barkentine of 314 tons register, sailed from Sackville, N.B., to Conway, Wales, and was wrecked at Cumberland Bay on August 5. Her port of registry was Skein, Norway. Cause: anchor chains parted. Value of vessel was $9,500.

210

ANNA MARIA, a schooner of 67 tons register, sailed from St. Pierre to Quebec and was wrecked at Black Brook, Victoria Co., C.B., on November 8. Her port of registry was Quebec. Cause: a leak. Value of schooner unknown.

ALARIC, a brigantine of 210 tons register, sailed from Boston to Liverpool and was wrecked at Seal Island on July 30. Her port of registry was Liverpool, N.S. Cause: error in judgment. Value of vessel was $5,000.

BUSY WILLIAM, a schooner of 65 tons register, sailed from Halifax to Cow Bay and was wrecked at Ecum Secum on July 8. Her port of registry was Halifax. Cause: struck a reef. Value of schooner was $1,800.

BACHELORS, a barque of 655 tons register, sailed from Buenos Aires to Yarmouth and was wrecked at entrance of Yarmouth Harbour on November 8. Her port of registry was Yarmouth. Cause: a gale. Value of vessel was $5,000.

C.B. MANNING, a schooner of 68 tons register, sailed from Gloucester for fishing and was wrecked at entrance of Yarmouth Harbour on April 7. Her port of registry was Gloucester. Cause: becalmed. Value of schooner was $3,880.

CHARLES P. THOMPSON, a schooner of 69 tons register, sailed from Gloucester to fishing grounds and was wrecked at Bonde Rock on July 3. Her port of registry was Gloucester. Cause: mistook a light. Value of schooner was $1,500.

CLIFFORD, a schooner of 88 tons register, sailed from Halifax to Shelburne and was wrecked near Lockeport on June 15. Her port of registry was Shelburne. Cause: haze. Value of schooner was $7,000.

DAISY, a schooner of 35 tons register, sailed from Halifax to Bay of Islands, Newfoundland, and was wrecked at Cat Harbour, Bras d'Or Lake, on October 10. Her port of registry was Halifax. Cause: water logged. Value of schooner was unknown.

ETTA WHITTEMORE, a brigantine of 390 tons register, sailed from Belliveau, N.S., to Weymouth and was wrecked at St. Mary's Bay, N.S., on May 26. Her port of registry was New York. Cause: a gale. Value of schooner was $1,900.

FLORA B., a schooner of 70 tons register, sailed from Cornwallis to Boston and was wrecked at Port George, N.S., on March 26. Her port of registry was Parrsboro. Cause: rudder went adrift. Value of schooner was $2,000.

GLADYS, a schooner of 144 tons register, sailed from New York to Halifax and was wrecked at Chaggogin Point, near Yarmouth, on January 21. Her port of registry was Shelburne. Cause: mistook a light. One life was lost and the value of schooner was $7,000.

HENRY BATTYE, a schooner of 57 tons register, sailed from Bank of Islands to Halifax and was wrecked at Meat Cove on January 18. Her port of registry was Halifax. Cause: a snow strom. Value of schooner was $3,500.

HENRIETTA, a schooner of 34 tons register, sailed from Saint John to Westport and was wrecked at Brier Island on October 20. Her port of registry was Yarmouth. Cause: poor judgment. Value of schooner was $800.

HARMONY, a schooner of 102 tons register, sailed from Cow Bay to Halifax and was wrecked near Lake Advice, N.S., on September 27. Her port of registry was Windsor. Cause: bad weather. Value of schooner was $1,000.

IRELAND, a barque of 973 tons register, sailed from Saint John, N.B., to Carnarvon and was wrecked at Brier Island on October 20. Her port of registry was Liverpool, G.B. Cause: fog. Value of vessel was $15,000.

JOE READ, a barque of 585 tons register, sailed from Bordeaux to Summerside and was wrecked at Canso reef on March 30. Her port of registry was Charlottetown. Cause: a gale. Value of vessel was unknown.

LAURA BELLE, a schooner of 74 tons register, sailed from Halifax to North Sydney and was wrecked between St. Esprit and Point Miscou on May 5. Her port of registry was Halifax. Cause: ice. Value of schooner is unknown.

LOTHAIR, a barque of 481 tons register, sailed from Newfoundland to Cow Bay and was wrecked in this Bay on November 16. Her port of registry was Sydney. Cause: a storm. Value of vessel was $12,000.

MARY ANN, a schooner of 66 tons register, sailed from Sydney to Halifax and was wrecked at Bass Rock on January 13. Her port of registry was Halifax. Cause: parting of chains. Value of schooner was $400.

MIZPAH, a barque of 898 tons register, sailed from Philadelphia to Quebec and was wrecked at Simon's Point, C.B., on May 26. Her port of registry was Yarmouth. Cause: strong currents. Value of vessel was $10,000.

MERRIMACK, a steamer of 1,119 tons register, sailed from Halifax to Boston and was wrecked at Little Hope Island on

212

July 10. Her port of registry was U.S.A. Cause: fog. Value of vessel was $150,000.

PETREL, a schooner of 12 tons register, sailed from Advocate to Parrsboro and was wrecked at McLaughlin's Head on October 13. Her port of registry was Windsor, N.S. Cause: grounded. Value of schooner was $160.

S.G.MORTON, a schooner of 44 tons register, sailed from Shut-in-Harbour, near Halifax, and was wrecked at Key Island on April 13. Her port of registry was Halifax. Cause: drifted ashore. Value of schooner was $2,000.

SUNBEAM, a schooner of 69 tons register, sailed from Port Philip to St. Pierre and was wrecked at Pugwash Harbour on October 22. Her port of registry was St. John's, Newfoundland. Cause: unknown. Value of schooner was $4,000.

TIBER, a schooner of 60 tons register, sailed from Arichat to Cow Bay on April 28 and, on May 6, was wrecked at Rocky Bay, C.B. Her port of registry was Halifax. Cause: heavy seas. Value of schooner was $1,200.

VILLAGE BELLE, a schooner of 40 tons register, sailed from Pubnico to Halifax and was wrecked at Michael Rock on January 4. Her port of registry was Shelburne. Cause: parting of hawser. Value of schooner was $900.

WINNIE, a schooner of 37 tons register, sailed from Cow Bay and was wrecked at Frying Pan, Canso, on August 25. Her port of registry was Charlottetown. Cause: a leak. Value of schooner was $600.

ELEY ELVY, a schooner of 18 tons register, sailed from Sand Harbour to Lunenburg and was wrecked at Ginlet Reef on September 15. Her port of registry was Halifax. Cause: a storm. Value of schooner was $600.

LIGHT FOOT, a schooner of 56 tons register, sailed from Halifax to Barrington and was wrecked at Clark's Harbour Reef on December 25. Her port of registry was Barrington. Cause: a gale. Value of schooner is unknown.

MINNIE, a schooner of 40 tons register, sailed from Georgetown, P.E.I., to Cape Broyle and was wrecked at Bras d'Or Lake, C.B., on December 28. Her port of registry was St. John's, Newfoundland. Cause: bad steering. One life was lost and the value of schooner was $800.

PRIZE, a schooner of 92 tons register, sailed from Lunenburg to fishing grounds and was wrecked at entrance to Lunenburg Harbour on August 15. Her port of registry was Lunenburg. Cause: rough seas. Value of schooner was $7,000.

SEA SLIPPER, a schooner of 55 tons register, sailed from Halifax to Shelburne and was wrecked at Lunenburg Harbour on December 5. Her port of registry was Halifax. Cause: snow storm. Value of schooner is unknown.

VIOLA, a schooner of 55 tons register, sailed from a place unknown and was wrecked at Bay of Fundy on December 16. Her port of registry was St. Andrews. Cause: a squall. Value of schooner is unknown.

WELCOME, a schooner of 32 tons register, sailed from French Village to Halifax and was wrecked at French Village on December 26. Her port of registry was Halifax. Cause: parting of cables. Value of schooner was $500.

ACTIVE, a schooner of 71 tons register, sailed from Louisburg to Halifax and was wrecked off Gabarus Bay on December 24. Her port of registry was Halifax. Cause: a wave. Value of schooner was $1,200.

ARTHUR, a schooner of 142 tons register, sailed from Port Hawkesbury to Boston and was wrecked on a bar in Liverpool Harbour on December 29. Her port of registry was Shelburne. Cause: a gale. Value of schooner was $6,000.

GENERAL GORDON, a schooner of 100 tons register, sailed from Louisburg to Halifax and was wrecked east side of White Head Harbour, N.S., on December 24. Her port of registry was Halifax. Cause: misstayed. Value of schooner was $8,000.

HEBE, a brig of 236 tons register, sailed from Rio de Janerio and was wrecked at Bryon Island, N.S., on October 10. Her port of registry was Jersey, G.B. Cause: currents. Value of vessel was $15,000.

JAMES, a schooner of 17 tons register, sailed from Beckerton to Montague, P.E.I., and was wrecked at Indian Harbour on October 20. Her port of registry was Halifax. Cause: parting of chains. Value of schooner was $900.

MAYFLOWER, a schooner of 23 tons register, sailed from Machias to Saint John and was wrecked at Seal Island. Her port of registry was Saint John. Cause: fog. Value of schooner was $600.

ROBERT BOAK, a schooner of 28 tons register, sailed from Charlottetown to Port Hawkesbury and was wrecked at Antigonish Bay on December 19. Her port of registry was Halifax. Cause: a snowstorm. Value of schooner was $1,000.

(1888)—ASHANTEE, a barque of 699 tons register, sailed from Liverpool to Pictou and was wrecked three miles off Harbour au Bouche on May 11. Her port of registry was Halifax. Cause: ice. Value of vessel was $15,000.

AMELIA, a schooner of 54 tons register, sailed from Halifax to Charlottetown and was wrecked at St. George's Bay, N.S., on May 11. Her port of registry was Halifax. Cause: ice. Value of schooner was $600.

A. CARCAUD, a schooner of 78 tons register, sailed from North Sydney to Halifax and was wrecked at New Harbour Head, N.S., on September 1. Her port of registry was Arichat. Cause: fog. Value of schooner was $920.

COAST GUARD, a schooner of 52 tons register, sailed from Murray Harbour, P.E.I., to Boston and was wrecked at Long Island, Bay of Fundy on January 17. Her port of registry was Pictou. Cause: gales. Value of schooner was $2,750.

CORINNE, a brigantine of 123 tons register, sailed from Boston to Newfoundland and was wrecked at Mud Island on September 12. Her port of registry was Sydney. Cause: currents. Value of vessel was $1,500.

CARRIE, a schooner of 97 tons register, sailed from Bear River, N.S., to Rockland, Me., and was wrecked at Hurricane Ledge, N.S., on July 11. Her port of registry was Saint John. Cause: currents. Value of schooner was $1,700.

E. CHAMBERS, a schooner of 215 tons register, sailed from New York to Saint John and was wrecked at Hillsburn, N.S., on January 15. Her port of registry was Saint John. Cause: a gale. Value of schooner was $6,690.

ELLA MAUD, a schooner of 29 tons register, sailed from Ingonish to North Sydney and was wrecked at Sydney River on July 29. Her port of registry was Sydney, C.B. Cause: a gale. Value of schooner was $1,000.

HATTIE LEWIS, a schooner of 54 tons register, sailed from Spry Bay to Cow Bay and was wrecked off Guyon Island, C.B., on April 22. Her port of registry was Halifax. Value of schooner was $3,500.

J.W. RUSSEL, a schooner of 52 tons register, sailed from Halifax to Sydney and was wrecked at Grand River, C.B., on April 22. Her port of registry was Port Medway. Cause: ice. Value of schooner was $1,600.

JOHN PURNEY, a schooner of 66 tons register sailed from Sheet Harbour to Shelburne and was wrecked at Wood Island on August 18. Her port of registry was Shelburne. Cause: bad weather. Value of schooner was $6,800.

MAY BRENT, a schooner of 110 tons register sailed from Parrsboro to Newbury Port and was wrecked at Seal Island on January 20. Her port of registry was Parrsboro. Cause: fire. Value of schooner was $4,800.

MYSTIC, a schooner of 79 tons register sailed from Halifax to Yarmouth and was wrecked at Port Mouton, Island Ledges, on February 19. Her port of registry was Yarmouth. Cause: currents. Value of schooner was $4,000.

MAZEPPA, a barkentine of 474 tons register sailed from Saint John to Cork and was wrecked at Seal Island on July 4. Her port of registry was Norway. Cause: tides. Value of vessel was $4,000.

MATHEW M. MURRAY, a schooner of 75 tons register sailed from Sydney to Gloucester and was wrecked at Louisburg on October 6. Her port of registry was U.S.A. Cause: unknown. Value of schooner was $5,000.

MAGGIE M., a barque of 429 tons register sailed from Glace Bay to Saint John and was wrecked at Cape Negro Island on November 11. Her port of registry was Saint John. Cause: currents. Value of vessel was $5,900.

SAINVAL COIPEL, a brigantine of 290 tons register sailed from Bear River to Trinidad and was wrecked at Mud Island on January 19. Her port of registry was Digby. Cause: ice. Value of vessel was $5,700.

THOR, a barque of 345 tons register, sailed from Liverpool, G.B., to Halifax and was wrecked at Musquodoboit on July 30. Her port of registry was Norway. Cause: fog. Value of vessel was $1,400.

WARREN J. CROSSLY, a schooner of 107 tons register, sailed from Placentia to Gloucester Bay and was wrecked at entrance of Louisbourg Harbour on January 5. Her port of registry was Gloucester. Cause: winds. Value of schooner was $14,500.

W.M. MacKAY, a schooner of 97 tons register, sailed from New York to Saint John and was wrecked at New London, N.S., on February 7. Her port of registry was Saint John. Cause: collision with *City of Truro*. Value of schooner was $22,500.

BEATRICE, a schooner of 109 tons register, sailed from G.B. fishing grounds to Yarmouth and was wrecked at Hill Point, N.S., on November 3. Her port of registry was Yarmouth. Cause: fog. Value of schooner was $7,500.

DALLAS HILL, a schooner of 109 tons register, sailed from Saint John to Providence and was wrecked at Thompson's Island, N.S., on November 25. Her port of registry was Saint John. Cause: a gale. Value of schooner was $3,900.

EFFORT, a schooner of 110 tons register, sailed from Halifax to Jordan River and was wrecked at LaHave Harbour on

December 12. Her port of registry was Port Hawkesbury. Cause: a gale. Value of schooner was $7,200.

J.W. RUSSEL, a schooner of 53 tons register, sailed from Grand River to Sydney, C.B., and was wrecked at Grand River on April 16. Her port of registry was Port Medway. Cause: a gale. Value of schooner was $1,000.

J.J. LOCKE, a schooner of 54 tons register, sailed from Boston to Barrington and was wrecked at Scituate Beach, N.S., on November 26. Her port of registry was Yarmouth. Cause: a gale. Value of vessel was $3,900.

LILY OF CLYDE, a schooner of 61 tons register, sailed from Sydney to Aspy Bay and was wrecked at White Point, C.B., on October 1. Her port of registry was Shelburne. Cause: parting of chains. Value of schooner was $2,700.

NAIAD, a schooner of 56 tons register, sailed from Joggins to Saint John and was wrecked at Cumberland Bay. Her port of registry was Parrsboro. Cause: dragging of anchors. Value of schooner was $400.

SWIFT CURRENT, a schooner of 63 tons register, sailed from Halifax to Ingonish Harbour and was wrecked at the entrance of this Harbour on December 3. Her port of registry was Halifax. Cause: tides. Value of schooner was $3,000.

SARAH CARLIN, a schooner of 148 tons register, sailed from Halifax to Bridgewater and was wrecked south west of Little Duck Island on November 4. Her port of registry was Halifax. Cause: winds. Value of schooner was $5,000.

TEAZER, a schooner of 31 tons register, sailed from Halifax to Spry Bay and was wrecked at Pleasant Harbour on October 29. Her port of registry was Halifax. Cause: dragging of anchors. Value of schooner was $300.

VESTA, a brigantine of 148 tons register, sailed from Harbour Grace to North Sydney and was wrecked at Cranberry on October 29. Her port of registry was St. John's, Newfoundland. Cause: fog. Value of vessel was $2,000.

W. WRIGHT, a schooner of 59 tons register, sailed from Grand Narrows to Charlottetown and was wrecked on east side of Smith's Island, N.S., on December 12. Her port of registry was Charlottetown. Cause: a gale. Value of schooner was $1,500.

WHITE WINGS, a schooner of 93 tons register, sailed from Liscomb to Boston and was wrecked at Liscomb Light on November 29. Her port of registry was Charlottetown. Cause: winds. Value of schooner was $9,000.

WILLOW, a schooner of 19 tons register, sailed from

Westport to Maitland and was wrecked at Maitland. Her port of registry was Yarmouth. Cause: a gale. Value of schooner was $300.

(1889)—ANNA B., a schooner of 16 tons register, sailed from Rose Blanche on a fishing trip and was wrecked at St. Paul's Island on March 5. Her port of registry was Saint John. Cause: hit another vessel while at anchor. Value of schooner was $400.

BARTIE PIERCE, a schooner of 90 tons register, sailed from St. Pierre Miquelon to Gloucester and was wrecked off Cape Canso on January 24. Her port of registry was Gloucester. Cause: a gale. Value of schooner was $5,000.

BESSIE, a schooner of 33 tons register, sailed from Halifax to Chester and was wrecked at Ketch Harbour on July 20. Her port of registry was Halifax. Cause: fog. Value of schooner was $600.

DUNROBIN, a schooner of 55 tons register, sailed from Rockland, Maine, to Quaco, N.B., and was wrecked at Port George, N.S., on March 30. Her port of registry was Saint John, N.B. Cause: non control of schooner. Value of schooner was $1,000.

FESTINE LENTE, a schooner of 80 tons register, sailed from Shelburne to Halifax and was wrecked at Bryon Island on August 4. Her port of registry was Shelburne. Cause: currents. Value of schooner was $5,000.

GLIDE, a schooner of 66 tons register sailed from Canning to Boston and was wrecked at Pereaux Beach, N.S., on November 17. Her port of registry was Windsor, N.S. Cause: fire. Value of schooner was $2,000.

HELENA, a schooner of 16 tons register, sailed from Lower Prospect on fishing trip and was wrecked at Jacob's Rock, N.S., on March 21. Value of schooner was $600.

JOHN SOMES, a schooner of 62 tons register, sailed from Georgetown, P.E.I., to fishing banks and was wrecked off Port Hood, N.S., on May 1. Her port of registry was Portland, N.S. Cause: fog. Value of schooner was $1,700.

JAMES DWYER, a schooner of 99 tons register, sailed from Halifax to Grand Narrows and was wrecked at Cape Roser, C.B., on June 5.

JEANNE D'ARCH, a schooner of 52 tons register, sailed from Halifax to New London, P.E.I., and was wrecked at White Head, N.S., on July 15. Her port of registry was in France. Cause: fog. Value of schooner was $1,500.

KESTREL, a schooner of 70 tons register, sailed from Cow

Bay to Halifax and was wrecked at Louisburg Harbour on October 25. Her port of registry was Halifax. Cause: hit a rock. Value of schooner was $2,000.

MAGELLAN, a schooner of 89 tons register, sailed from Halifax to Canso and was wrecked off Cape Canso on May 20. Her port of registry was Shelburne. Cause: error. Value of schooner was $3,500.

MAUD AND BESSIE, a schooner of 75 tons register, sailed from Boston to Joggins, N.S., and was wrecked at Maccan River on July 20. Her port of registry was Saint John. Cause: fog. Value of schooner was $500.

NEW ERA, a barkentine of 314 tons register, sailed from Pictou to Saint John, N.B., and was wrecked at Cape Negro, N.S., on June 27. Her port of registry was Charlottetown. Cause: fog. Value of vessel was $4,000.

NEVA, a schooner of 190 tons register, sailed from Bayfield to Cape George and was wrecked at Cape George Breakers on September 19. Her port of registry was Halifax. Cause: a squall. Value of schooner was $800.

OLIVER A. O'MULLIN, a schooner of 148 tons register, sailed from Cow Bay to Halifax and was wrecked off Jeddore, N.S., on March 26. Her port of registry was Parrsboro. Cause: ice. Value of schooner was $1,875.

THETIS, a schooner of 44 tons register, sailed from Lockeport to Lunenburg and was wrecked at Lockeport Harbour on September 13. Her port of registry was Lunenburg. Cause: misstayed. Value of schooner was $750.

MATILDA, a schooner of 80 tons register, sailed from Canso to Barrington and was wrecked at Cape Sable Island on November 20. Her port of registry was Barrington. Cause: bad weather. Value of schooner was $3,000.

MAUDE, a schooner of 14 tons register, sailed from Indian Harbour to Modesty Cove and was wrecked at Patty's Head, N.S., on September 17. Her port of registry was Lunenburg. Cause: heavy seas. Value of schooner was $700.

REGINA, a schooner of 57 tons register, sailed from Lunenburg to Pubnico and was wrecked at Raynes Point, N.S., on December 6. Her port of registry was Yarmouth. Cause: fog. Value of schooner was $1,200.

UNION B., a schooner of 20 tons register, sailed from Apple River to Port Lorne and was wrecked at Port Lorne. Her port of registry was Windsor, N.S. Cause: steering gear broke. Value of schooner was $300.

ANNIE, a schooner of 62 tons register, sailed from Glace Bay to St. John's, Newfoundland, and was wrecked at Glace Bay on November 28. Her port of registry was St. John's, Newfoundland. Cause: a leak. Value of schooner was $1,200.

KELSO, a schooner of 111 tons register, sailed from Liverpool to Yarmouth and was wrecked at West Head, N.S., on December 14. Her port of registry was Yarmouth. Cause: fire. Value of schooner was $2,300.

LARK, a schooner of 17 tons register, sailed from Mahone Bay to Halifax and was wrecked at Shad Bay on September 14. Her port of registry was Halifax. Cause: bad weather. Value of schooner was $400.

LODI, a schooner of 49 tons register, sailed from Summerside to Pictou and was wrecked at Malagash Point, N.S., on November 26. Her port of registry was Pictou. Cause: misstayed. Value of schooner was $700.

(1890)—ALGERIA, a barque of 620 tons register, sailed from Belfast,Ireland, to Sydney, C.B., and was wrecked at Cape Dauphin, C.B., on October 12. Her port of registry was Saint John, N.B. Cause: loss of canvas due to bad weather. Value of vessel was $8,000.

ANGELINE, a schooner of 67 tons register, sailed from Barrington to Pubnico and was wrecked at John's Island Ledge, Lobster Bay, on July 26. Her port of registry was Yarmouth. Cause: faulty compass. Value of schooner was $2,250.

HENRY A. BURNHAM, a barquentine of 473 tons, out of New York for Halifax with a cargo of coal, was wrecked at Seal Island on September 14.

NEW ENGLAND, a schooner of 60 tons register, sailed from River Hebert to Saint John, N.B., and was wrecked at River Hebert on May 15. Her port of registry was Saint John, N.B. Cause: ice. Value of schooner was $300.

SIR C. TUPPER, a schooner of 81 tons register, sailed from North Sydney to Catalina, Newfoundland, and was wrecked near Glace Bay Harbour on October 17. Her port of registry was St. John's, Newfoundland. Cause: a gale. Value of schooner was $1,850.

SUSIE E., a schooner of 98 tons register, sailed from Glace Bay to Saint John, N.B., and was wrecked off Marie Joseph, C.B., on July 31. Her port of registry was Halifax. Cause: fog. Value of schooner was $4,000.

TIOGO, a schooner of 93 tons register, sailed from Boston to Liverpool, N.S., and was wrecked in this harbour on March 6. Her port of registry was Lunenburg. Cause: unknown. Value of

schooner was $5,000.

TWILIGHT, a schooner of 49 tons register, sailed from Port Greville to Advocate Harbour and was wrecked in this harbour on August 27. Her port of registry was Parrsboro. Cause: a gale. Value of schooner was $700.

ULUNDA, a steamer of 1,160 tons register, sailed from Saint John to Halifax and was wrecked at Brier Island, N.S., on August 26. Her port of registry was West Harthlepool, G.B. Cause: fog and currents. Value of vessel was $125,000.

UNIQUE, a schooner of 75 tons register, sailed from Gloucester to the fishing grounds and was wrecked at Tusket Islands on July 5. Her port of registry was Boston, Mass. Cause: fog. Value of schooner was $7,000.

ANNIE S., a schooner of 34 tons register, sailed from Richibucto to Halifax and was wrecked at Richibucto Harbour on July 3. Her port of registry was Halifax. Cause: hit oyster beds. Value of schooner was $5,000.

BEN HUR, a schooner of 100 tons register, sailed from Gloucester, Mass., to the fishing grounds and was wrecked at Barrington on January 13. Her port of registry was U.S.A. Cause: bad judgment. Value of schooner was $15,000.

DAVID TAYLOR, a barque of 599 tons register, sailed from Londonderry, Ireland, to Saint John, N.B., and was wrecked 12 miles east of Lockeport, N.S., on May 20. Her port of registry was Saint John, N.B. Cause: off course. Value of vessel was $30,000.

ELECTRIC, a schooner of 58 tons register, sailed from Pictou to Cow Bay and was wrecked near Pictou on October 6. Her port of registry was Guysboro. Cause: main boom broke. Value of schooner was $1,000.

ELLEN ELIZA, a schooner of 21 tons register, sailed from Gabarus to Halifax and was wrecked at Point Michaux, C.B., on May 5. Her port of registry was Halifax. Cause: bad weather. Value of schooner was $1,300.

FINN, a brigantine of 170 tons register, sailed from Bristol to Quebec and was wrecked at Gabarus Bay, C.B., on August 24. Her port of registry was Norway. Cause: unknown. Value of vessel was $6,000.

GALAXY, a schooner of 33 tons register, sailed from Liverpool to Arichat and was wrecked at Thrum Cap, Halifax Harbour, on July 18. Her port of registry was Liverpool. Cause: mistook buoy. Value of schooner was $800.

HARRIET, a schooner of 26 tons register, sailed from

Pictou to Pugwash and was wrecked at Fraser's Cove, Pugwash, on October 12.

HENRY A BURNHAM, a brigantine of 473 tons register, sailed from New York to Halifax and was wrecked at Seal Island Light on September 14. Her port of registry was Boston. Cause: misjudgment. Value of vessel was $4,100.

JOHN TILTON, a schooner of 65 tons register, sailed from Pownal, P.E.I., to Glace Bay, C.B., and was wrecked at Chedabucto Bay, N.S., on May 12. Her port of registry was Charlottetown. Cause: fire. Value of schooner was $1,190.

LAURA, a schooner of 125 tons register, sailed from Rockland, Me., to Weymouth, N.S., and was wrecked at Gull Rock on June 21. Her port of registry was Digby. Cause: tides. Value of schooner was $1,500.

LAUREL, a schooner of 43 tons register, sailed from Moncton to Apple River and was wrecked at Pudsey's Reef on May 19. Her port of registry was Windsor. Cause: bad weather. Value of schooner was $250.

LENNIE, a schooner of 99 tons register, sailed from Antigua to Yarmouth and was wrecked at Digby Neck on December 27. Her port of registry was Yarmouth. Cause: a gale. Two lives were lost and the value of schooner was $4,500.

LIMA, a schooner of 27 tons register, sailed from Bass River, N.B., to Joggins, N.S., and was wrecked at Isle Haute, Bay of Fundy, on October 20. Her port of registry was Saint John, N.B. Cause: loss of sails and anchors. Value of schooner was $275.

LITTLE FRED, a schooner of 25 tons register, sailed from Westport to Belliveau's Cove and was wrecked on south side of Peter's Island on April 29. Her port of registry was Digby. Cause: tides. Value of schooner was $400.

MARIE ANNA, a brig of 250 tons register, sailed from Halifax to Cow Bay and was wrecked in this Bay on October 12. Her port of registry was Turk's Island. Cause: parting of chains. Value of vessel was $3,500.

MARION, a schooner of 78 tons register, sailed from Gloucester to the fishing grounds and was wrecked about eight miles east of Grand River, C.B., on August 6. Her port of registry was Gloucester. Cause: fog. Value of schooner was $4,700.

NAPOLEON 111, a steamer of 749 tons register, sailed from Cape Ray to Sydney and was wrecked on north side of Glace Bay entrance on October 18. Her port of registry was Quebec.

Cause: a gale. Value of vessel was $50,000.

OSSIPEE, a schooner of 69 tons register, sailed from Gloucester for fishing trip and was wrecked at South East Breakers, Country Harbour, on May 5. Her port of registry was Gloucester. Cause: hit a rock in thick of fog. Value of schooner was $30,800.

PARKER M. WHITEMORE, a ship of 2,205 tons register, sailed from Bristol, England, to Delaware Breakwater and was wrecked at Shelburne County on August 25. Her port of registry was U.S.A. Cause: bad weather. Value of vessel was $85,000.

PRINCESS BEATRICE, a steamer of 270 tons register, sailed from Halifax to Isaac's Harbour and was wrecked near Isaac's Harbour on September 16. Her port of registry was Glasgow, G.B. Cause: currents. Value of vessel was $20,000.

RICHARD THOMPSON, a schooner of 53 tons register, sailed from Pictou to Summerside and was wrecked along Northumberland Straits on date unknown. Her port of registry was Charlottetown. Cause: unknown. Four lives were lost and the value of the schooner was $800.

SCYLLA, a schooner of 102 tons register, sailed from Liscomb to Fortune Bay and was wrecked at Guysboro on December 22. Her port of registry was Lunenburg. Cause: bad weather. Value of schooner was $4,000.

VELOCIPEDE, a schooner of 104 tons register, sailed from Gloucester for a fishing trip and was wrecked at Louisburg Harbour on October 18. Her port of registry was Gloucester, Mass. Cause: a gale. Value of schooner was $6,500.

(1891)—ARDELLA, a schooner of 93 tons register, sailed from Lockeport on a fishing trip and was wrecked at Green Island, St. Peter's Bay, C.B., on May 16. Her port of registry was Shelburne. Cause: fog. Value of schooner was $6,750.

B.C. SMITH, a schooner of 98 tons register, sailed from St. Pierre to Lunenburg and was wrecked at Owen's Reef, Lunenburg Bay, on March 9. Her port of registry was Lunenburg. Cause: fog and tide. Value of schooner was $6,500.

BISMARK, a schooner of 54 tons register, sailed from Cheticamp to Pleasant Bay, C.B., and was wrecked in this bay on October 13. Her port of registry was Halifax. Cause: a gale. Value of schooner was $1,500.

BARBARONE, a schooner of 93 tons register, sailed from Halifax to Carbonnear, Newfoundland, and was wrecked at Cow Bay on November 6. Her port of registry was St. John's, Newfoundland. Cause: bad storm. Value of schooner is not known.

CYGNET, a schooner of 95 tons register, sailed from Halifax to Canso and was wrecked at Point Michaud on January 11. Her port of registry was Pictou. Cause: a gale. Value of schooner was $3,800.

SAMOA, a schooner under Captain Gelbert was lost in Manchester Bay in Guysborough County.

JOHN McLEOD, a vessel which sank sixteen miles S.S.E. of Devil's Island.

CAMELIA, a barque of 187 tons register, sailed from Bahia to Sydney, C.B., and was wrecked at Tin Cove, off Scatarie Island, on October 13. Her port of registry was Beddeford. Cause: a gale. Value of vessel is not known.

CHAMPION, a schooner of 16 tons register, sailed from Louisburg to Halifax and was wrecked at Grand Battery Shoal on December 17. Her port of registry was Halifax. Cause: unknown. Value of schooner was $250.

DOLPHIN, a schooner of 36 tons register, sailed from Halifax to Arichat and was wrecked at Arichat Harbour on October 13. Her port of registry was Jersey, G.B. Cause: broke from moorings. Value of schooner is unknown.

ENDEAVOUR, a schooner of 64 tons register, sailed from Parrsboro to Hillsboro and was wrecked at Cape Chignecto, Cumberland County, N.S., on November 6. Her port of registry was Saint John, N.B. Cause: winds. Value of schooner was $700.

EUREKA, a schooner of 94 tons register, sailed from Port George, N.S., to Rockland, Me., and was wrecked at Port George on December 2. Her port of registry was Parrsboro. Cause: unknown. Value of schooner was $1,200.

FESLAND, a brigantine of 138 tons register, sailed from Port Mulgrave to Digby and was wrecked at Spectacle Isle, N.S., on August 18. Her port of registry was Annapolis. Cause: fog. Value of vessel was $6,000.

FERNOT, a brigantine of 92 tons register sailed from Sheet Harbour to Halifax and was wrecked off Jeddore on September 8. Her port of registry was Halifax. Cause: misjudgment. Value of vessel was $2,550.

GORDON BELT, a schooner of 63 tons register, sailed from Caledonia, N.S., to Yarmouth and was wrecked at Peases Island on December 10. Her port of registry was Shelburne. Cause: currents. Value of schooner was $1,000.

HALEY ANN, a schooner of 55 tons register, sailed from Sydney, C.B., Chatham, N.B., and was wrecked at Poulet Bay, C.B., on December 17. Her port of registry is unknown. Cause: a gale. Value of schooner was $500.

ISAAC BURPEE, a schooner of 169 tons register, sailed from New York to Saint John and was wrecked two miles north east of Petit Light, Digby County, N.S., on January 26. Her port of registry was Saint John, N.B. Cause: breaking of boom. Value of schooner was $5,000.

J.L. CROSSLEY, a schooner of 170 tons register, sailed from Gabarus, C.B., to Halifax and was wrecked by gas wharf, Halifax, on October 13. Her port of registry was Windsor. Cause: a hurricane. Value of schooner was $2,500.

JOHN M. INGLIS, a schooner of 78 tons register, sailed from Louisburg to Halifax and was wrecked at Battery Island reefs, entrance to harbour, on December 26. Her port of registry was Liverpool, N.S. Cause: hit another schooner. Value of schooner unknown.

LEONARD B. SNOW, a schooner of 36 tons register, sailed from Belliveau's Cove to Weymouth and was wrecked near the wharf at Weymouth Bridge on April 16. Her port of registry was Digby. Cause: fire. Value of schooner was $2,300.

LINDA, a schooner of 57 tons register, sailed from Kingsport to Wolfville and was wrecked off Kingsport, N.S. Her port of registry was Parrsboro. Cause: schooner filled with water. Value of schooner was $300.

L.B. HATCH, a schooner of 89 tons register, sailed from Thomas Cove to Boston and was wrecked at South Seal Island, seven miles east of it, on December 17. Her port of registry was Annapolis. Cause: dismasted. Value of schooner is unknown.

MORRIS WILSON, a schooner of 98 tons register, sailed from Canso to Lunenburg and was wrecked 40 miles south south west from Cape Canso on October 13. Her port of registry was Lunenburg. Cause: a gale. Value of schooner was $3,500.

MARGARET JANE, a schooner of 65 tons register, sailed from Pictou to Charlottetown and was wrecked at Bay View off Pictou Harbour on October 13. Her port of registry was Charlottetown. Cause: a leak. Value of schooner was $250.

NEPTUNE, a schooner of 34 tons register, sailed from Amherst to Cow Bay and was wrecked on west side of the breakwater of Cow Bay on October 13. Her port of registry was Amherst. Cause: unknown. Value of schooner is unknown.

WILD BRIAR, a schooner of 80 tons register, sailed from Sydney to Chatham and was wrecked at Grandique Ferry Beach, Lennox Passage, on June 17. Her port of registry was Miramichi. Cause: a leak. Value of schooner was $850.

WILLIE A. JEWEL, a schooner of 67 tons register, sailed from Yarmouth to Clark's Harbour and was wrecked at Noddy Island on October 13. Her port of registry was Princetown, N.S. Cause: unknown. Value of schooner was $1,200.

STRANGER, a schooner of 35 tons register, sailed from Souris, P.E.I., on a fishing trip and was wrecked at Meat Cove on October 13. Her port of registry was Halifax. Cause: drifted. Value of schooner was $2,000.

STAR, a schooner of 118 tons register, sailed from Boston to Annapolis and was wrecked off Briar Island on June 7. Her port of registry was Annapolis. Cause: collision with another vessel. Value of schooner was $3,000.

TROJAN, a schooner of 557 tons register, sailed from Windsor, N.S., to New York and was wrecked at Harding's Ledge, S.W. Harbour, N.S., on December 23. Her port of registry was Parrsboro. Cause: a squall. Value of schooner was $25,051.

RIVER QUEEN, a schooner of 32 tons register, sailed from Sydney on a fishing trip and was wrecked at White Point on December 2. Her port of registry was Sydney. Cause: a gale. Value of schooner is unknown.

SARAH E. LEE, a schooner of 98 tons register, sailed from Gloucester on a fishing trip and was wrecked at Little Harbour, N.S., on February 7. Her port of registry was Gloucester. Cause: a snowstorm. Value of schooner was $9,000.

SAILOR'S FANCY, a schooner of 16 tons register, sailed from Glen Margaret to Peggy's Cove and was wrecked at Shut-In-Island in St. Margaret's Bay on October 13. Her port of registry was Halifax. Cause: misstayed. Value of schooner was $1,400.

POCAHONTAS, a schooner of 63 tons register, while at Parrsboro was wrecked on March 1. Her port of registry was Parrsboro. Cause: ice. Value of schooner was $400.

PAUL AND ESSIE, a schooner of 63 tons register, while fishing off shore at Shelburne was wrecked at Black Point on November 13. Her port of registry was Gloucester. Cause: bad weather. Value of schooner was $6,200.

QUICKSTEP, a schooner fo 28 tons register, sailed from Halifax to Port Hood and was wrecked 5 miles west of White Head Light on October 18. Her port of registry was Liverpool. Cause: a leak. Value of schooner was $700.

A.J. LLOYD, a schooner of 26 tons register, sailed from Green Harbour to Lunenburg and was wrecked 4 miles south east of Port Mouton Island on November 16. Her port of registry was Shelburne. Cause: unknown. Value of schooner was $800.

A.H. LENNOX, a schooner of 68 tons register, sailed from Georgetown to Portland, Me., and was wrecked north end of Dolino Island at White Head, N.S., on December 1. Her port of registry was U.S.A. Cause: unknown. Value of schooner was $1,800.

ALICE, a schooner of 75 tons register, sailed from Gloucester on a fishing trip and was later wrecked at Lingan, C.B., on December 1. Her port of registry was Gloucester, Mass. Cause: a gale. Value of schooner was $3,700.

A. ELLIOTT, a schooner of 30 tons register sailed from Pereau to Saint John, N.B., and was wrecked near Isle Haute, Bay of Fundy, on November 13. Her port of registry was Annapolis. Cause: gales. Value of schooner was $800.

BELLA MAY, a schooner of 79 tons register, sailed from Halifax to Sydney and was wrecked at Gabarus Harbour on December 1. Her port of registry was Halifax. Cause: high seas. Value of schooner was $3,000.

GETEWAYO, a schooner of 20 tons register, sailed from Glace Bay to Gabarus, and was wrecked in this harbour on December 1. Her port of registry was Halifax. Cause: gales. Value of schooner was $700.

DANIEL MAREY, a schooner of 109 tons register, sailed from Boston to Port Williams and was wrecked off Harborville, N.S., on December 1. Her port of registry was Boston. Cause: capsized. Six lives were lost and the value of schooner was $4,500.

EUXINE, a schooner of 38 tons register, sailed from Souris to Halifax and was wrecked at Canso Harbour on December 1. Her port of registry was Arichat. Cause: a gale. Value of schooner was $400.

EURYDICE, a ship of 1,247 tons register, sailed from Liverpool to Pensacola and was wrecked off Shelburne on December 20. Her por of registry was Saint John, N.B. Cause: a gale. Value of vessel was $10,000.

EMERALD, a schooner of 27 tons register, sailed from Halifax to Blandford and was wrecked in Prospect Basin on December 26. Her port of registry was Lunenburg. Cause: a snow storm. Value of schooner was $1,400.

EMERALD, a schooner of 25 tons register, sailed from Pictou to Georgetown and was wrecked at Murray Harbour on October 6. Her port of registry was P.E.I. Cause: a gale. Value of schooner was $500.

FLORENCE, C., a schooner of unknown tonnage, sailed from Marble Mountain to Boston and was wrecked off southern coast of N.S. on December 9. Her port of registry was Pictou.

Cause: fire. Value of schooner was $7,950.

GEORGE WILLIAMS, a schoner of 17 tons register, sailed from Little Glace Bay to Whycocomagh and was wrecked at entrance of Big Bras d'Or on November 13. Her port of registry was Sydney, C.B. Cause: collision. Value of schooner was $250.

HYACINTHE, a schooner of 29 tons register, sailed from Cow Bay to North Sydney and was wrecked at Little Bras d'Or Reef on December 27. Her port of registry was St. John's, Newfoundland. Cause: hit reef. Value of schooner was $900.

J.W. DURANT, a schooner of 147 tons register, sailed from Shulie to Barbados and was wrecked at Shulie, N.S., on December 1. Her port of registry was Parrsboro. Cause: a gale. Value of schooner was $8,100.

LETITIA MAY, a schooner of 41 tons register, sailed from Whitehead on a fishing trip and was wrecked at Rocky Ledge a half mile west of Whitehead Lighthouse on October 8. Her port of registry was Lunenburg. Cause: winds. Value of schooner was $700.

LADY KEY, a schooner of 31 tons register, sailed from Jeddore to Port Hawkesbury and was wrecked 150 yards S.S.W. of Whitehead Lighthouse on November 6. Her port of registry was Halifax. Cause: bad weather. Value of schooner was $1,347.

LORD MAYO, a schooner of 97 tons register, sailed from Calais, Maine, to Parrsboro and was wrecked at entrance to Parrsboro River on October 12. Her port of registry was Halifax. Cause: misstayed. Value of schooner was $1,300.

LADY FRANKLIN, a schooner of 63 tons register, sailed from Halifax to Antigonish and was wrecked at Meagher's Beach on December 1. Her port of registry was St. John's, Newfoundland. Cause: a hurricane. Value of schooner was $3,400.

MARIE, a barque of 663 tons register, sailed from Barrow, G.B., to Charlottetown, P.E.I., and was wrecked at Aspy Bay, C.B., on November 12. Her port of registry was Norway. Cause: heavy gales. Value of vessel was $40,000.

OCEAN BRIDE, a schooner of 20 tons register, sailed from Murray Harbour to Port Medway and was wrecked at Carrigan Pier, Guysboro County, on December 1. Her port of registry was Lunenburg. Cause: a gale. Value of schooner was $750.

OSCEOLA, a schooner of 83 tons register, sailed from Halifax to Glace Bay and was wrecked at Gabarus Harbour on December 1. Her port of registry was Halifax. Cause: a storm Value of schooner was $2,000.

RIVAL, a schooner of 31 tons register, sailed from Halifax

to Glace Bay and was wrecked at Simond's Point, Gabarus Bay, on November 8. Her port of registry was Halifax. Cause: a gale. Value of schooner was $650.

RATTLER, a schooner of 13 tons register, sailed from Liverpool to Port Herbert and was wrecked on east side of entrance to Port Herbert Harbour on September 26. Her port of registry was Liverpool, N.S. Cause: misstayed. Value of schooner was $800.

SCYLLA, a schooner of 102 tons register, sailed from Crapaud to Boston and was wrecked eight or nine miles S.E. of Cape George, Pictou County, on November 13. Her port of registry was Port Hawkesbury. Cause: hit another vessel. Value of schooner was $6,500.

SECOND, a schooner of 47 tons register, sailed from Saint John to Parrsboro and was wrecked at Eatonville River on November 20. Her port of registry was Parrsboro. Cause: fire. Value of schooner was $1,600.

SUNBEAM, a schooner of 68 tons register, sailed from Sydney to Halifax and was wrecked at Doewer's Cove on December 2. Her port of registry was Halifax. Cause: parting of chains. Value of shcooner was $1,560.

SILVER DART, a schooner of 30 tons register, sailed from Georgetown to Halifax and was wrecked at Murray Harbour Bar on October 10. Her port of registry was Halifax. Cause: a gale. Value of schooner was $925.

TRUE, a schooner of 60 tons register, sailed from Saint John, N.B., to Joggins, N.S., and was wrecked off Cape Maringum, Bay of Fundy, on October 27. Her port of registry was Saint John. Cause: sand bar. Value of schooner was $2,550.

TRAFFICK, a schooner of 41 tons register, sailed from Musquash to Rockland, Maine, and was wrecked at Little Musquash Harbour on April 21. Her port of registry was Annapolis. Cause: weather. Value of schooner was $300.

TRIAL, a schooner of 13 tons register, sailed from Halifax to Margaree and was later wrecked in this Harbour on December 1. Her port of registry was Halifax. Cause: weather. Value of schooner was $250.

WARRIOR, a schooner of 52 tons register, sailed from Pictou to Cow Bay and was wrecked at east side Ghost Beach, Judique, on December 13. Her port of registry was Pictou. Cause: a gale. Value of schooner was $800.

MABLE, a schooner of 43 tons register, sailed from Main-a-Dieu to Scatarie and was wrecked at Eastern Rock, Scatarie

Island, on November 20. Her port of registry was Guysboro. Cause: tides. Value of schooner was $1,490.

MARIE MATILDA, a schooner of 96 tons register, sailed from Arichat to Petit de Grat and was wrecked at Petit de Grat Inlet on December 15. Her port of registry was Arichat. Cause: filled with water and sank. Value of schooner was $610.

MAGGIE MILLARD, a schooner of 120 tons register, sailed from Sydney to Halifax and was wrecked at Gabarus. Her port of registry was Liverpool. Cause: a heavy storm. Value of schooner was $3,000.

METEOR, a schooner of 62 tons register, sailed from Placentia to Glace Bay and was wrecked off Louisburg Breakers, Rock Island, on December 17. Her port of registry was St. John's, Newfoundland. Cause: a gale. Value of schooner was $2,000.

NELLIE B., a schooner of 87 tons register, sailed from Glace Bay to a place unknown and was wrecked at Rabbie Island, Chedabucto Bay, on December 27. Value of schooner was $3,200.

OMEGA, a schooner of 55 tons register, sailed from Buctouche to Pictou and was wrecked off Cocagne Bar on December 1. Her port of registry was Halifax. Cause: a leak. Value of schooner was $600.

ELIZABETH ANN, a schooner under Captain De Coste out of Cow Bay for Halifax, with a cargo of coal, went aground on Seal Ledges off Marie Joseph and became a total wreck. She was 173 tons register and built at Harbour Bouche in 1866. She was owned by William Garrior of Tracadie.

W.E. YOUNG, a schooner of 92 tons register, sailed from Halifax to Glace Bay and was wrecked on south side of Glace Bay on November 29. Her port of registry was Lunenburg. Cause: a gale. Value of schooner was $2,500.

(1892)—ALMEDA, a schooner of 83 tons register, sailed from Carter's Creek, N.S., to Rockland, Maine, and was wrecked at Carter's Creek, mouth of River Hebert, on January 20. Her port of registry was Saint John, N.B. Cause: hit a rock. Value of schooner was $2,530.

ABRAHAM, a schooner of 163 tons register, sailed from Sydney to Halifax and was wrecked at Walker's Ledge, Cape Canso, on July 2. Her port of registry was Glasgow. Cause: hit rocks. Value of schooner was $25,600.

ALFRED, a schooner of 46 tons register, sailed from Westport on a fishing trip and was wrecked at Dartmouth Point, Bryer Island, on October 8. Her port of registry was Yarmouth. Cause: hit reef. Value of schooner was $1,300.

ARBUTUS, a schooner of 79 tons register, sailed from

Sydney, N.S., to Annapolis and was wrecked at Old Prospect Shoals, Gannet Light, on November 10. Her port of registry was Liverpool, N.S. Cause: error in compass. Value of schooner was $3,800.

ATLANTIC, a barque a 465 tons register, sailed from Belfast to Miramichi, N.B., and was wrecked at Preston Beach, Mira Bay, on August 13. Her port of registry was Norway. Cause: weather. Value of vessel was $5,500.

(1892)—BONNIE DOON, a schooner of 13 tons register, sailed from Port Mulgrave to White Haven and was wrecked at Canso Bull on January 20. Her port of registry was Guysboro. Cause: unknown. Value of schooner was $240.

ENTERPRISE, a schooner of 28 tons register, while at anchor in North East Harbour caught fire and sank on date unknown. Her port of registry was Shelburne. Value of schooner was $1,200.

EMERALD, a schooner of 29 tons register, sailed from Halifax to Blandford and was wrecked at Prospect Basin on date unknown. Her port of registry was Lunenburg. Cause: snow storm. Value of schooner is not known.

EMMA MARR, a barque of 799 tons register, sailed from Little Glace Bay to Saint John, N.B., and was wrecked 10 miles N.W. of Seal Island on November 27. Her port of registry was Saint John, N.B. Cause: hit a sunken object. Value of vessel was $31,850.

FRANKLIN PIERCE, a schooner of 57 tons register, sailed from Parrsboro to Windsor and was wrecked at Avon River Bar, N.S., on September 3. Her port of registry was Windsor, N.S. Cause: grounded on bar. Value of schooner was $850.

GLENGARIFF, a schooner of 67 tons register, sailed from Parrsboro to Digby and was wrecked in Bay of Fundy on March 18. Her port of registry was Parrsboro. Cause: unknown. Value of schooner was $1,400.

H. B. GRIFFIN, a schooner of 117 tons register, sailed from Liverpool, N. S., to Gloucester, Mass., and was wrecked at Shag Harbour on February 19. Her port of registry was Gloucester. Cause: fire. Value of schooner was $3,500.

HELEN M. CROSBY, a schooner of 64 tons register, sailed from Port Hawkesbury to Pugwash and was wrecked at Cape Head, N.S., on October 28. Her port of registry was Port Hawkesbury. Cause: hit rocks. Value of schooner was $1,200.

JUNO, a barque of 999 tons register, sailed from Amsterdam to Sydney, N.S., and was wrecked in Sydney Harbour on May 29. Her port of registry was Porsground, Norway. Cause: hit by another vessel. Value of vessel is not known.

LAURA SEYWARD, a schooner of 65 tons register, sailed from Port Hood to Aspy Bay and was wrecked at Wolf Island, Cape Breton, on July 22. Her port of registry was Gloucester, Mass. Cause: weather. Value of schooner was $2,000.

LAURA, a schooner of 93 tons register, sailed from Canso to Halifax and was wrecked 12 miles south of Liscomb on June 18. Her port of registry was Guysboro. Cause: fire. Value of schooner was $3,000.

LUCY ANN, a schooner of 44 tons register, sailed from a fishing trip and was wrecked 3 miles S.W. of Seal Island on June 25. Her port of registry was Rockland, Maine. Cause: fire. Value of schooner is not known.

MARY KATE, a schooner of 42 tons register, sailed from Cow Bay to North Sydney and was wrecked at Peter's Ledge, Sydney Harbour on March 18. Her port of registry was Charlottetown. Cause: a storm. Value of schooner is not known.

MAGGIE WILLET, a schooner of 147 tons register, sailed from St. John's, Newfoundland, to Sydney, C. B., and was wrecked near Scatarie Island on October 25. Her port of registry was Saint John, N.B. Cause: a storm. Value of schooner was $5,000.

NEITLE PARKER, a schooner of 183 tons register, sailed from Halifax to New York and was wrecked at mouth of Mabou Harbour on September 4. Her port of registry was Saint John, N. B. Cause: grounded in shallow water. Value of schooner was $1,000.

ROSSIGNOL, a schooner of 1,463 tons register, sailed from Parrsboro to England and was wrecked at Scott's Bay, N. S., on October 8. Her port of registry was Yarmouth. Cause: weather. Value of schooner was $3,500.

SYLVAN, a barque of 996 tons register, sailed from Barbados, W.I., to Saint John, N. B., and was wrecked at Trinity Ledge, near Cape Fouchere, on April 2. Her port of registry was Maitland. Cause: weather. Value of schooner was $20,000.

SANDOLPHON, a schooner of 105 tons register, sailed from Lockeport to Canso and was wrecked at Bear Point, Richmond Co., on August 11. Her port of registry was Shelburne. Cause: weather. Value of schooner was $8,500.

THERESA, a schooner of tonnage unknown, sailed from Chatham, N. B., to port unknown and was wrecked at Sambro on July 3. Her port of registry was New York. Cause: a leak. Value of

schooner was $4,000.

LAWRENCE, a schooner of 63 tons register, sailed from Halifax to Gaspe and was wrecked at Canso Harbour on May 5. Her port of registry was Gaspe, Quebec. Cause: fire. Value of schooner is not known.

C.N.MADER, a schooner of 87 tons register, sailed from Mahone Bay to Glace Bay and was wrecked at Glace Bay on October 23. Her port of registry was Lunenburg. Cause: a gale. Value of schooner was $3,600.

(1893)—CREDIT, a schooner of 124 tons register, sailed from New York to Saint John, N. B., and was wrecked 2 miles east of Race Point, N. S., on February 26. Her port of registry was Saint John, N.B. Cause: a snow storm. Value of schooner was $3,750.

CITY OF ST. JOHN, a schooner of 447 tons register, sailed from Yarmouth to Barrington and was wrecked at Hospital Reef, Clark's Harbour, on April 14. Her port of registry was Gaspe, Quebec. Cause: fog. Value of schooner is unknown.

GRAGSIDE, a steamer of 1,278 tons register, sailed from England to Montreal and was wrecked six miles S.W. of Whitehead, N. S., on May 19. Her port of registry was London, England. Cause: hit submerged object. Value of vessel is not known.

CHAUTAUGUAY, a schooner of 97 tons register, sailed from Louisburg to Saint John and was wrecked near St. Esprit, C. B., on August 6. Her port of registry was Parrsboro. Cause: a leak. Value of schooner is not known.

COUNTY OF YARMOUTH, a ship of 2,154 tons register, sailed from London to Sydney, C.B., and was wrecked at Petres Ledge, Sydney Harbour, on October 11. Her port of registry was Yarmouth. Cause: weather. Value of vessel is not known.

DOMINION, a schooner of 410 tons register, sailed from Yarmouth to Halifax and was wrecked at Big Duck Island, N. S., on April 22. Her port of registry was Yarmouth. Cause: unknown. Value of schooner was $15,000.

EVA J. MOORE, a schooner of 99 tons register, sailed from River Hebert to Saint John, N. B., and was wrecked in Cumberland Bay on September 20. Her port of registry was Parrsboro. Cause: a leak. Value of schooner was $2,500.

FARRAGUT, a schooner of 48 tons register, sailed from Gloucester on a fishing trip and was wrecked at Kindricks Island, Shag Harbour, on August 21. Her port of registry was Gloucester, Mass. Cause: a gale. Value of schooner was $1,800.

MARY JANE, a schooner of 89 tons register, sailed from

Cow Bay to Halifax and was wrecked at Salmon Rocks, C. B., on August 19. Her port of registry was Sydney, C.B. Cause: heavy seas. Value of schooner was $2,200.

MAY FLOWER, a schooner of 70 tons register, sailed from Saint John, N. B., to Estorville, N. S., and was wrecked at Spicer's Cove, Cumberland Co., on August 31. Her port of registry was Saint John, N. B. Cause: a gale. Value of schooner was $645.

NOTILUS, a schooner of 11 tons register, sailed from Chipman's Brook to Apple River and was wrecked at Refugee Cove on January 6. Her port of registry was Windsor, N. S. Cause: a gale. Value of schooner was $300.

NELLIE SHAW, a schooner of 250 tons register, sailed from Liverpool, N.S., to Hillsboro and was wrecked at Apple River, Cumberland Co., on October 15. Her port of registry was Parrsboro. Cause: a gale. Value of schooner was $10,000.

OSCEOLA, a schooner of 80 tons register, sailed from Halifax to Gabarus, C. B., and was wrecked at this port on date unknown. Her port of registry was Halifax. Cause: weather. Value of schooner was $2,000.

PRICE BROTHERS, a schooner of 79 tons register, sailed from Canning to Boston and was wrecked at Apple River on September 6. Her port of registry was Parrsboro. Cause: fire. Value of schooner was $500.

PONTECORRO, a barque of tonnage unknown, sailed from Fleetwood, G. B., to Miramichi, N. B., and was wrecked at Green Cove, Ingonish, on August 29. Her port of registry was Norway. Cause: a storm. Value of vessel is not known.

THREE SISTERS, a schooner of 42 tons register, sailed from Parrsboro to West Bay and was wrecked in this Bay on August 21. Her port of registry was Saint John, N. B. Cause: a gale. Value of schooner was $250.

W. D. RICHARD, a schooner of 98 tons register, sailed from LaHave, N. S., to Halifax and was wrecked near Halifax. Her port of registry was Lunenburg. Cause: a squall. Value of schooner was $4,600.

MARY, a schooner of 24 tons out of Poulamont, was wrecked at Marble Mountain. She was owned by John MacKay.

FLORA McLEOD, a schooner of 48 tons register, sailed from St. Stephen, N. B., to Saint John, N. B., was wrecked at Mohawk Ledge, Petite Passage, on November 4. Her port of registry was Saint John, N. B. Cause: tides and wind. Value of schooner was $3,000.

LUCY ANN, a schooner of tonnage unknown, sailed from

234

Rockland on a fishing trip and was wrecked 3 miles S.W. from Seal Island on October 25. Her port of registry was Rockland, Maine. Cause: fire. Value of schooner was $800.

(1894)—DIADEM, a schooner of 162 tons register, sailed from Porto Rico to Lunenburg and was wrecked at Indian Island off LaHave Island on June 19. Her port of registry was Lunenburg. Cause: fog. Value of schooner is not known.

EVANGELINE, a schooner of 86 tons register, sailed from Bordeau to St. Pierre Miquelon and was wrecked at Scatarie Island on date unknown. Her port of registry was Grenville. Cause: ice. Value of schooner was $1,720.

ELLEN MAY, a schooner of 60 tons register, sailed from Canso to Pictou and was wrecked off Little Harbour, Pictou Co., on June 7. Her port of registry was Lunenburg. Cause: fog and high winds. Value of schooner was $800.

ELIZA B., a schooner of 40 tons register, sailed from Baddeck to Sydney and was wrecked in Sydney Harbour on June 8. Her port of registry was Arichat. Cause: weather. Value of schooner was $500.

LADY ABERDEEN, a schooner of 88 tons register, sailed from St. Pierre to Halifax, was wrecked at Gabarus Bay on December 12. Her port of registry was Sydney, C. B. Cause: bad weather. Value of schooner was $2,000.

MONITOR, a schooner which was lost at Whitehead near Argyle on November 7.

KEZIA, a schooner of 136 tons out of New York for Charlottetown, went aground at Petit de Grat and became a total wreck. She was owned by D. Landry and built at Conqueral in the year 1882.

AMELIA CORKUM, a schooner of 99 tons register, sailed from Lunenburg to Halifax and was wrecked at Farmville. Her port of registry was Lunenburg. Cause: stranded. Value of schooner was $4,000.

ANNIE G., a schooner of 38 tons register, sailed from Halifax to Sydney and was wrecked on the south side of Goose Island on December 20. Her port of registry was Halifax. Cause: stranded. Value of schooner was $1,023.

FLORIDA, a barque of 100 tons register, sailed from Bermuda to Yarmouth and was wrecked at West Cape, Fouchere, N. S., on April 20. Her port of registry was Yarmouth. Cause: weather. Value of vessel was $2,500.

GLENARCHY, a barque of 297 tons register, sailed from Bermuda to Halifax and was wrecked at Clam Point, C. B., on January 11. Her port of registry was Halifax. Cause: parting of chains. Value of vessel was $9,000.

MERTON, a schooner of 61 tons register, sailed from Parrsboro to River Hebert and was wrecked near Apple River, Cumberland Bay, on April 9. Her port of registry was Parrsboro. Cause: dragging of anchors. Value of schooner was $500.

NATIVE, a schooner of 52 tons register, sailed from Glace Bay to Halifax and was wrecked at Cow Bay, C. B. Her port of registry was Halifax. Cause: collision. Value of schooner is not known.

CRESCENT, a schooner of 26 tons register, sailed from Souris on trading mission and was wrecked at Eastern Harbour, Cheticamp, on August 22. Her port of registry was Arichat. Cause: dragging of anchors. Value of schooner was $600.

AMHERST, a schooner of 99 tons register, sailed from Port Williams, N. S., to Boston and was wrecked in Minas Basin on December 10. Her port of registry was Parrsboro. Cause: a leak. Value of schooner was $600.

BAMBORO, a vessel which was wrecked on the Half Moons during the month of April, was a steel steamer of 2,016 tons.

ST. MARY, a schooner of 15 tons register, sailed from Margaree to Halifax and was wrecked at Broad Cove, Inverness Co., on November 4. Her port of registry was Port Hawkesbury. Cause: bad weather. Value of schooner was $150.

MAY QUEEN, a schooner of 34 tons register, sailed from Aspy Bay to Ingonish and was wrecked off Green Cove, N. S., on November 4. Her port of registry was Barrington. Cause: a leak. Value of schooner was $5,000.

AMOS B., a schooner of 80 tons register, sailed from Halifax to Guysboro and was wrecked at Peart's Beach on date unknown. Her port of registry was Guysboro. Cause: weather. Value of schooner is not known.

TRUE LOVE, a schooner of 30 tons register, sailed from Salmon River to Ecum Secum and was wrecked at Rocky Point, N. S. Her point of registry was Halifax. Cause: misstayed. Value of schooner was $900.

(1895)—BLYTHE, a schooner of 80 tons register, sailed from Rockland to Belliveau's Cove and was wrecked at Peter's Island Ledge, Grand Passage, N.S., on November 27. Her port of registry was Digby. Cause: winds and tide. Value of schooner was $1,000.

BILLY BROWN, a schooner of 88 tons register, sailed from Lockeport to Canso and was wrecked at Mosher's Island, mouth of LaHave River, on December 27. Her port of registry was

Shelburne. Cause: fire. Value of schooner was $3,000.

DAYLIGHT, a barquentine of 227 tons register, sailed from New York to Halifax and was wrecked at Green Island, near Yarmouth, on September 23. Her port of registry was U. S. A. Cause: weather. Value of vessel was $2,500.

DONACONA, a schooner of 174 tons register, sailed from Pereaux to Havana and was wrecked at Pereaux River, N. S., on December 24. Her port of registry was Windsor, N. S. Cause: fire. Value of schooner was $5,000.

ELIZA JANE, a schooner of 22 tons register, sailed from Shelburne on a fishing trip and was wrecked at Chedabucto Bay on September 1. Her port of registry was Shelburne. Cause: weather. Value of schooner was $750.

ETTA STEWART, a barque of 787 tons register, sailed from Sydney to Halifax and was wrecked at Three Fathoms Harbour on August 21. Her port of registry was Saint John, N. B. Cause: a storm. Eight lives were lost and the value of vessel was $7,200.

EAGLE, a brig of 130 tons register, sailed from Halifax to Demerara and was wrecked at Pennant Point on June 28. Her port of registry was Halifax. Cause: weather. Value of vessel was $8,200.

FLORA E., a schooner of 80 tons register, sailed from Parrsboro to Calais and was wrecked off Eatonville, N. S., on December 29. Her port of registry was Parrsboro. Cause: weather. Value of schooner was $1,500.

HASTY, a schooner of 46 tons register, sailed from Alberton to Gaspe and was wrecked at Poulet's Cove, Inverness Co., on November 20. Her port of registry was Gaspe. Cause: loss of sails. Value of schooner was $1,600.

ICARUS, a barque of 282 tons register, sailed from Parrsboro to Preston, England, and was wrecked in Parrsboro Harbour on August 1. Her port of registry was Windsor, N. S. Cause: fire. Value of vessel was $2,500.

JOHN, a barque of 539 tons register, sailed from Helsinglearg to West Bay and on to Preston, G. B., and was wrecked at Gulliver's Cove, Digby Neck, on October 16. Her port of registry was Sweden. Cause: weather. Value of vessel is not known.

LEO, a schooner of 77 tons register, sailed from Parrsboro to Yarmouth and was wrecked four miles from the Yarmouth whistle on August 21. Her port of registry was Annapolis. Cause: fog. Value of schooner was $1,000.

LORD ELDON, a schooner of 58 tons register, sailed from Guysboro to Halifax and was wrecked at Middle Rock, east of Cape Canso, on October 7. Her port of registry was Guysboro. Cause: weather. Value of schooner was $3,600.

LIZZIE G., a schooner of 16 tons register, sailed from Digby to Sandy Cove and was wrecked at Digby Neck on November 16. Her port of registry was Digby. Cause: weather. Value of schooner was $500.

MARIE DELPHIN, a schooner of 76 tons register, sailed from Parrsboro to Weymouth and was wrecked at Hardy's Point, Sydney Harbour, on November 6. Her port of registry was Parrsboro. Cause: weather. Value of schooner was $1,400.

MARGELIN, a schooner of 45 tons register, sailed from Pictou to Charlottetown and was wrecked at Pictou Harbour on December 29. Her port of registry was New Carlisle. Cause: ice. Value of schooner was $875.

MATTIE F., a schooner of 91 tons register, sailed from Round Counter, Newfoundland, and on to Gloucester, Mass., and was wrecked at Point Marache, entrance to Arichat Harbour, on February 8. Her port of registry was U.S.A. Cause: a snow storm. Value of schooner was $4,000.

MOGUL, a ship of 52 tons register, sailed from Port Townsend to Victoria and was wrecked at Cape Flattery, N. S., on May 4. Her port of registry was Victoria, B. C. Cause: a collision. Value of vessel is not known.

S. A. MORASH, a schooner of 99 tons register, sailed from Halifax to Main-a-Dieu and was wrecked at this place on August 24. Her port of registry was Lunenburg. Cause: weather. Value of schooner was $2,700.

S. A. MORASH, a schooner of 99 tons register, sailed from Port Morien to Bridgewater and was wrecked at Shag Rock, Mira Bay, on August 23. Her port of registry was Lunenburg. Cause: weather. Value of schooner was $3,000.

SWIFT CURRENT, a schooner of 64 tons register, sailed from Alberton, P.E.I., to Newfoundland and was wrecked at Broad Cove, C. B., on December 23. Her port of registry was Halifax. Cause: weather. Value of schooner was $1,318.

STELLA, a schooner of 128 tons register, sailed from St. Pierre to Halifax and was wrecked at Louisburg Harbour on January 24. Her port of registry was France. Cause: a gale. Value of schooner was $8,000.

(1896)—HESPER, a schooner of 1,766 tons register, sailed from Las Palmas to Saint John, N. B., and was wrecked at Ram Island off Lockeport on July 5. Her port of registry was West Hartlepool, G. B. Cause: stranded. Value of schooner was $125,000.

JESSAMINE, a schooner of 69 tons register, sailed from Boston to Shelburne and was wrecked at Todd's Point on December 16. Her port of registry was Liverpool. Cause: stranded. Value of schooner was $3,000.

KEZIAH, a schooner of 136 tons register, sailed from Lunenburg to Halifax and was wrecked in Glasgow Harbour on date unknown. Her port of registry was Lunenburg. Cause: fire. Value of schooner was $3,400.

LITTLE DORRIT, a schooner of 64 tons register, sailed from Barrington to Halifax and was wrecked at Doctor's Cove, Barrington, on August 28. Her port of registry was Barrington. Cause: fire. Value of schooner was $4,000.

OSCEOLA, a schooner of 124 tons register, sailed from Saint John to Halifax and was wrecked at Sandy Point on November 15. Her port of registry was Windsor, N. S. Cause: grounded. Value of schooner was $6,500.

PILOT, a schooner of 16 tons register, sailed from Round Hill to Moncton, N. B., and was wrecked at Cropley Ledge, Annapolis Co., on November 8. Her port of registry was Saint John, N. B. Cause: stranded. Value of schooner was $700.

WILD ROSE, a schooner of 38 tons register, sailed from Saint John to Yarmouth and was wrecked at Tiverton Beach, Digby Co., on December 4. Her port of registry was Windsor, N. S. Cause: stranded. Value of schooner was $800.

AUREOLA, a barkentine of 250 tons register, sailed from St. John's, Newfoundland, to North Sydney and was wrecked at Sydney Harbour, N. S., on August 31. Her port of registry was St. John's, Newfoundland. Cause: stranded. Value of vessel was $12,000.

AVALON, a schooner of 121 tons register, sailed from Saint John, N. B., to Sydney, C. B., and was wrecked at Green Island, Cape Sable, on September 10. Her port of registry was Windsor, N. S. Cause: stranded. Value of schooner was $3,500.

ARTEMUS TERRILL, a schooner of 121 tons register, sailed from Boston to Margaret's Bay and was wrecked off Sambro in July. Her port of registry was U. S. A. Cause: stranded. Value of schooner was $405.

ADDIE, a schooner of 16 tons register sailed from Halifax to Newfoundland and was wrecked at L'Ardoise Bay on December 28. Her port of registry was Halifax. Cause: foundered. Value of schooner was $200.

THAMES, a schooner of 24 tons register, sailed from Montreal to North Sydney and was wrecked at Petrie's Ledge, Sydney Harbour, on November 21. Her port of registry was Quebec. Cause: stranded.

VULOROUS, a schooner of 57 tons register, sailed from White Head to Halifax and was wrecked at Beaver Light on July 9. Her port of registry was Lunenburg. Cause: a collision.

VALERIAN, a schooner of 64 tons register, sailed from Sydney, C. B., to Halifax and was wrecked in Fisherman's Harbour on October 10. Her port of registry was Halifax. Cause: ran ashore. Value of schooner was $3,000.

WINNIE L., a schooner of 31 tons register, sailed from Port Malcolm to Ingonish and was wrecked at entrance to Ingonish Harbour on October 2. Her port of registry was Halifax. Cause: stranded. Value of schooner was $1,450.

ADRIA, a schooner of 194 tons register, sailed from Newcastle to LaHave River and was wrecked at this River on October 28. Her port of registry was Saint John, N. B. Cause: stranded. Value of schooner was $4,186; six lives were lost.

ANNIE G., a schooner of 38 tons register, sailed from Halifax to Sydney and was wrecked on south side of Goose Island on December 20. Her port of registry was Halifax. Cause: stranded. Value of schooner was $1,023.

ALICE, a schooner of 115 tons register, sailed from Port Medway to Liverpool and was wrecked at Vision Head, Seal Island, on August 25. Her port of registry was Lunenburg. Cause: stranded.

AGRA, a brigantine of 931 tons register, sailed from Pensacola to Sydney, C. B., was wrecked six miles north of Louisbourg on May 18. Her port of registry was Sandfiord, Norway. Cause: weather conditions. Value of vessel was $9,000.

BELGRAVIA, a brigantine of 3,274 tons register, sailed from Saint John to Liverpool and was wrecked at Partridge Island, Bay of Fundy, on May 22. Her port of registry was Glasgow. Cause: stranded. Value of vessel was $86,313.

BRODRENE, a brigantine of 464 tons register, sailed from Avonmouth to Miramichi and was wrecked at St. Paul Island on May 26. Her port of registry was Norway.

BUDA, a brigantine of 312 tons register, sailed from Saint John, N. B., to Buenos Ayres and was wrecked in the Bay of Fundy on December 20. Her port of registry was Saint John, N. B. Cause unknown. Eight lives were lost and the value of vessel was $11,354.

BELLE OF ROME, a schooner of unknown tonnage, sailed from Gabarus to Louisburg and was wrecked in Gabarus Harbour on January 7. Her port of registry was Britain. Cause: gale winds. Value of vessel was $1,650.

ETHEL, a schooner of 78 tons register sailed from Parrsboro to Port-a-Pique River and was wrecked at this river on October 18. Her port of registry was Saint John, N. B. Cause: stranded. Value of schooner was $700.

ELLEN, a schooner of 29 tons register, sailed from Parrsboro to Moore River and on its return home was wrecked at Moose Creek, Parrsboro, on November 1. Her port of registry was Parrsboro. Cause: a storm. Value of schooner was $500.

EQUATOR, a barque of 1,228 tons register, sailed from Rio de Janeiro to Grindstone Island, N. B., and was wrecked on the south side of Long Island, Digby, on May 29. Her port of registry was Yarmouth. Cause: grounded in thick fog. Value of vessel was $8,000.

EALING, a steamer of 1,246 tons register, sailed from Pelley Island, Newfoundland, to New York and was wrecked at south east breaker off Isaacs Harbour in January. Her port of registry was London, England. Cause: stranded. Value of vessel was $8,000.

FREDRIKKA, a barque of 448 tons register, sailed from Havre France to Bay Verte, N. B., and was wrecked at Aspy Bay, N. S., on August 25. Her port of registry was Norway. Cause: bad weather and currents.

FANNY B., a schooner of unknown tonnage, sailed from Halifax to Glace Bay and was wrecked at north side of Cow Bay, C. B., on date unknown. Her port of registry was Halifax. Cause: stranded. Value of schooner was $950.

F. P. T., a schooner of 41 tons register, sailed from Liscomb to Halifax and was wrecked at entrance to Jeddore Harbour on date unknown. Her port of registry was Halifax. Cause: a snow storm. Value of schooner was $625.

GENEVA MYRTIS, a schooner of 32 tons register, sailed from Yarmouth to Woods Harbour and was wrecked at Woods Harbour on September 2. Her port of registry was Barrington. Cause: fire. Value of schooner was $2,000.

GEORGE E. DALE, a schooner of 218 tons register, sailed from Parrsboro to Gardiner, Maine, and was wrecked at Mines Channel, Cumberland Co., on December 2. Her port of registry was New York. Cause: a leak. Value of schooner was $2,134.

GAZELLE, a schooner of 264 tons register, sailed from

Porto Rico to Delaware Breakwater and was wrecked 1 1/2 miles off C.B. on March 5. Her port of registry was Saint John, N. B. Cause: hit upon rocks. Value of schooner was $10,000.

GLEANOR, a schooner of 116 tons register, sailed from Harrington River to Salem, Mass., and was wrecked at mouth of Harrington River on May 12. Her port of registry was Parrsboro. Cause: stranded. Value of schooner was $2,200.

GUNHILDA, a barque of 533 tons register, sailed from Copenhagen to Louisburg and was wrecked near White Point on May 27. Her port of registry was Copenhagen. Cause: stranded. Value of vessel was $6,000.

HOPE, a schooner of 31 tons register, sailed from Big Bras d'Or to North Sydney and was wrecked about a mile west of lighthouse at Sydney Harbour on December 6. Her port of registry was Halifax. Cause: a heavy gale. Value of schooner was $500.

HATTIE R., a schooner of 78 tons register, sailed from Parrsboro to Saint John, N.B., and was wrecked at Ogilvie's Wharf, Bay of Fundy, on March 5. Her port of registry was Parrsboro. Cause: stranded. Value of schooner was $1,850.

J.W. DEAN, a schooner of 85 tons register, sailed from Harrington River to Bear River and was wrecked at Middle Grounds, Harrington River, N.S., on May 23. Her port of registry was Saint John. Cause: stranded. Value of schooner was $300.

LLEWELYN, a schooner of 62 tons register, sailed from Economy to Eastport, Maine, and was wrecked at Five Islands, Colchester Co., on October 18. Her port of registry was Saint John, N.B. Cause: stranded. Value of schooner was $540.

LILIAN, a schooner of 14 tons register, sailed from Halifax and was wrecked at Sambro in May. Her port of registry was Halifax. Cause: rudder box torn away. Value of schooner was $600.

MOSELLE, a schooner of 117 tons register, sailed from Hantsport to Lynn, Mass., and was wrecked at Tusket River on November 10. Her port of registry was Windsor, N.S. Cause: unknown. Value of schooner was $3,700.

MARY FARNELL, a schooner of 90 tons register, sailed from Gloucester to Whitehead and was wrecked at Tree Top Island, Whitehead, N.S., on December 12. Her port of registry was U.S.A. Cause: stranded. Value of schooner was $6,000.

MARCELINE, a schooner of 45 tons register, sailed from Pictou to Charlottetown and was wrecked at Graveyard Point, Pictou Harbour, on December 29. Her port of registry was New Carlisle, Quebec. Cause: stranded. Value of schooner was $875.

MARY E. HARLOW, a schooner of 96 tons register, sailed from Lockeport to Turk's Island and was wrecked at Port Jollie Beach on February 2. Her port of registry was Shelburne. Cause: lights out of order. Value of schooner was $6,450.

MARY KATE, a schooner of 42 tons register, sailed from North Sydney to Cow Bay and was wrecked at Peter's Ledge, C.B., on date unknown. Her port of registry was Charlottetown. Cause: bad weather. Value of schooner was $520.

QUATRE LOURS, a schooner of 69 tons register, sailed from St. Pierre to Sydney and was wrecked at east side of Glace Bay Harbour on December 6. Her port of registry was St. Pierre. Cause: heavy gales.

RESOLUTE, a schooner of 90 tons register, sailed from Gloucester to Halifax and was wrecked at Loraine, C.B. Her port of registry was Gloucester, U.S.A. Cause: bad weather. Value of schooner was $12,000.

S.H. MOOSE, a schooner of 114 tons register, sailed from King's Cove to Halifax and was wrecked at Nag Rock at the entrance to Louisburg Harbour on December 8. Her port of registry was St. John's, Newfoundland. Cause: a collision. Value of schooner was $9,000.

HARVEST HOME, a schooner of 29 tons register, sailed from Souris to Halifax and was wrecked at Isaac Harbour on January 1. Her port of registry was Charlottetown. Cause: ran upon a breaker. Value of schooner was $500.

HUNGARIAN, a schooner of 1,612 tons register, sailed from Gaspe Bay to Cape North, C.B., and was wrecked at Cape North on July 2. Her port of registry was Norway. Cause: deviation of compass.

IRENE, a schooner of 12 tons register, sailed from Arichat to Petit de Grat and was wrecked at Cape Rouge on April 25. Her port of registry was Arichat. Cause: stranded. Value of schooner was $125.

(1897)—MINNIE PIERCE, a schooner of 69 tons register, sailed from North Sydney to Bridgeport, Conn., and was wrecked at the entrance to Arichat Harbour on August 31. Her port of registry was St. John's, Newfoundland. Cause: hit upon a rock. Value of schooner was $250.

EMMA B., a schooner of 94 tons register, sailed from Boston to New Glasgow and was wrecked near Egg Island Light on May 14. Her port of registry was Barrington. Cause: foundered. Value of schooner was $1,600.

PRIMROSE, a schooner of 16 tons register, sailed from

Windsor to Cheticamp and was wrecked in Minas Basin on October 17. Her place of registry was Parrsboro. Cause: parting of moorings. Value of schooner was $100.

SUSANNAH R., a schooner of 43 tons register, sailed from Windsor to Parrsboro and was wrecked at East Bay, near Parrsboro, on November 19. Her place of registry was Parrsboro. Cause: parting of chains and drifted ashore. Value of schooner was $2,900.

SIRIUS, a brigantine of 115 tons register, sailed from Halifax to P.E.I. and was wrecked at Pictou Island on November 14. Her place of registry was Charlottetown. Cause: strong winds. Value of vessel was $1,000.

SCUD, a brig of 300 tons register, sailed from Lunenburg to Rockland, Maine, and was wrecked on the south side of St. Peter's Bay, Cape Breton, on December 7. Her place of registry was Boston. Cause: stranded. Value of vessel is unknown.

WILLIE CRAIG, a schooner of 48 tons register, sailed from Sydney to Charlottetown and was wrecked at St. Acone, C.B., on November 4. Her place of registry was Sydney, C.B. Cause: a leak. Value of schooner was $975.

GENESTA, a schooner of 79 tons register, sailed from Alberton, P.E.I., to St. John's, Newfoundland, and was wrecked at Grand Etang, Inverness Co., on December 14. Her port of registry was St. John's, Newfoundland. Cause: stranded. Value of schooner was $2,500.

HUNGARIAN, a schooner of 1,612 tons register, sailed from Gaspe Bay to Cape North and was wrecked at Cape North on July 2. Her port of registry was Norway. Cause: deviation of compass. Value of schooner unknown.

IRENE, a schooner of 12 tons register, sailed from Petit de Grat to Cape Rouge and was wrecked at Cape Rouge on April 25. Her port of registry was Arichat. Cause: stranded. Value of schooner was $125.

MAGNOLIA, a steamer of 260 tons register, while at a wharf in Sydney Harbour, caught fire and was totally wrecked. Her port of registry was Sydney. Value of vessel was $5,000.

POLAR STAR, a schooner of 75 tons register, sailed from Halifax to North Sydney and was wrecked at St. Peter's Canal on May 25. Her port of registry was Liverpool, N.S. Cause: foundered. Value of schooner is unknown.

ROY, a schooner, drifted ashore at Bald Tusket and became a total loss on March 21.

OTIS P. LORD, a schooner under Captain Lemuel

Goodwin, collided with schooner *Annie* in dense fog off Seal Island on August 5 and foundered immediately.

ADDIE, a schooner of 16 tons register, sailed from Halifax to Newfoundland and was wrecked at L'Ardoise Bay on date unknown. Her port of registry was Halifax. Cause: foundered. Value of schooner was $200.

DORIS, a barque of 187 tons register, sailed from Lunenburg to Bahamas and was wrecked off the coast of Nova Scotia on May 17. Her port of registry was Lunenburg. Cause: stranded. Value of vessel was $6,550.

EMMA B., a schooner of 94 tons register, sailed from Boston to New Glasgow and was wrecked near Egg Island Light on May 14. Her port of registry was Barrington. Cause: foundered. Value of schooner was $1,600.

GULNARE, a steamer of 120 tons register, sailed from North Sydney to Halifax and was wrecked at White Point on August 24. Her port of registry was Sydney. Cause: compass out of order. Value of vessel was $7,500.

GERONA, a vessel of 2,035 tons under Captain Dakers out of Portland, Maine, for London, England, with a cargo of livestock and produce, struck the wreck of *Assaye* at Blonde Rock and foundered on December 31. The carcasses of livestock washed ashore at Cape Islands. Value of cargo was $236,000.

SWALLOW, a schooner of unknown tonnage, while sailing along the coast of N.S., was wrecked at Pleasant Bay on September 17. Her port of registry was Arichat. Cause: stranded. Value of schooner was $2,500.

MINNIE PIERCE, a schooner of 69 tons register, sailed from North Sydney to Bridgeport, Conn., and was wrecked at the entrance to Arichat Harbour on August 31. Her port of registry was St. John's, Newfoundland. Cause: hit upon a rock. Value of schooner was $250.

WILLIAM C. ALLAN, a schooner of 12 tons register, sailed from Meteghan to Cape St. Mary's and was wrecked at Big Cove, Digby Co., on October 23. Her port of registry was Yarmouth. Cause: foundered. Value of schooner was $450.

EMMA B., a schooner of 94 tons register, sailed from Boston to New Glasgow and was wrecked near Egg Island Light on May 14. Her port of registry was Barrington. Cause: foundered. Value of schooner was $1,600.

EVANGELINE, a brig of tonnage unknown, sailed from Halifax to Kingsport and was wrecked in Minas Basin on date unknown. Her place of registry was Halifax. Cause: unknown.

Value of vessel is not known.

ELLEN ELIZA, a schooner of 21 tons register, sailed from Arichat to fishing grounds and was wrecked at Gabarus on date unknown. Her place of registry was Arichat.

GOLDEN EAGLE, a schooner of 13 tons register, sailed from Canning to Cape Blomidon and was wrecked at Big Eddy, near Cape Blomidon, on November 9. Her place of registry was Parrsboro. Cause: ran ashore. Value of schooner was $500.

GLEANER, a schooner of 19 tons register, sailed from Parrsboro to Cheverie and was wrecked at this port on November 13. Her place of registry was Parrsboro. Cause: heavy gales. Value of schooner was $150.

GYPSUM EMPRESS, a schooner of 723 tons register, sailed from Windsor to New York and was wrecked at St. Croix River during the month of July. Her place of registry was Windsor. Cause: stranded on a bar. Value of vessel was $2,500.

ANGELIQUE, a schooner of 20 tons register sailed from Marble Mountain to Sydney, C.B., and was wrecked at Grand Narrows Bridge during the month of November. Her place of registry was Halifax. Cause: stranded. Value of schooner was $700.

ATLANTA, a schooner of 94 tons register, sailed from Louisburg to Yarmouth and was wrecked between St. Joseph and Liscomb on March 13. Her place of registry was Halifax. Cause: ran upon the rocks. Value of schooner is not known.

CHINA, a barque of 718 tons register, sailed from Parrsboro to Dublin and was wrecked in Minas Channel on June 23. Her place of registry was Norway. Cause: stranded. Value of vessel was $7,000.

DESSIE M., a schooner of 99 tons register, sailed from Boston to New Glasgow and was wrecked at Liverpool Bar. Her place of registry was Port Medway. Cause: stranded. Value of schooner was $2,000.

DONALD CANN, a schooner of 99 tons register, sailed from Parrsboro to Yarmouth and was wrecked at Brier Island in the Bay of Fundy on October 31. Her place of registry was Yarmouth. Cause: stranded. Value of schooner was $4,000.

EUGENIA, a schooner of 196 tons register, sailed from St. Pierre to Sydney, C.B., and was wrecked at Lingan Bay during the month of October. Her place of registry was Quebec. Cause: ran ashore. Value of schooner is not known.

L.H. DAVIES, a schooner of 33 tons register, sailed from Halifax to Alberton, P.E.I., and was wrecked off Horsehead in the Northumberland Straits on date unknown. Her place of registry was Charlottetown.   Cause: stranded.   Value of schooner was $640.

LUPIN, a schooner of 47 tons register, sailed from St. Pierre to North Sydney and was wrecked thirty miles off Cape Smoky during the month of August.   Her place of registry was Newfoundland.   Cause: a leak.   Value of schooner was $600.

MAY, a brig of 148 tons register, sailed from Turk's Island to Lunenburg and was wrecked at Kingsbury Reef on March 6. Her place of registry was Lunenburg. Cause: stranded. Value of vessel was $500.

MAGGIE, a schooner of tonnage unknown, sailed from Louisburg to P.E.I. and was wrecked at the Strait of Canso. Value of schooner was $500.

MARIA CASAPONA, a barque of 624 tons register, sailed from Miramichi, N.B., to Spain and was wrecked on the south west point of St. Paul Island on October 13. Her place of registry was Italy.   Cause: ran on the rocks.

PRODITOR, a schooner of 54 tons register sailed from Halifax to Cheticamp and was wrecked at Mabou Mouth on August 8.   Her port of registry was Halifax.   Cause: stranded. Value of schooner was $700.

JENNIE B. THOMAS, a schooner under Captain John Apt, was driven ashore on the south side of Peters Island in Grand Passage, between Digby Neck and Long Island, and became a total loss.   She was owned by Joseph Snow.

AGNES, a schooner of 21 tons register, sailed from Cape Breton to Halifax and was wrecked at the mouth of Sheet Harbour during the month of April.   Her place of registry was Halifax. Cause: broke from its anchor.   Value of schooner was $750.

(1898)—AMIEL CORKUM, a schooner of 52 tons register, sailed from Lunenburg and was wrecked at North East Harbour, Shelburne Co., on November 27.   Her place of registry was Lunenburg. Cause: broke from moorings. Value of schooner was $900.

ANNIE G., a schooner of 99 tons register, sailed from Bridgetown to New York and was wrecked in the Bay of Fundy in the month of December.   Her place of registry was Yarmouth. Cause: a storm.

BLUE BELL, a schooner of 25 tons register, sailed from Bras d'Or Lake, C.B., to Sydney, C.B., and was wrecked at Point Aconi on September 27. Her place of registry was Sydney. Cause: a storm.

BALANCE, a schooner of 63 tons register sailed from New

Campbellton to Pictou and was wrecked three miles east of Pictou Light on September 27. Her place of registry was Halifax. Cause: a gale.

BRISK, a schooner of 33 tons register sailed from North Sydney to Newfoundland and was wrecked ten miles off Low Point Light, C.B., on October 12. Her place of registry was Lunenburg. Cause: collision. Value of schooner was $1,000.

SUNSHINE, a schooner of 86 tons register, sailed from Louisburg to Wolfville and was wrecked a half mile from Baccaro Light on October 17. Her place of registry was Windsor. Cause: stranded.

SAXON, a schooner of 119 tons register, sailed from Wallace to Boston and was wrecked at Green Island near Cape Sable Island on December 9. Her place of registry was Saint John, N.B. Cause: misstayed. Value of schooner was $3,000.

SURPRISE, a schooner of 60 tons register, sailed from Parrsboro to Hillsboro, N.B., and was wrecked at Parrsboro River on December 7. Her place of registry was Parrsboro. Cause: stranded. Value of schooner was $690.

SAMOA, a schooner of 89 tons register, sailed from Lunenburg to Georgetown and was wrecked along the coast of Guysboro on May 28. Her place of registry was Lunenburg. Cause: high winds. Value of schooner was $3,300.

JOS. C. MORGAN, a schooner of 36 tons register, sailed from Lockeport to Liverpool, N.S., and was wrecked at Black Rock, La Have, on August 20. Her place of registry was Shelburne. Cause: fog. Value of schooner was $500.

JOHN B. DOLLIVER, a schooner of 35 tons register, sailed from Halifax to Louisburg and was wrecked near Round Island, C.B., during the month of December. Value of schooner was $500.

JOSAPHINE, a steamer of 617 tons register, sailed from Buffalo to Shelburne and was wrecked at Yarmouth Harbour on January 20. Her place of registry was U.S.A. Cause: hit upon the rocks. Value of vessel was $34,000.

MARGARET J., a schooner of 56 tons register, sailed from Sydney to Wine Harbour and was wrecked at Wedge Island during the month of December. Her place of registry was Halifax. Cause: unknown. Value of schooner was $1,800.

PARISIAN, a schooner of 107 tons register, sailed from Louisburg to Halifax and was wrecked at Whitehead on December 16. Her place of registry was Lunenburg. Cause: stranded.

SPRING BIRD, a schooner of 92 tons register, sailed from

Pugwash to Margaree and was wrecked at Margaree Harbour on September 10. Her place of registry was Halifax. Cause: bad weather. Value of schooner was $200.

BERMA, a schooner of 95 tons register, sailed from Joggins to Saint John, N.B., and was wrecked at Apple River on November 27. Her place of registry was Dorchester. Cause: a gale. Value of schooner was $800.

CHARLES, a ship of 1,456 tons register, sailed from Saint John, N.B., to England and was wrecked near Cape Sable, Seal Island, on July 1. Her place of reigstry was Yarmouth. Cause: a proper watch not kept. Value of vessel was $9,000.

CONFEDERATE, a schooner of 49 tons register, sailed from Kelly's Cove, C.B., to Charlottetown and was wrecked in Northumberland Strait on October 11. Her place of registry was Charlottetown. Value of schooner was $308.

EXPRESS, a schooner of 298 tons register, sailed from Halifax to Barrington and Yarmouth and was wrecked at Bon Portage Island on September 16. Her place of registry was Lancaster, England.

ELLEN, a schooner of 32 tons register, sailed from Pictou to Margaree and was wrecked at Margaree Harbour on December 6. Her place of registry was Halifax. Cause: strong currents and high seas. Value of schooner was $200.

IRMA, a schooner of 233 tons register, sailed from England to Halifax and was wrecked at Halifax on November 22. Her place of registry was England. Cause: stranded. Value of schooner is not known.

S.S. GERONA, a vessel, with a cargo weighing up to 2,035 tons, foundered in Lobster Bay.

SARAH F., a schooner of 89 tons register, sailed from Parrsboro to Seal Island and was wrecked off Green Island on September 15. Her port of registry was Parrsboro. Cause: a leak. Value of schooner was $1,650.

S.G. IRWIN, a schooner of 98 tons register, sailed from Louisburg to Yarmouth and was wrecked along the south shore on September 8. Her place of registry was Arichat. Cause: a leak. Value of schooner was $500.

VINTON, a schooner of 94 tons register, sailed from Weymouth and was wrecked in the Bay of Fundy. Her place of registry was Weymouth. Six lives were lost.

WILLIE D., a schooner of 98 tons register, sailed from Parrsboro to Calais, Maine, and was wrecked in the Bay of Fundy on January 2. Her place of registry was Parrsboro. Cause: ran aground.

(1899)—ANNA McGEE, a steamer of 47 tons register, was wrecked at Gannet Rock Ledge on May 30. Her place of registry was Quebec. Cause: stranded. Value of vessel was $2,500.

AMORETTE, a schooner of 18 tons register, sailed from St. Peter's to Arichat and was wrecked on the Herring Rocks at the entrance to Arichat Harbour on May 3. Her place of registry was Charlottetown. Cause: stranded. Value of schooner was $200.

CRESTLINE, a schooner of 94 tons register, sailed from Sydney to Halifax and was wrecked twenty-five miles from Liscomb on June 19. Her place of registry was Port Hawkesbury. Cause: a leak. Value of schooner was $1,000.

MARTHA D. MELAIN, a schooner of 49 tons register, sailed from Digby to fishing grounds and was wrecked at Sulis Point, Annapolis Basin, on November 12. Her place of registry was Digby. Cause: a heavy storm. Value of schooner was $1,500.

MARY E. WHORF, a schooner of 77 tons register, sailed from Tiverton to Parrsboro and was wrecked at Petit Passage, Digby Co., on November 12. Her place of registry was Digby. Cause: a heavy gale. Value of schooner was $1,000.

NANCY ANNA, a schooner which was wrecked at Diligent River, Nova Scotia, on July 19.

NADID, a vessel which was wrecked four miles east of Pugwash Light on September 6.

TWO SISTERS, a schooner which was wrecked at Cheverie, Nova Scotia, possibly in the month of October.

YUKON, a schooner of 79 tons register, sailed from Spencer's Island, N. S., to Saint John, N. B., and was wrecked twelve miles west of Digby Gut in the Bay of Fundy on November 11. Her place of registry was Parrsboro. Cause: a storm. Value of schooner was $2,000.

SEA NYMPH, a schooner of 41 tons register, sailed from North Sydney to St. Pierre and was wrecked three miles off Low Point on July 30. Her place of registry was Halifax. Cause: a leak. Value of schooner was $880.

ELLA MAY, a schooner of 96 tons register, sailed from Parrsboro to Grand Manan and was wrecked at Beaver Harbour in the Bay of Fundy on January 7. Her port of registry was Parrsboro. Cause: dragging of its anchors. Value of schooner was $2,800.

GALAKA, a schooner of 98 tons register, sailed from Lunenburg to Burin, Newfoundland, and was wrecked off Main-a-Dieu, near Scatarie Island, on September 15. Her place of registry was Lunenburg. Cause: currents. Value of schooner was $6,500.

250

JERSEY LILY, a schooner of 96 tons register, sailed from Lockeport to Halifax and was wrecked twenty miles from Scatarie Island on January 29. Her place of registry was Shelburne. Cause: bad weather. Value of schooner was $2,800.

LAURENCE, a schooner of 65 tons register, sailed from Sydney to Charlottetown and was wrecked at Cape George on December 12. Her place of registry was Britain. Cause: grounded.

LEADER, a schooner of 97 tons register, sailed from Lunenburg to Placentia Bay, Newfoundland, and was wrecked at Beaver Harbour on January 14. Her place of registry was Lunenburg. Cause: bad weather. Value of schooner was $6,000.

MATILDA HOPEWELL, a schooner of 89 tons register, sailed from Sydney to Halifax and was wrecked at Black Rock at Great Bras d'Or, N. S., on May 13. Her place of registry was Sydney, N. S. Cause: fog. Value of schooner was $1,000.

OLIVER ELDRIDGE, a schooner of 48 tons register, sailed from Gloucester to Louisburg and was wrecked at St. Peter's Island on September 22. Her place of registry was Gloucester. Cause: unknown. Value of schooner was $2,000.

ORION, a schooner of 77 tons register, sailed from St. Pierre to Souris, P.E.I., and was wrecked at Louisburg on January 7. Her place of registry was Charlottetown. Cause: stranded.

SAMOA, a schooner of 89 tons register, sailed from Lunenburg to Georgetown and was wrecked along the coast of Guysboro Co. on May 28. Her place of registry was Lunenburg. Cause: strong winds. Value of schooner was $3,300.

DRUMALIS, a ship of 2,450 tons register, sailed from Dunkirk to New York and was wrecked on the south west ledge near Cape Sable on August 10. Her port of registry was Liverpool, G. B. Cause: stranded.

JUNO, a schooner of 92 tons register, sailed from Joggins to Digby and was wrecked at Port George, N. S., on December 31. Her place of registry was Saint John, N. B. Cause: heavy seas. Value of schooner was $1,350.

IONA, a schooner of 29 tons register, sailed from Saint John to Maitland, N. S., and was wrecked in Cobequid Bay on October 1. Her place of registry was Parrsboro. Cause: stranded. Value of schooner $275.

DAISY, a schooner of tonnage unknown, sailed from Arichat to fishing grounds and was wrecked along the Cape Breton coast on date unknown. Value of schooner was $1,000.

MARY GRACE, a schooner of 20 tons register, sailed from Cheverie, N. S., to Summerville and was wrecked in the Minas

Basin, Cambridge Creek, on April 30. Her place of registry was Parrsboro. Cause: a snow storm. Value of schooner was $200.

MAGGIE LYNDS, a schooner of 67 tons register, sailed from Moncton, N. B., to Parrsboro, N. S., and was wrecked at Advocate Harbour on November 13. Her port of registry was Saint John. Cause: dragging of her anchors. Value of schooner was $600.

MELINDA, a schooner of 88 tons register, sailed from Yarmouth to Parrsboro and was wrecked at Dartmouth Point, · Freeport, N.S., on December 1. Her place of registry was Parrsboro. Cause: hit upon a ledge. Value of schooner was $1,500.

(1900)—CATHERINE, a schooner of 61 tons register, sailed from Pictou to Arichat and was wrecked at West Arichat in the month of November. Her port of registry was Arichat. Cause: a leak. Value of schooner was $200.

RIPPLE, a schooner of 20 tons register, sailed from Arichat to Petite de Grat and was wrecked at Petite de Grat on October 13. Her port of registry was Halifax. Cause: unknown. Value of schooner was $150.

NEWFIELD, a ship of 509 tons register, sailed from Ottawa to White Cove and was wrecked on the north side of Digby Neck on September 22. Her port of registry was Ottawa. Cause: hit a ledge at the entrance to White Cove. Value of ship was $30,000.

NELLIE BLANCHE, a schooner of 89 tons register, sailed from Sackville to Parrsboro and was wrecked off Apple River on December 21. Her port of registry was Parrsboro. Cause: a leak. Value of schooner was $800.

ROBINETTA, a schooner of 14 tons register, sailed from Canso to the fishing grounds and was wrecked at Bald Rock near Canso on date unknown. Her port of registry was Halifax. Cause: hit upon the rocks. Value of schooner was $350.

THREE BROTHERS, a schooner of 23 tons register, sailed from Pictou to Kelly's Cove and was wrecked at Port Felix, N. S., on October 11. Her port of registry was Halifax. Cause: broke from moorings. Value of schooner was $225.

VIKING, a vessel which was lost somewhere around Seal Island.

PLANET MERCURY, a steel haul ship of 2,092 tons, was lost somewhere between Sandford and Seal Island.

CLYDE, a barque of 237 tons register, sailed from Bridgewater to Quebec and was wrecked at Margaree, C. B., on September 13. Her port of registry was Lunenburg. Cause: bad weather. Value of vessel was $7,000.

ELSIE, a schooner of 47 tons register, sailed from Lunenburg to Halifax and was wrecked off Cape Fourchu on July 28. Her port of registry was Lunenburg. Cause: capsized. Four lives were lost and the value of schooner was $1,450.

E.M.G. HARDY, a schooner of 90 tons register, sailed from North Sydney to Halifax and was wrecked at the entrance to Louisburg Harbour on November 15. Her port of registry was Sydney, N. S. Cause: stranded. Value of schooner was $2,300.

HATTIE McKAY, a schooner of 74 tons register, sailed from Parrsboro to Saint John, N. B., and was wrecked at Isle Haute in the Bay of Fundy on July 26. Her port of registry was Parrsboro. Cause: loss of sails. Value of schooner was $2,500.

IGOMAR, a barquentine of 1,182 tons register, sailed from West Hartlepool, G. B., to Grindstone Island, N. B., and was wrecked south west of Grindstone Island in the Bay of Fundy on September 12. Her port of registry was Norway. Cause: fog. Value of vessel was $12,000.

LENA MAY, a schooner of 18 tons register, left Digby for the fishing grounds and was wrecked in the Bay of Fundy during the month of June. Her port of registry was St. Andrews, N. B. Cause was unknown.

MARY AMANDA, a schooner of 42 tons register, sailed from Halifax to North East Harbour and was wrecked at North East Harbour in Shelburne Co. on November 8. Her port of registry was Shelburne. Cause: dragging of anchors. Value of schooner was $1,500.

MARIE ANNE, a schooner of tonnage unknown, sailed from North Sydney to fishing grounds and was wrecked at White Point in Aspy Bay in the month of September. Her port of registry was Amherst. Cause: weather.

MORNING LIGHT, a schooner of 46 tons register, sailed from Sydney to Point du Chene, N. B., and was wrecked at King's Head, Pictou Co., in the month of September. Her port of registry was Chatham, N. B. Cause: grounded.

G.H.B., a schooner of 36 tons register, sailed from Pictou to a place unknown and was wrecked at Janvrins Island, N. S., on October 20. Her port of registry was Arichat. Cause: parting of chains.

(1901)—RAMBLER, a schooner of 98 tons register, sailed from Burin, Newfoundland, to Lunenburg and was wrecked at St. Esprit Island near the light on March 6. Her port of registry was Lunenburg. Cause: stranded on the rocks. Value of schooner was $8,500.

WILLIE D., a schooner of 65 tons register, sailed from Cheverie to Parrsboro and was wrecked off Refuge Cove in the Bay of Fundy on April 26. Her port of registry was Parrsboro. Cause: a leak. Value of schooner was $1,500.

HARRY L. BELDUC, a schooner of 117 tons register, sailed from fishing grounds to Yarmouth and was wrecked at Green Island, at the entrance to Yarmouth Harbour, on December 30. Her port of registry was U.S.A. Cause: stranded.

JOSEPH ROWE, a schooner of unknown tonnage, sailed from Gloucester to Nova Scotia and was wrecked at Three Top Island near White Head on date unknown. Her port of registry was Gloucester. Cause: foundered. Value of schooner was $8,000.

JOHANNE, a barquentine of 473 tons register, sailed from Norway to Sydney, N. S., and was wrecked at Green Cove, C.B., on date unknown. Her port of registry was Norway. Cause: grounded. Value of vessel was $9,000.

MONITOR, a schooner of 99 tons register, sailed from Charlottetown, P.E.I., to Port Hood and was wrecked at Cole's Reef on the west side of Pictou Harbour on December 18. Her port of registry was Lunenburg. Cause: stranded. Value of schooner was $5,000.

OLIVER WENDELL HOLMES, a schooner of 102 tons register, sailed from Gloucester to Newfoundland and was wrecked south west of Seal Island on December 30. Her port of registry was U.S.A. Cause: misjudgement.

SUSAN AND ANNIE, a schooner of 79 tons register, sailed from Digby to Joggins and was wrecked on Western Head, Cape Enrage, on July 4. Her port of registry was Parrsboro. Cause: stranded. Value of schooner was $1,030.

CURLEW, a brigantine of 307 tons register, sailed from Liverpool, England, to North Sydney and was wrecked 1 1/2 miles from Point Aconi, C.B., on April 6. Her port of registry was Norway. Cause: bad weather. Value of vessel was $35,000.

ARMENIA, a ship of 2,218 tons register, sailed from Glasgow, G.B., to Saint John, N.B., and was wrecked at Negro Head in the Bay of Fundy on January 29. Her port of registry was Glasgow. Cause: stranded.

EPES TARR, a schooner of 48 tons register, sailed from Shag Harbour to Gloucester and was wrecked at Mud Island on October 6. Her port of registry was U.S.A. Cause: stranded. Value of schooner was $1,500.

EMMA C., a schooner of 29 tons register, sailed from LaHave to Halifax and was wrecked at Pennant Point on October

25. Her port of registry was Lunenburg. Cause: stranded. Value of schooner was $2,900.

E. N. MERCHANT, a schooner of 48 tons register, while at Digby Harbour she went aground and became a total loss. Her port of registry was Digby. Cause: unknown. Value of schooner was $100.

GLENDALE, a schooner of 37 tons register, sailed from Montague to Chezzetcook and was wrecked at Red Rock Ledge on November 22. Her port of registry was Lunenburg. Cause: a storm. Value of schooner was $900.

GOULD MILLER, a schooner of 99 tons register, sailed from Gloucester to the fishing grounds and was wrecked at North Sydney. Her port of registry was U.S.A. Cause: unknown. Value of schooner was $28,000.

WILL CARLETON, a schooner of 88 tons register, sailed from Port Hood to Port La Tour and was wrecked at Liscomb Light on Black River Ledge on October 25. Her port of registry was Barrington. Cause: hit upon the ledge. Value of schooner was $2,056.

WESTFIELD, a schooner of 80 tons register, sailed from Point Wolf to Saint John, N. B., and was wrecked 12 miles north of Digby Gut on December 4. Her port of registry was Saint John, N. B. Cause: dragging of anchors. Four lives were lost and the value of schooner was $1,000.

WILLIE, a schooner of 22 tons register, sailed from Westport to Halifax and was wrecked on Gannet Rock Ledges on August 21. Her port of registry was Yarmouth. Cause: stranded. Value of schooner was $1,000.

(1902)—GLADSTONE, a vessel out of Sherbrooke to New York, was wrecked at Sandwich Point, near Halifax Harbour, in the month of January. Her port of registry was Moncton, N. B. Cause: grounded.

MARION, a schooner of 124 tons register, sailed from Saint John, N. B., to Parrsboro and was wrecked in Minas Channel on January 1. Her port of registry was Saint John, N. B. Cause: grounded. Value of schooner was $10,500.

RELIANCE, a schooner of 83 tons register, sailed from Gloucester to the fishing grounds and was wrecked at Indian Point, 10 miles from Lockeport, on March 2. Her port of registry was Gloucester. Cause: stranded. Value of schooner was $12,000.

SUSAN, a schooner of 15 tons register, sailed from River Inhabitants to Arichat and was wrecked near Arichat on date unknown. Her port of registry was Port Hawkesbury and the cause was due to a gale.

TIBER, a ship of 1,134 tons register, sailed from Louisburg to Halifax and was wrecked off Canso on December 25. Her port of registry was Montreal and the cause was due to foundering. (Twenty-one lives were lost.)

THISTLE, a schooner of 114 tons register, sailed from North Sydney to Quebec and was wrecked at St. Paul Island on May 28. Her port of registry was Quebec and the cause was due to fog. Value of schooner was $3,500.

GRENADA, a schooner of 93 tons register, sailed from Sydney to Liverpool and was wrecked five miles south of Cape LaHave, N. S., on December 15. Her port of registry was Lunenburg. Cause: foundered. Value of schooner was $1,700.

(1903)—METROPOLIS, a schooner of 66 tons register, sailed from Noel, N.S., to Campobello, N. B., and was wrecked in Minas Basin on September 25. Her port of registry was Saint John, N. B. Cause: unforeseen conditions. Value of schooner was $350.

ROSEMARY, a schooner of 94 tons register, sailed from Sydney, N. S., to Summerside, P.E.I., and was wrecked at Cape George three miles off Bras d'Or Lake on May 24. Her port of registry was Charlottetown. Cause: unforeseen conditions. Value of schooner was $2,500.

HENRY HOOVES, a schooner of 37 tons register, sailed from Halifax to Gowing and was wrecked in Halifax Harbour on November 2. Her port of registry was Halifax. Cause: collision with another schooner. Value of schooner was $5,000.

MILETUS, a schooner of 95 tons register, sailed from Sydney, C. B., to Chatham, N. B., and was wrecked at Cape North, C. B., on August 8. Her port of registry was Lunenburg. Cause: a leak.

ELLIOT, a schooner of 227 tons register, sailed from Halifax to Channel, Newfoundland, and was wrecked at St. Pauls Island on March 26. Her port of registry was Charlottetown. Cause: ice. Value of schooner was $30,000.

SEA LILLY, a schooner of 37 tons register, sailed from Port Hood to Sambro and was wrecked north west of Beaver Light on September 26. Her port of registry was Lunenburg. Cause: stranded. Value of cargo was $525.

ISABELLA, a schooner of 85 tons register, was wrecked at Port Bevis in Bras d'Or Lake, C. B., on January 3. Her port of registry was Sydney. Cause: foundered. Value of schooner was $1,000.

GEORGINA, a schooner of 34 tons register, sailed from Burnt Island, Newfoundland, to Halifax and was wrecked 45 miles south east of Sheet Harbour on August 1. Her port of registry was St. John's Newfoundland. Cause: collision with the *B.K. Birgitte.*

HAVELOCK, a schooner of 78 tons register, sailed from Port Hastings to Bridgetown and was wrecked at Sable River Bar on May 15. Her port of registry was Halifax. Cause: unforeseen conditions. Value of schooner was $1,350.

(1904)—AGATHA, a schooner of 92 tons register, sailed from Shelburne to the fishing grounds and was wrecked at Indian Bay on September 14. Her port of registry was Shelburne. Cause: stranded. Value of schooner was $7,400.

ARIEL, a schooner of 249 tons register, sailed from St. John's, Newfoundland, to Sydney, C.B., and was wrecked off Cranberry Head on November 1. Her port of registry was Liverpool, England. Cause: stranded. Value of schooner was $12,000.

BOBS, a schooner of 107 tons register, sailed from Halifax to Louisburg and was wrecked at Glace Bay on December 24. Her port of registry was St. John's, Newfoundland. Cause: stranded. Value of schooner was $8,500.

BESSIE M. DEVINE, a schooner of 91 tons register, sailed from Gloucester to Bay of Islands, Newfoundland, and was wrecked at Collis Cove, east of White Head, on November 30. Her port of registry was Gloucester, Mass., US.A. Cause: fire.

MAGGIE SULLIVAN, a schooner of 123 tons register, sailed from Boston to Lunenburg and was wrecked at Owens Point on September 12. Her port of registry was Boston. Cause: stranded. Value of schooner was $9,150.

ROBERT EWING, a schooner of 399 tons register, sailed from Louisburg to Yarmouth and was wrecked two miles south west of Bald Tusket, Bay of Fundy, on September 14. Her port of registry was Parrsboro. Cause: stranded. Value of schooner was $3,000.

SAILOR'S HOME, a schooner of 93 tons register, sailed from Halifax to Beckerton and was wrecked at Beckerton Head on December 2. Her port of registry was Halifax. Cause: stranded. Value of schooner was $3,500.

VOLUNTEER, a schooner of 99 tons register, sailed from Harbour Grace, Newfoundland, to Sydney, C.B, and was wrecked at Lingan Bar near Old Bridgeport on November 2. Her port of registry was St. John's, Newfoundland. Cause: stranded. Value of schooner was $3,000.

WATER LILY, a schooner of 71 tons register, sailed from Saint John, N.B., to Parrsboro Basin and was wrecked at McKay's

Head on September 21. Her port of registry was Saint John, N.B. Cause: weather. Value of schooner was $1,500.

HIGHLAND LASS, a schooner of 19 tons register, sailed from Point Morien to the fishing grounds and, on its return, was wrecked at Morien on October 1. Her port of registry was Sydney, C.B. Cause: stranded. Value of schooner was $400.

HARRY TROOP, a schooner of 199 tons register, sailed from Aurno to Shelburne and was wrecked at McNutt's Island on October 16. Her port of registry was Liverpool, N.S. Cause: stranded. Value of schooner was $10,000.

KATE B., a schooner of 24 tons register, sailed from Louisburg to the fishing grounds and, on its return, was wrecked at the entrance to Louisburg Harbour on October 13. Her port of registry was Sydney, C.B. Cause: broke steering wheel. Value of schooner was $500.

LEONE, a schooner of 79 tons register, sailed from Sydney to Halifax and was wrecked at Scatarie Island. Her port of registry was Lunenburg. Cause: stranded. Value of schooner was $1,000.

LADY OF AVON, a schooner of 249 tons register, sailed from Cambridge, N.S., to New York and was wrecked at West Bay, Parrsboro, Bay of Fundy, on September 11. Her port of registry was Windsor, N.S. Cause: a collision with the schooner *Chacma*. Value of schooner was $500.

LAURA, a schooner of 53 tons register, sailed from Sheet Harbour to Halifax and was wrecked at Mushaboom Point on November 19. Her port of registry was Halifax. Cause: stranded. Value of schooner was $400.

WARRIOR, a schooner of 93 tons register, sailed from North Sydney to Annapolis and was wrecked at Digby on December 18. Her port of registry was Halifax. Cause: loss of sails. Value of schooner was $1,500.

WILLIE A., a schooner of 70 tons register, sailed from Halifax to Sydney, C.B., and was wrecked at Whitehaven on November 14. Her port of registry was Arichat. Cause: stranded. Value of schooner was $1,350.

YUBA, a barquentine of 557 tons register, sailed from Mossal Bay, South Africa, to Weymouth and was wrecked at New Whale Cove, Digby Neck, on July 29. Her port of registry was Larwick, Norway. Cause: stranded.

TRIUMPH, a schooner of 38 tons register, sailed from Halifax to Port Medway, N.S., and was wrecked at Volgers Cove, N.S., on May 13. Her port of registry was Halifax. Cause: stranded. Value of schooner was $300.

WELLIMAN HALL, a schooner of 136 tons register, sailed from Parrsboro to New York and was wrecked in Minas Basin on October 30. Her port of registry was Parrsboro. Cause: fire. Value of schooner was $4,000.

WANITA, a schooner of 42 tons register, sailed from Saint John to Windsor and was wrecked at Cape Chignecto, Advocate Bay, on November 28. Her port of registry was Windsor, N.S. Cause: stranded. Value of schooner was $500.

J.H. BOWERS, a barque of 655 tons register, sailed from Weymouth to Buenos Aires and was wrecked at St. Mary's Bay on March 4. Her port of registry was Sydney, N.S. Cause: a leak. Value of vessel was $4,500.

INDEPENDENCE, a schooner of 102 tons register, sailed from Gloucester to Bay of Islands, Newfoundland, and was wrecked at Schooner Pond, C. B., on December 27. Her port of registry was Gloucester. Cause: weather conditions. Value of schooner was $10,100.

JOHN LAWRENCE, a schooner of 23 tons register, sailed from Larry's River, Sherbrooke, to Wine Harbour and was wrecked at Wine Harbour Bar on April 3. Her port of registry was Halifax. Cause: unforeseen conditions. Value of schooner was $400.

J. W. RAYMOND, a schooner of 35 tons register, sailed from Annapolis to Liverpool and was wrecked at Pease Island on April 24. Her port of registry was Liverpool, N. S. Cause: unforseen conditions. Value of schooner was $750.

GRANADA, a schooner of 60 tons register, sailed from Mulgrave to D'Escousse, St. Peter's, and was wrecked at Grand Grave St. Peter's Bay, in July. Her port of registry was Port Hawkesbury. Cause: fire.

HAZEL GLEN, a schooner of 95 tons register, sailed from Saint John, N.B. to Halifax and was wrecked at Troops Point, Annapolis River on June 24. Her port of registry was Yarmouth. Cause: river conditions. Value of schooner was $1,200.

HERMOD, a schooner of 1,918 tons register, sailed from Sunderland to Sydney, C.B., and was wrecked at Flint Isle, C.B., on July 10. Her port of registry was Bremen, Germany. Cause: stranded.

(1905)—BLENHEIM, a brigantine of 199 tons register, sailed from New York to Chatham, N.B., and was wrecked fifteen miles south of Cape Sable on June 12. Her port of registry was Paspebiac, Quebec. Cause: a collision. Value of vessel was $850.

COLUMBIA, a schooner of 87 tons register, sailed from Gloucester to North Sydney and was wrecked two miles north of Low Point, C.B., on June 25. Her port of registry was Gloucester,

Mass. Cause: collision with *S.S. Sverre.* Value of schooner was $8,000.

EDWARD A. PERKINS, a schooner of 58 tons register, sailed from Gloucester to Bay of Islands and was wrecked at Black Rock off Louisburg on January 19. Her port of registry was Gloucester, Mass. Cause: stranded. Value of schooner was $7,500.

PREMIER, a schooner of 99 tons register, sailed from LaHave to Magdalen Islands and was wrecked at Red Head Shoal, Strait of Canso, on June 6. Her port of registry was Lunenburg. Cause: stranded. Value of schooner was $7,000.

RIVAL, a schooner of 31 tons register, sailed from Jeddore to Halifax and was wrecked at Lawrencetown on June 15. Her port of registry was Halifax. Cause: stranded. Value of schooner was $500.

ALPH B. PARKER, a schooner of 47 tons register, sailed from Freeport, N.S., and was wrecked at Cape Cove Sand Flats, Digby Co., on October 16. Her port of registry was Saint John, N.B. Cause: stranded. Value of schooner was $1,300.

BASIL M. GELDERT, a schooner of 99 tons register, sailed from Halifax to Bay of Islands, Newfoundland, and was wrecked at Owl's Head Harbour on January 10. Her port of registry was Lunenburg. Cause: stranded. Value of schooner was $5,000.

IDA M. SHAFNER, a schooner of 139 tons register, sailed from New York to Sydney, N.S., and was wrecked on the south east ledge of Isaac's Harbour on December 9. Her port of registry was Annapolis. Cause: stranded. Value of schooner was $8,000.

J.W. HILL, a schooner of 78 tons register, sailed from Chatham, N.B., to Sydney and was wrecked at Sydney Harbour on September 9. Her port of registry was Halifax. Cause: fire. Value of schooner was $1,200.

L.M.B., a schooner of 99 tons register, sailed from Windsor, N.S., to Red Beach, Maine, and was wrecked at La Tete Passage, Bay of Fundy, on July 14. Her port of registry was Maitland. Cause: stranded. Value of schooner was $2,000.

LEIF, a ship of 1,137 tons register, sailed from Cork, Ireland, to Nova Scotia and was wrecked at Bridgewater Harbour on December 2. Her port of registry was Norway. Cause: grounded. Value of vessel was $10,000.

MARY MAY, a schooner of 23 tons register, sailed from Dover to Canso and was wrecked at Glasgow Head, near Canso Harbour, on October 9. Her port of registry was Halifax. Cause: stranded. Value of schooner was $500.

HORLAND, a vessel which was lost on Black Point during the month of July.

MAUD M. STORY, a schooner of 78 tons register, sailed from Gloucester, Mass., to Wood's Harbour and was wrecked in the breakers off Sambro on November 20. Her port of registry was St. Andrew, N.B.   Cause: stranded.   Value of schooner is unknown.

PRO. PATRIA, a steamer of 380 tons register, sailed from St. Pierre Miquelon to North Sydney and was wrecked near Fourchu on May 29.   Her port of registry was France.   Cause: stranded.

PURITAN, a schooner of 62 tons register, sailed from Canos to the fishing banks and, on its return home, was wrecked at Shag Rocks, St. Andrews Channel, Strait of Canso, on September 18. Her port of registry was Gloucester, U.S.A. Cause: stranded. Value of schooner was $4,000.

SAMUEL DRAKE, a schooner of 68 tons register, sailed from Port Morien to Halifax and was wrecked off Scatarie on September 21.   Her port of registry was Charlottetown, P.E.I. Cause: foundered.

SAINTE MARIE, a schooner of 148 tons register, sailed from New York to Yarmouth and was wrecked at Bunker Island near Yarmouth on March 22. Her port of registry was Lunenburg. Cause: stranded.   Value of schooner was $4,000.

PETER MITCHELL, a schooner of 26 tons register, sailed from Ship Harbour to Halifax and was wrecked at Three Fathom Harbour   on   October   6.   Her   port   of   registry   was   Port Hawkesbury. Cause stranded.   Value of schooner was $1,200.

(1906)—BEATRICE, a schooner of 353 tons register, sailed from North Sydney to St. John, N.B., and was wrecked at Cranberry Head on December 24.   Her port of registry was Cardiff, G.B. Cause: a leak.   Value of schooner was $35,000.

EMILIE ANDRIE, a schooner of 116 tons register, sailed from St. Pierre Miquelon to Sydney, N.S., and was wrecked at Little Loraine, C.B., on April 12.   Her port of registry was St. Pierre Miquelon.   Cause: stranded.   Value of schooner was $2,500.

EMMA R. HARVEY, a schooner of 300 tons register, sailed from Apple River, N.S., to Boston and was wrecked five miles east of Digby Gut on December 5. Her port of registry was U.S.A. Cause: a leak.

FLORA TEMPLE, a schooner of 55 tons register, sailed from Halifax to Margaree and was wrecked five miles north east of Port   Hood   on   December   1.   Her   port   of   registry   was   Port Hawkesbury. Cause: stranded.

FLORENCE MAY, a schooner of 74 tons register, sailed from Sydney, C.B., to Buctouche, N.B., and was wrecked at Cape Tormentine on August 30. Her port of registry was Chatham, N.B. Cause: stranded.

HARLYN, a schooner of 928 tons register, sailed from Frapani to Gloucester, Mass., and was wrecked at Black Point, Shelburne Co., on July 8. Her port of registry was West Hartlepool. Cause: stranded.

IVANHOE, a schooner of 100 tons register, sailed from Perth Amboy, N.J., for Popes Harbour and was wrecked at Middle Ledge off Isaac Harbour on November 6. Her port of registry was Lunenburg. Cause: stranded. Value of schooner was $5,100.

JESSIE, a schooner of 36 tons register, sailed from Port Hastings for Guysboro and was wrecked at Medford Haven, at old bridge in Guysboro Co., on date unknown. Her port of registry was Halifax. Cause: foundered. Value of schooner was $480.

KEEWAYDIN, a schooner of 187 tons register, sailed from Providence, R.I., to Parrsboro and was wrecked off Tarpoulin Cove, N.S., on June 7. Her port of registry was Parrsboro. Cause: a collision.

LENA M., a schooner of 27 tons register, sailed from Souris, P.E.I., for White Haven, Conn., and was wrecked at Ball Breaker south west of Cranberry Island light on August 5. Her port of registry was Halifax. Cause: stranded. Value of schooner was $2,000.

LEVOSE, a schooner of 86 tons register, sailed from Rockport, Maine, to Digby and was wrecked two miles west of Weymouth on July 10. Her port of registry was Weymouth. Cause: stranded. Value of schooner was $600.

MAGGIE, a schooner of 13 tons register, sailed from Arichat to Canso and was wrecked in Canso Harbour on October 13. Her port of registry was Lunenburg. Cause: fire. Value of schooner was $1,500.

MAGIC, a schooner of 27 tons register, sailed from Port La Tour to Yarmouth and was wrecked at Bear Point, Barrington Harbour, on November 23. Her port of registry was Digby. Cause: stranded.

NELLIE CARTER, a schooner of 78 tons register, sailed from Apple River to Parrsboro and was wrecked at Pudsey's Point, at the mouth of Apple River, on July 30. Her port of registry was Parrsboro. Cause: ran ashore during the fog.

NORTH STAR, a schooner of 35 tons register, sailed from

Milon to Cheticamp, N.B., and was wrecked on the west side of Port Hood Harbour on November 3. Her port of registry was Charlottetown. Cause: stranded. Value of schooner was $850.

RIPPLES, a schooner of 34 tons register, sailed from Georgetown, P.E.I., to Sherbrooke and was wrecked at Port Bickerton, N.S., on date unknown. Her port of registry was Port Hawkesbury. Cause: fire. Value of schooner was $900.

TERENCE C. LOCKWOOD, a schooner of 98 tons register, sailed from Lockeport to Newark and was wrecked at Soldier's Ledge at Tusket, Yarmouth Co., on November 18. Her port of registry was Shelburne. Cause: stranded.

WALLULA, a schooner of 82 tons register, sailed from Saint John to Parrsboro and was wrecked at Bald Rock in Cumberland Bay on November 1. Her port of registry was Saint John, N.B. Cause: water logged condition. Value of schooner was $200.

BLUENOSE, a schooner of 166 tons register, sailed from Hantsport, N.S., for New York and was wrecked at Parrsboro River on June 12. Her port of registry was Windsor. Cause: fire. Value of schooner was $300.

CARRIE EASTER, a schooner fo 179 tons register, sailed from Port Hastings to Yarmouth and was wrecked 20 miles east of Halifax on March 18. Her port of registry was Port Medway. cause: foundered. Value of schooner was $2,750.

DARBY, a barque of 882 tons register, sailed from Weymouth to Canary Islands and was wrecked at Campbell's wharf at Sissiboo River in the month of December. Her port of registry was Norway.

ANGOLA, a ship of 1,811 tons register, sailed from Progress to Sydney, C.B., and was wrecked at Howick Point, N.S., on July 10. Her port of registry was London, G.B. Cause: stranded.

ATRATO, a schooner of 215 tons register, sailed from Philadelphia for St. John's, Newfoundland, and was wrecked at Liverpool, N.S., on February 10. Her place of registry was Belze. Cause: stranded.

ATLANTIC, a schooner of 80 tons register, sailed from LaHave to Halifax and was wrecked at Goose Island in Isaacs Harbour on December 12. Her port of registry was Lunenburg. Cause: stranded. Value of schooner was $5,800.

(1907)—EDITH, a schooner of 45 tons register, sailed from Port Herbert to Liverpool and was wrecked one mile south of Liverpool Harbour on September 12. Her port of registry was Maitland. Cause: foundered. Value of schooner was $500.

FLEET WING, a schooner of 54 tons register, sailed from Annapolis Royal to Port George and was wrecked on the west side of Digby Gut on November 5. Her port of registry was Annapolis Royal. Cause: stranded. Value of schooner was $500.

FLORENCE, a schooner of 19 tons register, sailed from Saint John, N. B., to Yarmouth and was wrecked at Sandford, N. S., in the Bay of Fundy on October 1. Her port of registry was Yarmouth. Cause: stranded. Value of schooner was $500.

FOUR BROTHERS, a schooner of 26 tons register, sailed from Murray Harbour, P.E.I., to New Glasgow and was wrecked at Merigomish on November 20. Her port of registry was Halifax. Cause: stranded. Value of schooner was $600.

GURDIAN, a schooner of 99 tons register, sailed from Camalene, Newfoundland, to Sydney, C. B., and was wrecked off Cranberry Head on May 1. Her port of registry was St. John's, Newfoundland. Cause: stranded. Value of schooner was $4,000.

I. B. HAMBLIN, a schooner of 22 tons register, sailed from White Haven to Canso and was wrecked in Canso Harbour on December 3. Her port of registry was Lunenburg. Cause: fire. Value of schooner was $1,500.

JAMES R., a schooner of 51 tons register sailed from St. Pierre Miquelon to Cheticamp and was wrecked at Queens Ledges, off Glace Bay, on November 21. Her port of registry was Halifax. Cause: stranded. Value of schooner was $1,000.

KATE, a schooner of 10 tons register, sailed from Louisburg to Charlottetown and was wrecked at St. Esper't, C. B., on November 6. Her port of registry was Sydney, C. B. Cause: stranded. Three lives were lost and the value of schooner was $1,000.

CHELSON, a vessel which was wrecked at Viceroy Cove.

ANNIE ETHEL, a schooner under Captain George Harris, was wrecked on the rocks just off Harbour Point on the south side of Gabarus Bay. Apparently it was a cold and dreary day, with the sea full of small pieces of ice, known as 'lolly'. Because of the strong winds and tide, the vessel was driven ashore and became a total wreck. Close by, another vessel, under Captain Weatherbee, was wrecked some years earlier.

MARY E. SMITH, a schooner of 99 tons register, sailed from Windsor, N. S., to Sydney, C. B., and was wrecked along the south shore of N.S. on September 25. Her port of registry was Lunenburg. Cause: foundered. Value of schooner was $4,500.

MOOWEENA, a schooner of 10 tons register, sailed from Port La Tour for the fishing grounds and was wrecked at Phoebecs Point on November 7. Her port of registry was Yarmouth. Cause: stranded.

NEW DOMINION, a brigantine of 133 tons register, sailed from Isaac Harbour to Louisburg and was wrecked at Round Island near Gabarus on June 10. Her port of registry was Quebec. Cause: dragging of anchors. Value of vessel was $1,500.

NEW ERA, a schooner of 115 tons register, sailed from Port Hastings to Clarks Harbour and was wrecked at Sandwich Point in Halifax Harbour on December 15. Her port of registry was Liverpool, N. S. Cause: ran aground. Value of schooner was $5,300.

ORINOCO, a ship of 1,550 tons register, sailed from Saint John, N.B., to Halifax and was wrecked on the western part of Seal Island on July 26. Her port of registry was London, England. Cause: stranded. Value of vessel was $225,000.

PARTHENIA, a schooner of 99 tons register, sailed from Shelburne to Liverpool and was wrecked at Brooklyn, in Liverpool Bay, on November 7. Her port of registry was Port Medway. Cause: stranded. Value of schooner was $2,540.

BLANCHE, a schooner of 78 tons register, sailed from Gloucester to Canso and was wrecked at Kalbacks Head, near Lunenburg Harbour, on April 8. Her port of registry was Gloucester, Mass. Value of schooner was $1,200.

CANDID, a schooner of 35 tons register, sailed from Halifax to Port Mouton and was wrecked in Liverpool Harbour on January 12. Her port of registry was St. John's, Newfoundland. Cause: stranded.

DEETA M., a schooner of 81 tons register, sailed from Halifax to Souris, P.E.I., and was wrecked at West Quoddy Ledge on May 18. Her port of registry was Lunenburg. Cause: stranded. Value of schooner was $4,000.

ALICE, a schooner of 55 tons register, sailed from Five Islands to West Bay and was wrecked at West Bay on October 7. Her port of registry was Parrsboro. Cause: stranded. Value of schooner was $525.

ARIZONA, a schooner of 99 tons register, sailed from Louisburg to Lockeport and was wrecked forty miles south south west of Cape Sable Island on February 18. Her port of registry was Liverpool. Cause: stranded.

UNIVERSE, a ship of 1,635 tons register, sailed from New York to Pictou and was wrecked at Seal Cove, White Haven, N.S., on April 25. Her port of registry was Norway. Cause: stranded. Value of ship was $13,000.

ARGO, a schooner of 80 tons register, sailed from Gloucester to Sydney and was wrecked at Whale Cove at the entrance to White Head Harbour on December 10. Her port of registry was St. John's, Newfoundland. Cause: stranded. Value of schooner was $4,500.

BASUTOLAND, a schooner of 190 tons register, sailed from Point Du Chene to Vineyard Haven and was wrecked at White Point, Canso Harbour, on November 13. Her port of registry was Liverpool, N. S. Cause: stranded. Value of schooner was $5,000.

CHAMPION, a schooner of 79 tons register, sailed from Labrador to Halifax and was wrecked at Dead Mans Cove, C.B., on December 5. Her port of registry was Saint John, N. B. Cause: stranded. One loss of life and the value of schooner was $12,000.

CRYSTAL, a schooner of 15 tons register, sailed from Halifax to Ingraham and was wrecked at Chebucto on September 9. Her port of registry was Halifax. Cause: a collision.

DECORRA, a schooner of 150 tons register, sailed from Perth to Eastport, Maine, and was wrecked one mile west of Gulliver's Cove in the Bay of Fundy on September 7. Her port of registry was Machias, Maine. Cause: sinking condition. Value of schooner was $1,200.

R.N.B., a schooner of 37 tons register, sailed from Parrsboro to Canning, N. S., and was wrecked at Kingsport Beach in the Minas Basin on October 15. Her port of registry was Windsor, N.S. Cause: stranded. Value of schooner was $300.

SCEPTER, a schooner of 91 tons register, sailed from Gloucester to the fishing grounds and was wrecked at Scatarie Island on October 21. Her port of registry was Gloucester, Mass. Cause: stranded.

THISTLE, a schooner of 34 tons register, sailed from Wycocomagh to Glace Bay and was wrecked at Black Rock Light, C.B., in the month of October. Her port of registry was Charlottetown, P.E.I. Cause: stranded.

VOLUND, a steamer of 671 tons register, sailed from Windsor to New York and was wrecked on Blomidon Shore in Minas Basin on October 5. Her port of registry was Bergen, Norway. Cause: stranded. Value of vessel was $12,200.

YANKEE, a schooner of 3 tons register, sailed from Yarmouth to Tusket Island and was wrecked on Whales Back Ledge on August 8. Her port of registry was Yarmouth. Cause:

stranded.

(1908)—DOLPHIN, a schooner of 4 tons register, sailed from Tusket Wedge to Tusket and was wrecked at Deep Cove Island on February 1. Her port of registry was Yarmouth. Cause: stranded. Value of schooner was $1,000.

PANSY, a schooner of 76 tons register, sailed from Diligent River to Saint John, N.B., and was wrecked at the entrance to Minas Channel on March 21. Her port of registry was Saint John, N.B. Cause: stranded. Value of schooner was $2,540.

MAGGIE SMITH, a schooner of 83 tons register, sailed from Halifax to North Sydney and was wrecked at St. Esprit on December 10. Her port of registry was Port Hawkesbury. Cause: stranded. Value of schooner was $1,450.

MARCELINE, a barquentine of 112 tons register, sailed from Bordeaux to St. Pierre Miquelon and was wrecked forty miles east of Port Main, C.B., on December 17. Her port of registry was France. Cause: foundered. Value of vessel was $5,000.

MARY KATE, a schooner of 13 tons register, sailed from Port Mouton to Halifax and was wrecked off Port Medway on July 28. Her port of registry was Shelburne. Cause: foundered. Value of schooner was $800.

MURDOCK FINLAYSON, a schooner of 80 tons register,sailed from River Bourgoise to Halifax and was wrecked one and a half miles east of Devil's Island on November 1. Her port of registry was Arichat. Cause: stranded. Value of schooner was $2,700.

OCEAN, a ship of 2,459 tons register, sailed from Montreal to Sydney, N.S., and was wrecked at Petre Ledge, North Sydney, on July 10. Her port of registry was Norway. Cause: hit the ledge. Value of vessel was $22,000.

CORINTO, a schooner of 98 tons register, sailed from Parrsboro to Machias Seal Island Light and was wrecked at Seal Island on August 17. Her port of registry was Parrsboro. Cause: stranded. Value of schooner was $3,000.

DIDO, a schooner of 59 tons register sailed from Halifax to Musquodoboit and was wrecked at Sheet Harbour on May 20. Her port of registry was Guysboro. Cause: foundered. Value of schooner was $700.

DOMINION, a schooner of 96 tons register, sailed from Halifax to Louisburg and was wrecked at Ship Harbour on August 21. Her port of registry was Lunenburg. Cause: fire. Value of schooner was $1,500.

ETHEL BLANCHE, a schooner of 17 tons register, sailed from fishing grounds to Port Hawkesbury and was wrecked at a wharf in Port Hawkesbury in the month of May. Her port of registry was Pictou. Cause: stranded.

GEORGE L. SLIPP, a schooner of 98 tons register, sailed from Hantsport to Boston and was wrecked at Gullivars Cove, N.S., on October 18. Her port of registry was Saint John, N.B. Cause: stranded. Value of schooner was $4,500.

GOLDEN RULE, a schooner of 148 tons register, sailed from Portland, Maine, to Yarmouth and was wrecked at Barrington, N.S., on August 19. Her port of registry was Shelburne. Cause: hit a rock. Value of schooner was $6,800.

JULIA FARSEY, a schooner of 63 tons register, sailed from Sydney, C.B., to Lamatime, Newfoundland, and was wrecked at Cranberry Head, C.B., on May 31. Her port of registry was St. John's, Newfoundland. Cause: stranded. Value of schooner was $1,250.

ADA MILDRED, a schooner of 99 tons register, sailed from Sherbrooke to Louisburg and was wrecked near White Head on January 20. Her port of registry was Pictou. Cause: stranded. Value of schooner was $5,000.

BONNIE LIN, a schooner of 10 tons register, sailed from Yarmouth to Grand Harbour and was wrecked 15 miles west of Brice Island on October 13. Her port of registry was Barrington. Cause: foundered. Value of schooner was $600.

ETHEL G., a schooner of 11 tons register, sailed from Port Hastings to White Haven, N.S., and was wrecked at White Haven on August 2. Her port of registry was Arichat. Cause: stranded. Value of schooner was $500.

JENNIE C., a schooner of 16 tons register, sailed from Saint John, N.B., and was wrecked at Seeleys Cove, N.S., in the month of January. Her port of registry was Yarmouth. Cause: stranded. Value of schooner was $500.

ARCOLA, a ship of 1,651 tons register, sailed from Preston, G.B., to Chatham, N.B., and was wrecked at Hay Cove, St. Paul Island, on July 8. Her port of registry was Saint John, N.B. Cause: stranded.

CALABRIA, a barge of 451 tons register, sailed from New York to Windsor, N.S., and was wrecked near Margaretsville on December 2. Her port of registry was Windsor. Cause: broke from her tow and drifted ashore. Value of barge was $5,000.

CALUNA, a schooner of 15 tons register, sailed from Point Duchene to Saint John and was wrecked at Seal Rock, Pictou Co., on November 10. Her port of registry was Richibucto, N.B. Cause: stranded. Value of schooner was $3,500.

CARRIE MAY, a schooner of 25 tons register, sailed from Shag Harbour and was wrecked at Mud Island, Yarmouth Co., on April 9. Her port of registry was Yarmouth. Cause: stranded. Value of schooner was $500.

PRUDENT, a schooner of 117 tons register, sailed from Windsor, to West Chester and was wrecked one mile west of Harbourville on August 1. Her port of registry was Saint John, N.B. Cause: stranded. Value of schooner was $2,000.

UTOPIA, a schooner of 98 tons register, sailed from Charlottetown to Sydney and was wrecked off Cape Jack on September 19. Her port of registry was Charlottetown, P.E.I. Cause: stranded. Value of schooner was $1,800.

VERA, a schooner of 77 tons register, sailed from Gloucester to Canso and was wrecked at Walkers Ledge three miles west of Cranberry Head on December 30. Her port of registry was Gloucester, Mass. Cause: hit ledge. Value of schooner was $10,000.

ZULERKA, a schooner of 8 tons register, sailed from Mira Gut to Loarine and was wrecked at Black Rock, C.B., on September 1. Her port of registry was Sydney, C.B. Cause: foundered. Value of schooner was $500.

VENTURER, a schooner of 256 tons register, sailed from Yarmouth to Louisburg and was wrecked at Port Le Herbert, Lat. 43. 47' W long 64 53', on October 26. Her port of registry was Liverpool, N.S. Cause: stranded. Value of schooner was $3,500. (1909)—REGINA B., a schooner of 81 tons register, sailed from Port Hood to Halifax and was wrecked north of Gas Buoy, Halifax Harbour, on October 19. Her port of registry was Port Hawkesbury. Cause: a collision with the *John Irwin*. Value of schooner was $1,400.

ARTHUR BINNEY, a schooner of 80 tons register, sailed from Boston to Canso and was wrecked at Forchu, C.B., on April 27. Her port of registry was Boston. Cause: stranded. Value of schooner was $8,000.

COLUMBIA, a schooner of 99 tons register, sailed from St. John's, Newfoundland, to Louisburg and was wrecked at St. Esprit Island off C.B. on April 3. Her port of registry was St. John's, Newfoundland. Cause: stranded.

HORNET, a schooner of 26 tons register, sailed from Kingsport to Parrsboro and was wrecked at Kingsport, N.S., on January 6. Her port of registry was Windsor, N.S. Cause: stranded. One life was lost and the value of the schooner was $600.

OMEGA, a schooner of 82 tons register, sailed from Port Morin to Buctouche and was wrecked at Cape Hogan on June 6. Her port of registry was Charlottetown. Cause: stranded. Value of schooner was $1,000.

P.F. NO. 2, a schooner of 31 tons register, sailed from St. Pierre to the fishing grounds and was wrecked at White Point, C.B., on May 25. Her port of registry was St. Pierre Miquelon. Cause: stranded. Value of schooner was $1,000.

ACACIA, a schooner of 98 tons register, sailed from New York to Clarke's Harbour and was wrecked at Clarke's Harbour on October 15. Her port of registry was Barrington. Cause: stranded. Value of schooner was $800.

ARGOSY, a schooner of 84 tons register, sailed from Halifax to St. Peters, C.B., and was wrecked at Black Point at Grand River, Richmond Co., on November 16. Her port of registry was Lunenburg. Cause: stranded. Value of schooner was $1,200.

BELMONT, a schooner of 98 tons register, sailed from North Sydney, C.B., to Pubnico and was wrecked at Barrington Passage, N.S., on November 13. Her port of registry was Lunenburg. Cause: stranded. Value of schooner was $3,100.

CANADIENNE, a schooner of 53 tons register, sailed from North Sydney to St. Paul Island and was wrecked at north east end of the island on October 26. Her port of registry was Halifax. Cause: stranded. Value of schooner was $1,000.

DORA A LAWSON, a schooner of unknown tonnage, sailed from Gloucester, Mass., to the fishing grounds and was wrecked at Canso Harbour on December 20. Her port of registry was U.S.A. Cause: stranded. Value of schooner was $8,000.

H.J. LOGAN, a schooner of 772 tons register, sailed from Halifax to Dartmouth and was wrecked on the Dartmouth side of the Harbour on August 6. Her port of registry was Parrsboro. Cause: fire. Value of schooner was $31,000.

HOPE, a schooner of 22 tons register, sailed from Port La Tour to Barrington and was wrecked at Calm Point, Cape Sable Island, on May 1. Her port of registry was Barrington. Cause: stranded. Value of schooner was $450.

LEDEE ADELE, a schooner of 50 tons register, sailed from Souris, P.E.I., to Pictou and was wrecked four miles north east of Pictou Island on August 18. Her port of registry was Magdalen Islands. Cause: stranded. Value of schooner was $300.

LEWANIKA, a schooner of 298 tons register, sailed from Sydney, N.S., to Saint John, N.B., and was wrecked east by south of Betty Island, N.S., on October 25. Her port of registry was

Bridgetown, Barbados. Cause: dragging of anchors. Value of schooner was $5,500.

MYRTLE V. HOPKINS, a schooner of 158 tons register, sailed from Halifax to Sydney and was wrecked at the entrance to Sydney Harbour on November 16. Her port of registry was Liverpool,N.S. Cause: stranded. Value of schooner was $4,500.

(1910)—ACADIAN, a schooner of 32 tons register, sailed from Meteghan to Pubnico and was wrecked at St. Mary's Bay on May 24. Her port of registry was Weymouth. Cause: capsized. Value of schooner was $600.

BORGHILD, a barque of 725 tons register, sailed from Fredrikshald to Jeddore and was wrecked at Castor Ledge near Beckerton, N.S., on June 1. Her port of registry was Fredrikshald, Norway. Cause: stranded. Two lives were lost.

NIAGARA, a schooner of 78 tons register, sailed from Gloucester to Canso and was wrecked south west of Cranberry Island on April 27. Her port of registry was U.S.A. Cause: stranded.

VIVIAN B. WALTERS, a schooner of 86 tons register, sailed from Lunenburg to Canso and was wrecked near New Harbour, Guysboro, on April 8. Her port of registry was Lunenburg. Cause: stranded. Value of schooner was $8,800.

(1911)—A.K. MACLAN, a schooner of 176 tons register, sailed from Lunenburg to St. John's, Newfoundland, and was wrecked off St. Esprit, C.B., on April 16. Her port of registry was Lunenburg. Cause: foundered. Value of schooner was $8,000.

BEN EARN, a ship of 2,661 tons register, sailed from Glasgow to Saint John, N.B., and was wrecked at Half Moon Rock on July 16. Her port of registry was Glasgow. Cause: stranded.

BLEW WAVE, a schooner of 37 tons register, sailed from Parrsboro to Windsor and was wrecked at Cobequid Bay on August 22. Her port of registry was Parrsboro. Cause: stranded. Value of schooner was $300.

CHARLOTTE, a schooner of 79 tons register, sailed from Louisburg to Port Mouton and was wrecked at Port Mouton on July 23. Her port of registry was Lunenburg. Cause: hit upon the rocks. Value of schooner was $1,900.

ELECTRA, a schooner of 78 tons register, sailed from Pictou to Margaree Harbour and was wrecked at Margaree Harbour on October 25. Her port of registry was Charlottetown. Cause: stranded.

271

EFFIE MAY, a schooner of 49 tons register, sailed from Pictou to Halifax and was wrecked at Port Hood on November 16. Her port of registry was Lunenburg. Cause: stranded. Value of schooner was $2,500.

FLORA, a schooner of 64 tons register, sailed from Louisburg to Halifax and was wrecked at Egg Island on April 23. Her port of registry was Liverpool, N.S. Cause: a leak. Value of schooner was $1,500.

GEORGIA E., a schooner of 95 tons register, sailed from Barton to Briar Island and was wrecked at Briar Island on July 7. Her port of registry was Weymouth. Cause: stranded. Value of schooner was $1,500.

HARLOW, a schooner of 267 tons register, sailed from St. John's, Newfoundland, to St. Paul Island and was wrecked at this Island on April 7. Her port of registry was Windsor, N.S. Cause: abandoned. Value of schooner was $7,500.

J & L IRVING, a schooner of 79 tons register, sailed from Buctouche, N.B., to Port Hastings and was wrecked at Eastern Harbour on August 17. Her port of registry was Yarmouth. Cause: stranded. Value of schooner was $1,500.

LANGEN, a barque of 1,138 tons register, sailed from Bridgewater to Lunenburg and was wrecked at Port La Have on February 9. Her port of registry was Norway. Cause: a leak. Value of vessel was $8,000.

L'ETOILE, a schooner of 47 tons register, sailed from Sydney to Georgetown and was wrecked at Big Bras d'Or on July 28. Her port of registry was Port Hawkesbury. Cause: stranded.

LAURA E. FRANKLAND, a schooner of 46 tons register, sailed from Halifax to Campbell's Cove and was wrecked in this cove on December 23. Her port of registry was Halifax. Cause: stranded. Value of schooner was $600.

MARY F. SMITH, a schooner of 32 tons register, sailed from Boston to Clarke's Harbour and was wrecked at Green Island on September 6. Her port of registry was Boston. Cause: stranded. Value of schooner was $2,350.

MOOWEEN, a schooner of 83 tons register, sailed from Gloucester to Canso and was wrecked at Great Island on December 13. Her port of registry was Duxbury, Mass. Cause: stranded. Value of schooner was $12,600.

O.P. SILVER, a schooner of 70 tons register, sailed from Pictou to Canso and was wrecked at Chedabucto Bay on August 29. Her port of registry was Lunenburg. Cause: stranded.

RELIANCE, a schooner of 19 tons register, sailed from

Philadelphia to Yarmouth and was wrecked at Cape Fourchu on November 13. Her port of registry was Shelburne. Cause: stranded.

WALKYRIE, a schooner of 87 tons register, sailed from St. Malo to the fishing grounds and was wrecked at the strait of Canso on April 29. Her port of registry was St. Malo, France. Cause: stranded.

(1912)—ANNIE BLANCHE, a schooner of 68 tons register, sailed from Parrsboro to Machias Port, Maine, and was wrecked off Spencer's Island on March 29. Her port of registry was Parrsboro. Cause: foundered. Value of schooner was $1,200.

ARIZONA, a schooner of 85 tons registry, sailed from Rockport, Maine, to Blympton and was wrecked at Cranberry Island on August 12. Her port of registry was Yarmouth. Cause: stranded. Value of schooner was $4,000.

ABRAHAM LINCOLN, a schooner of 58 tons register, sailed from P.E.I. to Sydney, C.B., and was wrecked at the entrance of Strait of Canso on November 28. Her port of registry was Charlottetown. Cause: stranded.

BONAVISTA, a schooner of 837 tons register, sailed from Saint John, N.B., to Louisburg and was wrecked in the Bay of Fundy on March 16. Her port of registry was Montreal. Cause: stranded. Value of schooner was $25,000.

ENERGY, a schooner of 97 tons register, sailed from Campbellton, N.B., to Sydney, C.B., and was wrecked at Cranberry Head on June 12. Her port of registry was Lunenburg. Cause: stranded. Value of schooner was $1,500.

ETHEL, a schooner of 93 tons register, sailed from Perth to Halifax and was wrecked 25 miles S.S.W. off Cape Sable on October 2. Her port of registry was Yarmouth. Cause: foundered. Value of schooner was $3,400.

HENRY MAY, a schooner of 179 tons register, sailed from Portland, Maine, to Shulie, N.S., and was wrecked at Apple River on May 14. Her port of registry was U.S.A. Cause: stranded. Value of schooner was $2,000.

HUSTLER, a schooner of 39 tons register, sailed from Barrington to Clarke's Harbour and was wrecked on the east side of Clarke's Harbour on July 29. Her port of registry was Barrington. Cause: stranded. Value of schooner was $600.

JOHN HARVEY, a schooner of 99 tons register, sailed from Boston to St. Peter, Newfoundland, and was wrecked near the entrance to Gabarus, N.S., on January 9. Her port of registry was St. John's, Newfoundland. Cause: stranded.

J. A. SILVER, a schooner which was wrecked at Shenogue, N.S., on October 3.

MONICA A. THOMAS, a schooner of 46 tons register, sailed from Louisburg to the fishing grounds and was wrecked later in Louisburg Harbour on September 1. Her port of registry was Louisburg. Cause: stranded. Value of schooner was $3,000.

MYRTLE, a schooner of 10 tons register, sailed from Halifax to Liverpool, N. S., and was wrecked three miles off Lunenburg on October 12. Her port of registry was Halifax. Cause: foundered. Value of schooner was $675.

MAYFLOWER, a schooner of 26 tons register, sailed from St. Andrews, N.B., to Annapolis and was wrecked at Parker's Cove, N.S., on December 11. Her port of registry was Digby. Cause: stranded. Value of schooner was $700.

NINA S., a schooner of 18 tons register, sailed from Halifax to Terence Bay and was wrecked at Pennant Point on October 8. Her port of registry was Halifax. Cause: fire. Value of schooner was $2,000.

NEW HOME, a schooner of 31 tons register, sailed from Barrington to Halifax and was wrecked at the entrance to Halifax Harbour on November 13. Her port of registry was Barrington. Cause: stranded. Value of schooner was $2,700.

ST. ROCH, a schooner of 46 tons register, sailed from St. Pierre Miquelon to Sydney, C. B., and was wrecked at Scatarie Island on April 28. Her port of registry was France. Cause: stranded.

STELLA MAUD, a schooner of 99 tons register, sailed from Parrsboro to Windsor, N.S., and was wrecked in Avon River on December 17. Her port of registry was Saint John, N.B. Cause: stranded. Value of schooner was $950.

S.P. WILLARD, a schooner of 87 tons register, sailed from Gloucester to fishing grounds and was wrecked at Gabarus on December 30. Her port was Essex, U.S.A. Cause: stranded. Value of schooner was $5,000.

URBYE, a barque of 967 tons register, sailed from Genoa to Bridgewater and was wrecked at Port Beckerton on May 10. Her port of registry was Norway. Cause: stranded. Value of vessel was $50,000.

VIRGINIA, a schooner of 134 tons register, sailed from Halifax to LaHave and was wrecked at Rosehead, N.S., on January 9. Her port of registry was Lunenburg. Cause: stranded. Value of schooner was $4,000.

WARREN W., a schooner of 79 tons register, sailed from

Glace Bay to Chatham, N.B., and was wrecked at Big Bras d'Or on May 9. Her port of registry was Charlottetown, P.E.I. Cause: stranded. Value of schooner was $1,200.

(1913)—ALICE P. TURNER, a schooner of 166 tons register, sailed from Parrsboro to Boston and was wrecked at Black Rock in the Bay of Fundy on January 28. Her port of registry was Stonington. Cause: stranded. Value of schooner was $2,000.

AGNES G. DONAHUE, a schooner of 99 tons register, sailed from Annapolis to Saint John, N.B., and was wrecked at Point Prim, N.S., on September 9. Her port of registry was Lunenburg. Cause: unknown.

BRIDGEPORT, a ship of 3,380 tons register, sailed from Sydney to Montreal and was lost off Sydney on November 1. Her port of registry was London, G.B. Cause: unknown. Value of ship was $72,400, with a loss of 45 lives.

DIANA, a schooner of 89 tons register, sailed from Gloucester to the fishing grounds and was wrecked at Shag Harbour on November 12. Her port of registry was Gloucester. Cause: hit sunken rock. Value of schooner was $10,000.

EVELYN, a ship of 2,379 tons register, sailed from Nordenham to Savannah, Georgia, and was wrecked at Louisburg on January 9. Her port of registry was West Hartlepool, G.B. Cause: foundered.

FREIA, a ship of 1,593 tons register, sailed from Barbadoes to Bahia Blanca and was wrecked at Cape Fourchu, N.S., on May 31. Her port of registry was Norway. Cause: stranded. Value of vessel was $25,000.

GERALD TURNBULL, a ship of 1,967 tons register, sailed from Cardiff to Grindstone Island and was wrecked at Gannet Dry Ledge on May 19. Her port of registry Cardiff, G.B. Cause: stranded.

IONA W., a schooner of 77 tons register, sailed from Georgetown, P.E.I., to Liverpool, N.S., and was wrecked off Whitehead, N.S., on December 7. Her port of registry was Lunenburg. Cause: unknown. Six lives were lost and the value of the schooner was $5,000.

JUSTICE H., a vessel of unknown tonnage, sailed from Halifax to Fourchu, N.S., and was wrecked at Framboise Bay on February 18. Her port of registry was Halifax. Cause: stranded.

MAYFLOWER, a schooner of 45 tons register, while in Halifax Harbour caught fire and was destroyed on September 24. Her port of registry was Halifax. Value of the schooner was $4,000.

SURPRISE, a schooner of 15 tons register, sailed from

Margaree to Pictou and was wrecked at Lismore, N.S., on May 15. Her port of registry was Canso. Cause: stranded. Value of schooner was $550.

SHAMROCK, a schooner of 88 tons register, sailed from Bay of Ireland to Halifax and was wrecked five miles west of Cranberry Island Light on June 8. Her port of registry was Lunenburg. Cause: stranded. Value of schooner was $5,000.

THEODORE ROOSEVELT, a schooner of 90 tons register, sailed from Gloucester to Digby and was wrecked at Centreville, N.S., on October 31. Her port of registry was U.S.A. Cause: stranded.

(1914)—ANN LOUISE LOCKWOOD, a schooner of unknown tonnage, was wrecked at Walton River, N. S., during the month of May. Her port of registry was U.S.A.

ALICE GERTRUDE, a schooner of 81 tons register, sailed from Shelburne to the fishing grounds and was wrecked on the west side of Seal Island on May 24. Her port of registry was Shelburne. Cause: stranded. Value of schooner was $2,500.

ALICE J. CRABTREE, a schooner of 325 tons register, sailed from St. Andrews, N.B., to Bridgewater and was wrecked at Port Jollie Head on August 2. Her port of registry was New York. Cause: stranded. Value of schooner was $8,000.

BOBS, a schooner of 97 tons register, sailed from Parrsboro to Cheverie, N.S., and was wrecked at Light House Bar in Parrsboro River on November 3. Her port of registry was Dorchester, N.B. Cause: stranded. Value of schooner was $600.

HUGH JOHN, a schooner of 119 tons register, sailed from Pictou to Sherbrook and was wrecked off Liscomb on December 23. Her port of registry was Halifax. Cause: stranded.

J. L. COBWELL, a schooner of 99 tons register, sailed from Gaspereau, P.E.I., to Port Mulgrave and was wrecked in Canso Harbour on November 18. Her port of registry was Saint John, N.B. Cause: stranded. Value of schooner was $200.

KOLM, a schooner of unknown tonnage, sailed from Magdalen Islands to Machias, Maine, and was wrecked 15 miles south east of Sambro on June 5. Her port of registry was Machias. Cause: foundered.

LUELLA, a schooner of 99 tons register, sailed from Louisburg to Stonehaven, N.B., and was wrecked south of Cabbage Cove, N. S., on June 16. Her port of registry was Chatham, N.B. Cause: stranded. Value of schooner was $4,700.

LAHAVE, a schooner of 34 tons register, sailed from Halifax to Musquodoboit and was wrecked in Chebucto Bay on September 21. Her port of registry was Lunenburg. Cause: fire.

LIMELIGHT, a schooner of 126 tons register, sailed from St. Pierre Miquelon to Souris, P.E.I., and was wrecked at Wine Harbour on November 20. Her port of registry was Charlottetcwn. Cause: stranded. Value of schooner was $5,000.

LIGHTSHIP No. 19, out of Glasgow for Halifax, was wrecked off Liscomb on May 6. Her port of registry was Great Britain. There was a loss of 19 lives.

MINER, a schooner of 32 tons register, sailed from Liverpool, N.S., to Main a Dieu and was wrecked off the Cape Breton Coast on August 19. Her port of registry was Liverpool. Cause: foundered. Value of schooner was $2,000.

MARION C., a sloop of 10 tons register, sailed from Port Medway and was wrecked at Middle Island on September 13. Her port of registry was Liverpool. Cause: stranded.

NINA, a schooner of 101 tons register, sailed from Port Medway to Liverpool and was wrecked three miles east by north from Coffins Island on January 29. Her port of registry was Port Medway. Cause: foundered. Value of schooner was $350.

NAVARRA, a ship of 2,847 tons register, sailed from Saint John, N. B., to Havre, France, and was wrecked at Holmes Island, N. S., on December 30. Her port of registry was Glasgow. Cause: stranded.

ROY PENNY, a schooner of 26 tons register, sailed from Port Hood to Petite de Grat and was wrecked at Port Hood Harbour on September 26. Her port of registry was Port Hawkesbury. Cause: stranded. Value of schooner was $1,750.

SPECULATOR, a schooner of 99 tons register, sailed from Louisburg to Halifax and was wrecked at Framboise on May 26. Her port of registry was Lunenburg. Cause: stranded. Value of schooner was $6,400.

SPARMAKER, a schooner of 24 tons register, sailed from Parrsboro and was wrecked off Parrsboro lighthouse on June 10. Her port of registry was Saint John, N. B. Cause: foundered. Value of schooner was $100.

CLARENCE H. VENNER, a schooner of 814 tons register, sailed from Elizabeth Port, N.Y., to Halifax and was wrecked off Cape Sable Light station on July 17. Her port of registry was U.S.A. Cause: stranded. Value of schooner was $20,000.

CIENFUEGOS, a ship of 1,139 tons register sailed from Gulfport to Montreal and was wrecked at Scatarie Island on July 19. Her port of registry was Cuba. Cause: stranded.

DOLLY GREY, a schooner of 13 tons register, sailed from Lockeport to the fishing grounds and was wrecked 70 miles south east of Shelburne on February 16. Her port of registry was Lunenburg. Cause: unknown. Value of schooner was $900.

EGLANTINE, a schooner of 56 tons register, sailed from Gloucester to the fishing grounds and was wrecked at Taylor's Head on January 20. Her port of registry was Gloucester. Cause: stranded. Value of schooner was $5,800.

HARRY B., a schooner of 67 tons register, sailed from Crapaud, P.E.I., to Sydney, N.S., and was wrecked at Pictou Harbour on November 14. Her port of registry was Charlottetown. Cause: a collision with the *Dictator*. Value of schooner was $4,300.

ST. ANTHONY, a schooner of 100 tons register, sailed from Saint John, N.B., to Selmah and was wrecked at Advocate Harbour on November 14. Her port of registry was Parrsboro. Cause: stranded. Value of schooner was $6,400.

SIR WILFRID, a schooner of 39 tons register, sailed from Glace Bay and was wrecked 200 yards outside the breakwater at Glace Bay on November 22. Her port of registry was Pictou. Cause: stranded. Value of schooner was $500.

CAPELLA, a steamer that went down near Louisburg, was 1,023 tons register.

(1915)—A. W. PERRY, a steamer of 957 tons register, sailed from Boston to Halifax and was wrecked at Chebucto Head on June 8. Her port of registry was Halifax. Cause: stranded. Value of vessel was $100,000.

DONZELLA, a schooner of 99 tons register, sailed from Charlottetown to Sydney, N.S., and was wrecked at Guiou Island, N.S., on June 27. Her port of registry was Charlottetown. Cause: stranded. Value of schooner is unknown.

ELMER, a schooner of 15 tons register, sailed from Digby to fishing grounds and was wrecked at Parker's Cove in Bay of Fundy on May 27. Her port of registry was Digby. Cause: stranded. Value of schooner was $500.

ELSIE BIRDETT, a schooner of 90 tons register, sailed from Mahone Bay to Queensport, N.S., and was wrecked in Chebucto Bay on July 17. Her port of registry was Lunenburg. Cause: stranded.

EMPRESS, a schooner of 355 tons register, sailed from Bridgewater to New York and was wrecked at Barrington Passage on November 10. Her port of registry was Bridgetown, West Indies. Cause: fire.

ELIZABETH, a schooner of tonnage unknown, was wrecked at Green Cove, N. S., on December 2. Her port of registry was France. Cause: foundered.

FAVOURITE, a schooner of 28 tons register, sailed from Whitehead on a fishing trip and was wrecked six miles south east of Beaver Harbour light on September 13. Her place of registry was Liverpool, N.S. Cause: foundered. Value of schooner was $1,000.

GEO. LINWOOD, a schooner of 25 tons register, sailed from Halifax to East Chezzetcook and was wrecked at East Chezzetcook on September 2. Her port of registry was Digby. Cause: stranded. Value of schooner was $500.

HIAWATHA, a schooner of 98 tons register, sailed from Burin, Newfoundland, to Halifax and was wrecked in Halifax Harbour on September 10. Her port of registry was Lunenburg. Cause: fire. Value of schooner was $9,000.

JOHN MILLARD, a schooner of 69 tons register, sailed from a place unknown and was wrecked at Pictou on September 27. Her port of registry was Charlottetown. Cause: collision with a sunken wreck, the *A. Arsenault.* Value of schooner was unknown.

JENNIE B. HODGSONS, a schooner of 79 tons register, sailed from Brigus, Newfoundland, to North Sydney and was wrecked one mile north east of Cranberry Head. Her port of registry was Chatham. Cause: foundered.

KILHELL, a steamer of 56 tons register, sailed from Port Hastings to Halifax and was wrecked on Bald Rock Shoal on January 9. Her port of registry was Parrsboro. Cause: stranded. Value of schooner was $10,000.

LEO, a schooner of 93 tons register, sailed from Economy to Economy Point and was wrecked at this place on July 5. Her port of registry was Saint John. Cause: stranded. Value of schooner was $200.

LOUISE, a schooner of 34 tons register, sailed from Port Hastings to Barrington and was wrecked near Blanche Life Saving Station at North Sydney on July 10. Her port of registry was Barrington Passage. Cause: stranded. Value of schooner was $7,400.

LEVUKA, a schooner of 76 tons register, sailed from Windsor to Parrsboro and was wrecked in Minas Basin on December 14. Her port of registry was Parrsboro. Cause: stranded. Value of schooner was $200.

ORIGINAL, a schooner of 97 tons register, sailed from Lunenburg to fishing grounds and was wrecked at Ingonish on December 4. Her port of registry was Lunenburg. Cause: stranded. Value of schooner was $12,500.

ORLEANS, a schooner which sailed from Louisburg to

Montague, P.E.I., was wrecked at Big Dover, N.S., on December 14. Her port of registry is unknown. Cause: stranded.

PRISCILLA SMITH, a schoner of 77 tons register, sailed from Gloucester to Shelburne and was wrecked at the entrance to Jordan Bay on February 1. Her port of registry was Gloucester, Mass. Cause: stranded.

SENLAC, a steamer of 615 tons register, sailed from Saint John to Sydney and was wrecked in Sydney Harbour on December 13. Her port of registry was Saint John. Cause: fire.

YARMOUTH PACKET, a schooner of 77 tons register, sailed from Louisburg to Canso and was wrecked at the entrance to Chedabucto Bay on May 6. Her port of registry was Yarmouth. Cause: stranded.

(1916)—ANNIE COGGINS, a schooner of 22 tons register, sailed from Digby to Avonport and was wrecked off this place on June 20. Her port of registry was Digby. Cause: foundered.

ADA PEARD, a brigantine of 219 tons register, sailed from Barbadoes to Saint John, New Brunswick, and was wrecked near Salmon River in the Bay of Fundy on September 2. Her port of registry was Fowey, England. Cause: stranded. Value of vessel was $10,000.

ARNEAC, a schooner of 496 tons register, sailed from Chatham, New Brunswick, to Portland, Maine, and was wrecked twenty miles south east of Seal Island on October 1. Her port of registry was New York. Cause: foundered.

ALEX. ANDERSON, a schooner of 725 tons register, sailed from Chatham, New Brunswick, to Portland, Maine, and was wrecked twenty miles south west by west off Seal Island on October 1. Her port of registry was New York. Cause: foundered.

ANNIE PEARL, a schooner of 40 tons register, sailed from Hall's Harbour to Minas Basin and was wrecked at this place on October 13. Her port of registry was Moncton. Cause: stranded.

ALTONA, a schooner of 28 tons register, sailed from Halifax to Ingramport and was wrecked at Prospect on December 10. Her port of registry was Halifax. Cause: stranded. Value of schooner was $1,250.

ALEAEA, a schooner of 99 tons register, sailed from Liverpool, N.S., to Elizabeth Port, U.S.A., and was wrecked at Yarmouth on December 23. Her port of registry was Port Medway, N.S. Cause: stranded.

CORONA, a schooner of 76 tons register, sailed from Boston to the fishing grounds and was wrecked at Green Island,

N.S., on February 26. Her port of registry was Boston. Cause: stranded.

CLIFFORD J. WHITE, a steamer of 259 tons register, sailed from New York to Yarmouth and was wrecked at Lobster Bay, N.S., on August 16. Her port of registry was Machias, Maine. Cause: foundered.

DAWSON, a sloop of 17 tons register, sailed from place unknown and was wrecked at Lockeport on December 16. Her port of registry was Shelburne. Cause: stranded. Value of sloop was $3,500.

FLORENCE E. MELANCON, a steamer of 92 tons register, was wrecked off Brier Island during the month of November. Her port of registry was Weymouth. Cause: stranded.

H.R. SILVER, a schooner of 199 tons register, sailed from Bridgetown to Sydney, N.S., and was wrecked at Cape Spear Cove on January 17. Her port of registry was Bridgetown, Barbadoes. Cause: foundered. Value of schoner was $13,000.

HERCULES, a schooner of 737 tons register, sailed from Perth Amboy, N.J., to Halifax and was wrecked of Yarmouth Fairway buoy on August 12. Her port of registry was Philadelphia. Cause: a leak. Value of schooner was $37,200.

HIPPOLYTE, a ferry of 12 tons which sailed from Barrington to Claxton Harbour, was wrecked at Clark's Harbour on December 16. Her port of registry was Barrington. Cause: stranded. Value of ferry was $1,300.

ISLAND GEM, a schooner of 11 tons register, sailed from Bennett's Beach to Parrsboro Roads and was wrecked in Minas Channel on August 13. Her port of registry was Yarmouth. Cause: stranded. Value of schooner was $500.

L.T. WHITMORE, a schooner of 240 tons register, sailed from Port Greville to Tralie, Ireland, and was wrecked at Spencers Island on May 30. Her port of registry is unknown. Cause: fire. Value of schooner was $5,500.

LILLIE E. MELANCON, a schooner of 90 tons register, sailed from Parrsboro to Digby and was wrecked at Parkers Cove in the Bay of Fundy on October 12. Her port of registry was Weymouth. Cause: stranded. Value of schooner was $3,000.

LYDIA L., a schooner of 14 tons register, sailed from Yarmouth to Tiverton and was wrecked at Little Wood Island on December 16. Her port of registry was Yarmouth. Cause: stranded. Value of schooner was $100.

LENA F. OXNER, a schooner of 99 tons register, sailed from New York to Halifax and was wrecked forty miles south of

Liverpool on December 29. Her port of registry was Quebec. Cause: foundered.

LOUIS K. COTTINGHAM, an American vessel, was wrecked near Seal Island during the month of January.

MARJORIE McGLASKEN, a schooner of 109 tons register, sprang a leak in the Bay of Fundy and foundered during the month of January. Her port of registry was Lunenburg.

MAGGIE W., a vessel out of North Sydney for Newfoundland, was wrecked at Cape Smoky on September 1. Her port of registry is unknown. Cause: foundered.

MIKADO, a schooner of 48 tons register, sailed from Little River, N.S., to Weymouth and was wrecked at St. Mary's Bay on September 23. Her port of registry was Yarmouth. Cause: stranded. Value of schooner was $5,000.

NELLIE, a schooner of 59 tons register, sailed from Mahone Bay to Ship Harbour and was wrecked at Cape Sable on January 7. Her port of registry was Yarmouth. Cause: stranded. Value of schooner was $800.

PREMIER, a schooner of 97 tons register, sailed from Gloucester to Canso and was wrecked near Cranberry Island on November 29. Her port of registry was Gloucester. Cause: stranded. Value of schooner was $13,000.

PANSY, a schooner of 76 tons register, sailed from Parrsboro to Parrsboro Roads and was wrecked at this place on December 12. Her port of registry was Parrsboro. Cause: stranded.

STANLEY L., a schooner of 19 tons register, sailed from Saint John, N.B., to Advocate Harbour and was wrecked at Advocate Beach on January 17. Her port of registry was Parrsboro. Cause: stranded. Value of schooner was $500.

STORMOUNT, a schooner of 1,230 tons register, sailed from Philadelphia to Sydney and was wrecked at Gull Ledge on June 26. Her port of registry was Montreal. Cause: stranded. Value of schooner was $300,000.

VESTA, a schooner of 113 tons register, sailed from Liverpool, N.S., to New York and was wrecked five miles east of Seal Island on July 21. Her port of registry was New London. Cause: foundered. Value of schooner was $1,634.

WILLIAM MASON, a schooner of tonnage unknown, sailed from New York to Yarmouth and was wrecked four miles off Meteghan, N.S., on December 19. Her port of registry is unknown. Cause: foundered.

(1917)—ATLANTIC, a schooner of 67 tons register, sailed from Halifax to Fourchu, C.B., and was wrecked at Bad Neighbour

Shoal on June 14. Her port of registry was Lunenburg. Cause: stranded. Value of schooner was $10,00.

CORA MAY, a schooner of 117 tons register, sailed from Saint John, N.B., to Parrsboro and was wrecked in the Bay of Fundy on April 10. Her port of registry was Saint John, N.B. Cause: foundered. Value of schooner was $1,500.

CYRENE, a schooner of 95 tons register, sailed from Charlottetown to Pictou and was wrecked at the entrance to Pictou Harbour on August 27. Her port of registry was Lunenburg. Cause: a collision with the *Aranmore*. Value of schooner was $3,000.

DELIVERANCE, a schooner of 78 tons register, sailed from Halifax and, while sailing out of the harbour, was wrecked. Her port of registry was Liverpool, N.S. Cause: a collision with the *Regin*. Value of schooner was $125,000.

DOUGLAS ADAMS, a schooner of 99 tons register, sailed out of Halifax for Curling, Newfoundland, and was wrecked at Point Michaud, N.S., on December 10. Her port of registry was Lunenburg. Cause: stranded. Value of schooner was $15,800.

JOSEPH P. MASQUITA, a schooner of 78 tons register, sailed from Gloucester to the fishing grounds and was wrecked at White Head Harbour, N.S., on December 10. Her port of registry was Gloucester, U.S.A. Cause: stranded. Value of schooner was $17,500.

LOLA R., a schooner of 13 tons register, sailed from Herring Cove to Halifax and was wrecked in Halifax Harbour on December 6. Her port of registry was Lunenburg. Cause: explosion of *Mont Blan* and *Imo*. Value of schooner was $500.

MARK A. TOBIN, a schooner of 99 tons register, sailed from Lunenburg to Halifax and was wrecked off Sambro Island on May 6. Her port of registry was Lunenburg. Cause: stranded. Value of schooner was $27,000.

OREGON, a schooner of 46 tons register, sailed from Canso to Shelburne and was wrecked at the entrance to White Head, N.S., on July 16. Her port of registry was Charlottetown. Cause: stranded.

PREMIER, a schooner of 187 tons register, while sailing for the approaches to Halifax harbour, was wrecked off Sambro on June 2. Her port of registry was London. Cause: stranded.

ST. BERNARD, a schooner of 123 tons register, while in Halifax harbour, was blown to pieces on December 6. Her port of registry was Parrsboro. Cause: explosion of the *Mont Blanc* and

Imo. Value of schooner was $12,000.

TRIUMPH, a ketch of 124 tons register, sailed from Halifax to the fishing grounds and was wrecked at Lawrencetown Head on March 28. Her port of registry was Grimsby, B.C. Cause: stranded. Value of ketch was $10,000.

UNA, a sloop of 10 tons register, sailed from Lockeport to Liverpool, N.S., and was wrecked off Western Shaol on April 9. Her port of registry was Yarmouth. Cause: foundered. Two lives were lost.

WINNIE, a schooner of 17 tons register, sailed from Ker's Brook for Parrsboro and was wrecked two miles south of Sambro light on June 11. Her port of registry was Saint John, N.B. Cause: foundered. Value of schooner was $3,500.

(1918)—ALLISON H. MAXNER, a schooner of 92 tons register, sailed from Lunenburg and was wrecked at Black Rock on March 4. Her port of registry was Lunenburg. Cause: foundered. Value of schooner was $15,300.

BONNIE B., a schooner of 19 tons register, sailed from Canso to Mulgrave and was wrecked at this place on April 25. Her port of registry was Lunenburg. Cause: foundered. Value of schooner was $320.

BLANCHARD C., a schooner of 11 tons register, sailed from Liverpool, N.S., to Port Mouton and was wrecked off Port Mouton Island on November 24. Her port of registry was Liverpool. Cause: fire. Value of schooner was $1,500.

CARRIE, a schooner of 99 tons register, sailed from Sydney to Charlottetown and was wrecked at Pictou Island. Her port of registry was Lunenburg. Cause: stranded. Value of schooner was $2,500.

INVERNESS, a schooner of 46 tons register, sailed from Canso and was wreckd at Mulgrave on April 25. Her port of registry was Halifax. Cause: foundered. Value of schooner was $10,000.

LA HAVE, a schooner of 60 tons register, sailed from LaHave to Halifax and was wrecked off Big Tancook Island on May 14. Her port of registry was Halifax. Cause: stranded. Value of schooner was $20,000.

S.S. ANCOR, a vessel that went down at Seal Island.

LUX BLANCA, a ship of 3,086 tons register, sailed from Halifax to Tampica and was torpedoed off Halifax on August 5. Her port of registry was Toronto.

LEAH D., a schooner of 48 tons register, sailed from Saint John, N.B., to Scotch Bay, N.S., and was wrecked at

Margeretville, N.S., on October 10. Her port of registry was Saint John, N.B. Cause: stranded. Value of schooner was $1,600.

MARY E. McDOUGALL, a schooner of 98 tons register, sailed from Sydney, N.S., to Summerside, P.E.I., and was wrecked at the entrance to Bras d'Or, C.B., on June 9. Her port of registry was Charlottetown. Cause: stranded. Value of schooner was $3,000.

ONWARD, a schooner of 92 tons register, sailed from Parrsboro to Windsor and was wrecked at Cogmagun River on June 5. Her port of registry was Saint John, N.B. Cause: stranded.

OTOKIO, a schooner of 89 tons register, sailed from LaHave to the Eastern Shore and was wrecked off Sober Island on September 6. Her port of registry was Lunenburg. Cause: foundered. Value of schooner was $38,000.

OLIVE S., a schooner of 86 tons register, sailed from place unknown and was wrecked at Tangier Harbour in the month of September. Her place of registry was Charlottetown. Cause: stranded. Value of schooner was $350.

ROB ROY, a schooner of 77 tons register, sailed from Boston to the fishing grounds and was sunk by a submarine 35 miles west of Seal Island on August 3. Her port of registry was U.S.A. Value of schooner was $14,000.

VALMORE, a schooner of 11 tons register, foundered in Lockeport Harbour on September 6. Her port of registry was Halifax. Value of schooner was $400.

W.E. GLADSTONE, a schooner of 22 tons register, sailed from Port Maitland for Yarmouth and was wrecked at Brier Island on November 6. Her port of registry was Yarmouth. Cause: foundered.

(1919)—AUTHENTIE, a schoner of 22 tons register, sailed from Liverpool and was wrecked off Liverpool Harbour on August 14. Her port of registry was Liverpool. Cause: stranded. Value of schooner was $6,000.

AUDREY A., a schooner of 10 tons register, sailed from Barrington to the fishing grounds and was wrecked 20 miles south of Cape Sable on September 15. Her port of registry was Barrington Passage. Cause: abandoned. Value of schooner was $1,000.

ALICE, a schooner of 42 tons register, sailed from Halifax to Sheet Harbour and was wrecked at the entrance to Jeddore Harbour on November 4. Her port of registry was Liverpool. Cause: stranded. Value of schooner was $1,600.

ARABIA, a schooner of 80 tons register, sailed from Fortune, Newfoundland, to Gallouse, Newfoundland, and was wrecked at Little Round Shoal, St. Peters Bay, N.S., on November 19. Her port of registry was St. John's, Newfoundland. Cause: stranded.

BEDEQUE, a schooner of 34 tons register, sailed from Port Hawkesbury for Madame Island and was wrecked at this island on June 5. Her port of registry was Liverpool, N.S. Cause: foundered. Value of schooner was $5,000.

CURLEW, a schooner of 63 tons register, sailed from Yarmouth to the fishing grounds and was wrecked at Petit Passage on January 10. Her port of registry was Barrington Passage. Cause: stranded.

CHELSTON, a ship of 2,389 tons register, was wrecked at St. Paul Island on September 12. Her port of registry was Glasgow. Cause: stranded.

DELBERT D., a schooner of 16 tons register, sailed from Halifax to Liverpool and was wrecked off Port Medway on January 29. Her port of registry was Liverpool, N.S. Cause: stranded.

DAISY, a schooner of 69 tons register, sailed from Boston for Summerside, P.E.I., and was wrecked in the Northumberland Strait on September 16. Her port of registry was Charlottetown. Cause: foundered.

ETHERINGTON, a schooner of 28 tons register, sailed from Yarmouth to the fishing grounds and was wrecked at Swanse's Cove, N.S., on June 30. Her port of registry was Shelburne. Cause: fire.

JASSE HART 11, a schooner of 212 tons register, sailed from Eastport to Apple River, N.S., and was wrecked at Apple River on April 30. Her port of registry was Calais, Maine. Cause: foundered. Value of schooner was $6,000.

J.C. WILLIAMS, a schooner of 28 tons register, sailed from Halifax to Arichat and was wrecked at Ship Harbour on November 5. Her port of registry was Halifax. Cause: stranded. Value of schooner was $1,500.

KING MALCOLM, a ship of 1,304 tons register, sailed from Louisburg for Halifax and was wrecked at the entrance to Beaver Harbour on February 15. Her port of registry was St. John's, Newfoundland. Cause: stranded. Value of ship was $50,000.

LOUISE MAUD, a schooner of 21 tons register, sailed from Jeddore to Halifax and was wrecked 12 miles off Halifax on

December 18. Value of schooner was $950.

MARGEREY AUSTIN, a schooner of 112 tons register, sailed from Alma, N.B., to Saint John, New Brunswick, was wrecked near Apple River light, N.S., on January 2. Her port of registry was Saint John, New Brunswick. Cause: stranded. Value of schooner was $27,300.

MULGRAVE, a steamer of 330 tons register, sailed from Louisburg to Halifax and was wrecked at the entrance to Beaver Harbour on February 15. Her port of registry was Ottawa. Cause: stranded. Value of steamer was $100,000.

MERRIMAC, a schooner of 70 tons register, was wrecked in Halifax Harbour on November 9. Her port of registry was Sydney, N.S. Cause: foundered. Value of schooner was $950.

NORTH STAR, a schip of 1,999 tons register, sailed from Boston for Yarmouth and was wrecked at Green Island, N.S., on August 8. Her port of registry was Boston. Cause: stranded.

NILE, a schooner of 34 tons register, sailed from Lunenburg for Georgetown, P.E.I., and was wrecked off Cape George, N.S., on December 20. Her port of registry was Lunenburg. Cause: foundered.

OCEAN CHILD, a schooner of 19 tons register, sailed from Halifax Harbour and was wrecked in the harbour on November 6. Value of of schooner was $300.

POLAR LAND, a ship of 2,501 tons register, sailed from New York for Gibraltar and was wrecked off Scatarie Island on November 7. Her port of registry was Baltimore. Cause: foundered.

(1920)—ALBATROSS, a sloop of 80 tons register, sailed from Halifax to Portugal and was wrecked near Egg Island, N.S., on March 10. Her port of registry was Portugal. Cause: stranded. Value of sloop was $37,000.

ATTAINMENT, a schooner of 318 tons register, sailed from St. John's, Newfoundland, for Parrsboro and was wrecked at Bear Cove, Long Island, in the Bay of Fundy on April 25. Her port of registry was St. John's. Cause: stranded.

S.S. MONTARA, a vessel that went down at Gooseberry Cove.

BAY QUEEN, a schooner of 32 tons register, sailed from Shelburne to Halifax and was wrecked near Cape LaHave on May 19. Her port of registry was Barrington. Cause: foundered.

CAPE BRETON, a ship of 1,109 tons register, sailed from Halifax for Louisburg and was wrecked south east of Point Scatarie Island on March 7. Her port of registry was Montreal.

Cause: stranded.

CHARLES A. RITCEY, a schooner of 360 tons register, sailed from Lunenburg and was wrecked at Rose Head in Lunenburg Co. on September 13. Her port of registry was Lunenburg. Cause: stranded. Value of schooner was $50,000.

DIANTHUS, a schooner of 33 tons register, was wrecked in Halifax Harbour during a gale on February 11. Her port of registry was Liverpool, N.S. Value of schooner was $500.

GABRIELLA, a trawler of 285 tons register, sailed from St. Pierre for Sydney and was wrecked at Livingstone shoal on December 8. Her port of registry was Boulogne. Cause: stranded.

HOWARD D. TROOP, a schooner of 69 tons register, sailed from St. John on a cruise and was wrecked at Petit Passage, in the Bay of Fundy, on April 17. Her port of registry was Saint John, N.B. Cause: a collision with the *Canadian Voyageur*. Value of schooner was $15,000.

LAKE ELWIN, a ship of 1,658 tons register, sailed from Ecosse for New York and was wrecked at Gabarus Rock, N.S., on July 5. Her port of registry was U.S.A. Cause: stranded.

CASIS, a schooner of 62 tons register, sailed from Sheet Harbour to Sydney and was wrecked off Louisburg on July 19. Her port of registry was Halifax. Cause: stranded.

OHIO, a schooner of 42 tons register, sailed from Yarmouth for the fishing grounds and was wrecked eight miles south by west of Shelburne light on October 4. Her port of registry was Yarmouth. Cause: fire. Value of schooner was $6,000.

(1921)—BESSIE F. KEEFER, a schooner of 79 tons register, sailed from North Sydney for Charlottetown and was wrecked at Malmesley Beach on May 6. Her port of registry was Charlottetown. Cause: foundered.

BALEINE, a trawler of 154 tons register, sailed from Port Hawkesbury for the fishing grounds and was wrecked at Cape Hogon, N.S., on September 30. Her port of registry was St. John's, Newfoundland. Cause: stranded. Value of vessel was $125,000.

B & C, a sloop of 14 tons register, sailed from Tiverton to Meteghan and was wrecked at Petit Passage on December 7. Her port of registry was Digby. Cause: stranded. Value of sloop was $100.

EDITH McINTYRE, a schooner of 149 tons register, sailed from Meteghan to Saint John, N.B., and was wrecked one and a half miles off Timer Point in the Bay of Fundy on August 12. Her port of registry was Windsor. Value of schooner was $25,000.

INNOVATION, a schooner of 190 tons register, sailed

from Little Bras d'Or to Halifax and was wrecked thirty miles south east of Cape Canso on July 26. Her port of registry was LaHave. Cause: foundered. Value of schooner was $35,000.

MUSQUASH, a sloop of 64 tons register, sailed from Louisburg for Halifax and was wrecked seven miles south east of St. Esprit, C.B., on August 4. Her port of registry was Quebec. Cause: a collision. Value of sloop was $92,000.

MARY P. HARTY, a schooner of 77 tons register, sailed from Gloucester for the fishing grounds and was wrecked south of Seal Island Lighthouse on August 8. Her port of registry was Gloucester. Cause: stranded.

MONARCH, a schooner of 83 tons register, sailed from Gloucester for the fishing grounds and was wrecked nine miles south east from Cranberry Island Light on August 11. Her port of registry was Gloucester. Cause: stranded. Value of schooner was $4,000.

MARGARET H., a schooner of 75 tons register, sailed from LaHave to Lunenburg and was wrecked off Harrington Cove on November 25. Her port of registry was Louisburg. Cause: stranded. Value of schooner was $8,000.

VOLUNDA, a ship of 1,056 tons register, sailed from North Sydney to Montreal and was wrecked off Neil's Harbour, C.B., on July 29. Her port of registry was Pictou. Cause: stranded. Value of vessel was $264,858.

(1922)—ALEXANDRA, a schooner of 93 tons register, sailed from Ingonish to Gloucester and was wrecked at Black Point on January 3. Her port of registry was Lunenburg. Cause: unknown.

BELAND, a schooner of 35 tons register, sailed from Woods Harbour to Barrington and was wrecked off Cape Negro, N.S., on November 24. Her port of registry was LaHave. Cause: foundered.

DIEGO, a schooner of 27 tons register, sailed from Halifax to Jeddore and was wrecked at Dickies Rock on July 1. Her port of registry was Port Medway. Cause: stranded. Value of schooner was $800.

E. A. CHISHOLM, a schooner of 78 tons register, sailed from North Sydney to Charlottetown and was wrecked at Hillsborough Bay on October 18. Her port of registry was Lunenburg. Cause: stranded.

HARRY B., a schooner of 67 tons register, sailed from Sydney to Charlottetown, P.E.I., and was wrecked at Toney River, N.S., on August 20. Her port of registry was Charlottetown. Cause: foundered. Value of schooner was $1,500.

LUCY A., a schooner of 31 tons register, sailed from

Yarmouth and was wrecked 3 1/2 miles west of Cape Forchu on April 4. Her port of registry was Yarmouth. Cause: foundered. Value of schooner was $22,000.

LOREN B. SNOW, a schooner of 75 tons register, sailed from Yarmouth to the fishing grounds and was wrecked 25 miles west of Cape Fourchu on June 1. Her port of registry was Yarmouth. Cause: foundered.

SHANNON, a schooner of 51 tons register, while at Halifax was wrecked at Pennant Point on January 24. Her port of registry was Halifax. Cause: stranded. Value of schooner was $20,000.

STRATHCONA, a schooner of 88 tons register, sailed from Halifax to Port Hawkesbury and was wrecked at Bull Rocks in Fishermen's Harbour on May 8. Her port of registry was Lunenburg. Cause: foundered.

VICTORIA, a schooner of 99 tons register, sailed from Country Harbour to Sheet Harbour and was wrecked at Sheet Harbour on December 6. Her port of registry was Lunenburg. Cause: stranded.

WIN THE WAR, a schooner of 149 tons register, sailed from Digby to Lunenburg and was wrecked at Bon Portage Island, N.S., on July 2. Her port of registry was LaHave. Cause: stranded. Value of schooner was $10,000.

(1923)—ABERDEEN, a vessel that was lost on Limb Ledge near Seal Island on October 13. She was carrying a new light apparatus for the Cape Sable light at the time she went down.

(1924)—GEORGE M. COOK, a vessel of 133 tons register out of Lunenburg, ran ashore in the fog at Seal Island on June 29.

(1929)—JOSEPHINE DE COSTA, a vessel of 60 tons register out of Boston, Mass., foundered on Blonde Rock on September 21.

GUARD, a vessel of 212 tons register out of Halifax, was stranded on Limbs Point, Seal Island, on September 21.

(1930)—LINTON, a vessel which ran aground on West Cape, just outside of Yarmouth Harbour, on December 2. She was 137' in length, 23'across and 11' in the hold. She was a steel haul and 213 tons register.

(1932)—AZORES, a vessel of 53 tons register, was destroyed by fire southwest of Seal Island on June 1.

KEITH & ROBERTSON, a vessel of 14 tons register, out of Digby foundered ten miles east of Seal Island on July 9.

(1933)— a Norwegian vessel was wrecked at Neils Harbour on October 7.

PERYNEAS, a vessel of 582 tons register out of British